Contemporary International Business Communication

当代国际商务函电

主编　杨晋

天津大学出版社
TIANJIN UNIVERSITY PRESS

内容提要

本书讲授当今信息时代国际商务沟通的理念及其在具体涉外商务信函写作和沟通中的应用。结合典型国际商务和职业场合案例,系统讲解高效商务沟通的方式、技巧和信函写作。课文内容举一反三、实用性强。本书适用于双语教学、英语教学以及有一定英语基础的专业人士自学。

图书在版编目(CIP)数据

当代国际商务函电/杨晋主编.—天津:天津大学出版社,2011.10

ISBN 978-7-5618-4182-2

Ⅰ.①当… Ⅱ.①杨… Ⅲ.①国际贸易-英语-电报信函-写作 Ⅳ.①H315

中国版本图书馆 CIP 数据核字(2011)第 197865 号

出版发行 天津大学出版社
出 版 人 杨欢
地 址 天津市卫津路 92 号天津大学内(邮编:300072)
电 话 发行部:022-27403647 邮购部:022-27402742
网 址 www.tjup.com
印 刷 河北省昌黎县第一印刷厂
经 销 全国各地新华书店
开 本 185mm×260mm
印 张 17.75
字 数 443 千
版 次 2011 年 10 月第 1 版
印 次 2011 年 10 月第 1 次
印 数 1-4 000
定 价 34.00 元

前　言

信息技术领域科学技术的飞速发展使国际商务的沟通方式发生了巨大的变化。电子商务的日益普及给人们带来极大的便利的同时，也给人们的国际沟通能力提出了极大的挑战。

许多涉外工作人员每天需要处理来自世界各地、通过不同媒介发来的大量信息，需要与不同人种、操不同语言、属不同文化背景的商务人员进行沟通，而沟通的效果常成为商务及职业场合胜败的决定因素。事实上，当今的国际商务竞争在很大程度上体现在跨文化沟通能力的竞争，而这种竞争又具体表现在思维方式和语言表达方面。

为了使商科学子、涉外企业家、经管人员及从业人员增强国际商业沟通能力和英语表达能力，本书吸取英美沟通专业的专家提倡的最新沟通理念和沟通方式，根据涉外商务和职业场合的需要，系统地阐述了国际商务沟通的通用规则，各种跨时区、跨地域、跨文化的信函写作方式，并编写了典型范例。同时，摒弃了陈旧古板的商业套语，使商务函电写作和沟通更适合当今高效率和换位思考的要求和理念，以助于实现同国际接轨。

本书将现代英美沟通理念和方法融入英语语言的学习中，尤其是每课加入的“优化沟通效果”(Communication for Results)，意在使学生和读者领悟现代英美职业人员的思维习惯、表达方式、沟通语气，并增强英语语感。另外，意在使学生不仅能够表达出意思，而且懂得如何表达才能达到预期的效果。

作为商业和财经类大学重点课程教材，本书可用于双语教学和英语教学，以便培养学生直接用英语思维的习惯，从而提高表达效果。书中内容用于培养涉外复合型人才的主要教程，在近年教学实践中取得了显著的成效。

本书多年来用于天津财经大学精品课程“英文商务写作”教材，每课附有启发性的问题和相关练习及参考答案，使学生能够掌握信件、备忘录、合同及报告等国际商业文件的写作方法，同时精于对各种沟通媒介(如书面、电子和口头)的选择。

本书由天津财经大学教师杨晋主编(全部课文及第11、15、16、17、18、19、20课练习)，参编人员为该校教师：鲍杉(第1、2课练习)、杨祎(第3、4课练习)、张建东(第7、13课练习)、张秋英(第6、8课练习)、韩华(第9课练习)、李军育(第10课练习)、张君(第12课练习)、韩子钰(第14、5课练习)，该校教师骆媛负责本书教学多媒体课件设计。。全书由杨晋统稿，美籍专家Sonia R. Crockett主审。

编者

2011年7月

Contents

Lesson One

The Principles of Effective Business Communication

Business communication refers to all the messages that are sent and received for business purposes. In international business communication among people from different countries, messages can be transmitted by written and electronic correspondence (such as letter, memo, fax, e-mail) or through oral media (such as telephone, voice mail, teleconferencing).

Effective communication in international business can help you reach a deal, improve customers' satisfaction, promote the sale of your products, keep a good impression of your company and enhance your work efficiency. In addition, the correspondence and information exchanged during communication are often important documents kept for evidence of business arrangements. Whether a message is effectively produced can make the difference between success and failure of the business. Therefore, skills in effective communication are essential for business personnel.

The golden rules of effective business communication can be boiled down to the following 6 points:

1. Express ideas clearly

Clear expression is to insure that your reader will understand with little effort and be free from doubt and misunderstanding. On the other hand, you can only get the respond you need quickly from your reader when your meaning is crystal clear.

Clearness can be achieved by:

(1) Use familiar words with precise meanings. **e. g.** :

Instead of writing	Write
We have bimonthly direct cargo services sailing from Shanghai to San Francisco. ("Bimonthly" can mean either twice a month or every two months.)	We have two direct cargo services sailing from Shanghai to San Francisco every month. *or* We have direct sailing from Shanghai to San Francisco every two months.

(2) Avoid wordy expressions, jargon and clichés. **e. g.** :

Instead of writing	Write
in due course	today, tomorrow (or a specific time)
We wish to inform you that the meeting is put off.	The meeting is put off.
Attached please find the latest catalogue.	Enclosed is the latest catalogue.

续表

Instead of writing	Write
at this point in time	now
have the capacity of	can
in view of the fact that . . .	because

2. Keep the message concise

Before writing a business letter, for instance, you must have a clear and definite purpose in mind. Do not try to cover everything in your letter. Narrow the scope and keep to the point. Eliminate any unimportant and irrelevant sentences, phrases or words as they can make your message too long, or even worse, it may distract your reader from your main purpose and weaken your major points.

However, conciseness does not mean writing exclusively in short sentences or omitting necessary detail. It means making every word count. Compare the following examples.

Wordy with irrelevant information	Concise and to the point
I know you've had gorgeous spring weather, with sunny skies and fine days. But here in the U. S. it's been a spring of another color. We've been hammered with storms, flooding, and even late snow. Travel over here has been a nightmare, which is why you'll find my expenses a bit high this month.	Enclosed are my expense statement and receipts for March 2006. My expenses are higher than usual this month because unusual weather stranded me in Chicago for nearly five days. The airport was closed for four days, and we were forced to sleep in the terminal wherever we could find room.

3. Adopt a reader-focused approach

No matter what purpose your message has, it is the reader who decides whether you will achieve the result you intended. Consequently, it is important to put your reader first. To achieve this you must, first of all, have a clear picture of your reader when you prepare your message so that you will be able to adapt your tone, style and content to your readers' needs and establish a good relationship with them. Ask the following questions to learn about your reader.

(1) Who is my reader?

Try to put yourself in your reader's position and think from his/her point of view. In intercultural communication you have to adapt to your reader's way of expression, their culture and custom.

(2) What is the relation between my reader and me?

The answer to this question will help you adopt an appropriate tone and style. If the reader is a colleague with whom you've kept long-term friendly relations, for instance, you may use a direct approach and a less formal style. On the other hand, if it is a new customer you have had no contact with before, you may adopt a more formal style.

(3) What do my readers want to know, and what is already known?

Readers want relevant and accurate information in order to reach a certain goal or solve a certain problem. They don't want you to repeat what they have already known.

(4) What interests or motivates them?

In writing a persuasive message find out good reasons and evidence that is most persuasive to your readers. Write about the benefits your readers can receive if they accept your idea.

(5) What will be or might be the reaction of my readers to my message?

If you predict that your readers' reaction will be negative, that is, they will be displeased with, uninterested in your message, use an indirect approach — give your evidence or reasons before the main idea. Whereas, if your readers are likely to be positive to your message, use a direct approach — start a letter with a clear statement of the main idea followed by reasons and explanations. **e.g.**:

Direct	Indirect
We have to raise the prices of our goods because of the sharp increase in the price of raw materials.	As the prices of raw materials have sharply increased, we have to raise the price of our goods.

4. Get the right tone and style

In business messages, the tone most appealing to your reader is a tone that is friendly but efficient, a tone that makes your reader feel there's someone at the other end of the message who is taking notice and showing interest in his/her concerns. For this purpose write in a natural, friendly and sincere way instead of an impersonal, written style.

The trend in today's business writing is that people prefer style that is less formal and more natural. In many countries such as the US, business letters are often written in conversational style that looks like face-to-face talk.

Consider the following methods to write in the right tone and style.

(1) Active voice and passive voice

Sentences in active voice are easier to read and understand than passive voice. People using active voice sound more responsible and honest, while using passive voice seem to try to hide themselves behind the message. It is advisable to use active voice in routine messages.

Passive voice	Active voice
Our plan has been changed.	We've changed our plan.
Damaged goods can never be exchanged.	We cannot change damaged goods.
The new measures are considered by the managers to be effective.	The managers consider the new measures effective.
Problems have been found in this contract.	The contract has problems.
It is necessary that payment be effected next month.	We shall effect payment next month.

However, under circumstances when you want to point out your reader's faults and mistakes but don't want your message to sound accusing, or when you want to tell your reader what to do but don't want your message to read like an order, use passive voice, which helps you avoid using the word "you" and makes your message sounds more courteous, considerate and objective. Compare the following sentences.

Sentences with "you"	Sentences without "you"
You shouldn't load this kind of goods on deck.	This kind of goods cannot be loaded on deck.
You must not wash the wool sweater in hot water.	The wool sweater shrinks if washed in hot water.
You should never use that kind of paper in the copy machine.	That kind of paper does not work well in the copy machine.
You have to meet the deadline if you want your goods to be shipped before the end of the month.	The deadline must be met if the goods are to be shipped before the end of the month.
You must correct all these copies by noon.	All these copies must be corrected by noon.
You lost the shipment.	The shipment is lost.

(2) Emphasize the positive

As the saying goes "Every cloud has a silver lining", focus on the positive side rather than on the negative. Stress what can be done rather than what cannot be done. Your message will sound more sincere and friendly if you make your reader feel hopeful and optimistic.

Negative	Positive
We never exchange damaged goods.	We are happy to exchange goods that are returned to us in good condition.
It is impossible to fill your order this month.	Your order will be filled next month.
We apologize for inconveniencing you during the remodeling of our workshop.	The renovation now under way will enable us to serve you better.

(3) Use "you" attitude

Use "you" or "your" instead of "we" and "our", or "I" and "my". This "you" attitude shows that you see a problem or a matter from your reader's perspective. It shows your warmth and concern to your reader, while "I" or "we" attitude creates an impression of selfishness.

"We" attitude	"You" attitude
To help us process your order, we must ask for another copy of the inquiry.	So that your order can be filled promptly, please send another copy of the inquiry.
We offer T-shirts in different colors and styles.	Select your T-shirts from different colors and styles.
We allow 5 percent discount for payment within 10 days.	You earn 5 percent discount if you pay within 10 days.

(4) Be courteous

Writing in a polite and considerate tone is more effective to get your reader's reply and acceptance. Courtesy also involves a prompt reply after receiving a message seeking information from you. It is impolite to keep your reader waiting.

Impolite	Polite
Your letter is not clear at all. I cannot understand it.	If I understand your letter correctly, ...
You should give us more details on your products.	Will you give us more details on your products?

5. Have a good command of English

Foreign language is often used in international business, and English is the most widely used language. Good sentence structure and correct usage of grammar, spelling, words and punctuation in your letter leave a good impression of you and your company on your reader. Moreover, it improves readability of your letter and avoids ambiguity.

Poor punctuation	Good punctuation
We are sending you under separate cover two bags of samples for the goods you ordered by air as instructed.	We are sending you, under separate cover, two bags of samples by air for the goods you ordered.

Incorrect place of modifiers	Correct place of modifiers
Our new model desk is suitable for busy executives with thick legs and large drawers.	With its thick legs and large drawers, our new model desk is suitable for busy executives.
Please inform us the earliest shipment we can have as soon as possible.	Please inform us as soon as possible the earliest shipment we can have.

Incorrect use of noun and pronoun	Correct use of noun and pronoun
After two-months slump, we increased the sales.	After two months slump, sales increased.
Working as fast as possible, the goods are ready to be shipped.	Working as fast as possible, we have got the goods ready to be shipped.
Being a qualified expert in this field, I'm sure you can do the job.	Being a qualified expert in this field, you can surely do the job.

6. Have a good command of business knowledge

Business letters are often related to some special fields of knowledge, it is, therefore, important to learn business practices and special terms. For instance, some widely used abbreviations may involve complex business procedures and practices; some words and expressions that look familiar to you may have meanings quite different from what you have learned in everyday usage. Correct and accurate usage is the precondition in writing effectively. Let's look at a few examples:

(1) Short forms that are widely used and accepted in business practice

Ex-works (Delivery at the factory)

Ex-warehouse (Delivery at the warehouse)

F. O. T. (Free on truck)

F. O. B (Free on board)

F. A. S. (Free alongside ship)

C. I. F. (Cost, Insurance, and Freight)

(2) Special terms which are often misunderstood

A good example is "short delivery", which means that the delivered quantity of goods is less than that stipulated in the contract. It was once mistakenly misunderstood for "quick delivery".

Other business terms such as "Clean bill of lading", "All risks", and "With particular average", have specific meanings in international business practice. Incorrect usage and misunderstanding may result in disputes and loss.

New Words and Phrases

correspondence [ˌkɔriˈspɔndəns] *n.* 1) communication by the exchange of letters 通信联系
2) letters written or received 信件

transmit [trænzˈmit] *v.* send; convey 传送

Iron transmits heat. 铁传导热。

enhance [inˈhɑːns] *v.* to make greater in value, beauty, or reputation 提高;增进

Making dialogues in English can enhance students' practical application of English.

用英语做对话能增强学生的英语实际应用能力。

to enhance friendship 增进友谊

personnel [ˌpəːsəˈnel] *n.* (used with a pl. verb) persons employed by an organization, business, or service 全体员工;职员

golden [ˈgəuldən] *a.* 1) having the color of gold 金色的

golden crops 金色的庄稼

2) marked by peace and prosperity 兴隆的,昌盛的

a golden age 兴盛时期

3) of the greatest value or importance 绝好的,重要的

golden rules 重要规则

intercultural communication 跨文化交流

distract (from) *v.* to take (a person, a person's mind) off what he/she is doing 分散(注意力等),使分心

My attentions are distracted from my study. 我的注意力从学习中分散了。

free from 没有……的,免除……的,不受……拘束的

The advantage of the packing is that it keeps the goods free from dust.

这种包装的优点是它使商品不染灰尘。

He seems to be naturally free from flu. 他似乎天生不会得流感。

concise [kən'sais] *a.* clear and succinct 简明扼要的

respond [ri'spɔnd] *v.* reply 响应，答应，反应

Students responded by warm applause. 学生报以热烈的掌声。

ambiguous [ˌæm'bigjuəs] *a.* open to more than one interpretations 含糊的，模棱两可的

The meaning of this letter is ambiguous. 这封信的意思不清楚。

wordy ['wəːdi] *a.* using more words than necessary 话多的，唠叨的，冗长的

a wordy speaker 唠叨的讲话人

jargon ['dʒɑːgən] *n.* the specialized or technical language of a trade 行话

cliché ['kliːʃei;kliː'ʃei] *n.* a trite or overused expression 陈词滥调

eliminate [i'limineit] *v.* to get rid of;remove 除去，删除

to eliminate errors 消除错误

to eliminate the false and retain the true 去伪存真

irrelevant [i'reləvənt] *a.* unrelated to the matter at hand 不相关的

an irrelevant comment 毫不相关的评论

count [kaunt] *v.* 1) to recite numerals 计数

Let's count one two three. 我们来数1、2、3。

2) to have importance 有价值

Their opinions count for little. 他们的观点没有价值。

strand [strænd] *v.* 1) to drive or run ashore or aground 使搁浅

2) to be brought into or left in a difficult or helpless position 困住

I was stranded in the strange town without money or friends. 既无钱，也无朋友，我被困在了这个陌生的城镇。

persuasive [pə'sweisiv] *a.* having the power to persuade 有说服力，易使人信服的

a persuasive argument 令人信服的论点

a persuasive evidence 有说服力的证据

courteous ['kəːtiəs] *a.* characterized by gracious consideration toward others 有礼貌的，谦恭的

renovation [ˌrənəu'veiʃən] *n.* 革新

punctual ['pʌŋktjuəl] *a.* acting or arriving exactly at the time appointed 准时的，严守时间的，按期的

to be punctual for the class 准时上课

punctuality [ˌpʌŋktʃu'æləti] *n.* 准时；守时

stipulate ['stipjuleit] *v.* to lay down as a condition of an agreement 规定

The contract will stipulate a price and a date of payment. 合同将规定价格和付款日期。

appealing [ə'piːliŋ] *a.* having the power of attracting or of arousing interest 有感染力的，引人注意的

appealing scenes 引人注目的场景

refer to *v.* 1) to mention 提到

The contract refers to the means that deals with dispute. 合同中提到解决争议的方式。

2) to consult 参考;查资料

If you don't know the meaning of this word, refer to the dictionary. 如果你不知道这个词的意思,就查阅辞典。

3) to send to (sb.) for decision or action 交给(某人)做决定或采取行动

The seller referred the complaint to the carrier. 卖方把这项投诉交给承运方。

under way 在进行中

The project of subway is under way. 地铁正在修建之中。

Notes

1. **boil down to** 归结为

The lecture can be boiled down to the following points. 这个讲座可归纳为以下几点。

2. **voice mail** 语音留言

3. **teleconference** a conference held among people in different locations by means of telecommunication equipment, such as closed-circuit television 通过使用电信设备例如闭路电视而使位于不同地点的人召开的会议;电信会议

4. **Adopt a reader-focused *approach*** 采用以读者为中心的方式

approach 方式; 方法

e. g.: the right approach to dealing with such matters 处理这种事情的正确方法

5. **Your reader will respond quickly only if your meaning is *crystal clear*.**

crystal clear 易懂的,一清二楚的

6. **It means making every word count.** 那意味着每一个字都有价值。

7. **"Every cloud has a silver lining"** "黑暗中总有一线光明"

8. **When writing a business letter, the tone most *appealing to* your reader is a tone that is friendly but efficient...**

appeal to 有吸引力

e. g.: goods that not only *appeal to* the eye but also to the purse 物美价廉的商品

Good work *appeals to* everyone. 好的作品人人喜爱。

The idea never *appealed to* me very much. 这种想法从未引起我多大兴趣。

9. **have a (good) command of** 掌握

College students should have a command of English. 大学生应掌握英语。

Exercises

1. Answer the following questions.

1) What are the principles of writing a good business letter?

2) What is the direct approach to business letters? Under what circumstances would the writer be better use the direct approach? Give examples.

3) What is the appropriate tone in writing business letters?

4) Under what circumstances does one use passive voice and avoid using the subject "you"?

5) What is the trend of business letter writing in today's business world?

6) Why is it important to learn trade terms and business practices?

2. Choose the best answer to complete the following statements.

1) Writing letters clearly can be achieved by using ______ that can be easily understood.

A. detailed descriptions　　B. special terms

C. friendly tone　　D. familiar words and short sentences

2) Having a clear and definite purpose in mind when you write a letter means ______.

A. do not try to cover everything in your letter

B. narrow the scope and keep to the point

C. eliminate any unimportant and irrelevant points, sentences, phrases or words

D. all of the above

3) When writing a business letter, the tone most appealing to your reader is a tone that is ______.

A. friendly, natural and efficient　　B. formal but clear

C. impersonal and in written style　　D. humorous

4) When you expect your readers will be ______ with the message, you use indirect approach.

A. uninterested　　B. interested　　C. hesitant　　D. cheerful

5) Use passive voice and avoid using the subject "you" when ______.

A. you want to give an order to your reader

B. you want to make your reader feel guilty

C. you want to point out your reader's mistakes but don't want to make your reader feel embarrassed

D. you want to make your message more courteous and considerate

6) To be courteous when writing a letter you should ______.

A. respond as early as possible　　B. point out the mistakes your reader has made

C. use an indirect approach　　D. use correct language

7) Having a good command of English means ______.

A. using good sentences structure　　B. correct usage of English grammar

C. correct usage of spelling　　D. all of the above

8) Which of the following statements is incorrect?

A. Writing clearly is one of the golden rules in writing a letter.

B. Using a direct approach when writing a letter means starting a letter with facts and reasons followed by the main idea.

C. Use active voice in routine messages so that the sentences are easy to read.

D. Trade terms and abbreviations are sometimes used in writing business letters.

3. Decide whether the following statements are true or false. Write "T" for true, and "F" for false.

1) Clearness in writing letters can be achieved by using more words and giving more details. (　)

2) It is important to put your reader first because your reader is decisive of the efficiency of your message. (　　)

3) If your reader is a new customer with whom you have had no contact before, you may adopt an informal style to write your letter. (　　)

4) The trend in today's business world is that people prefer styles that are formal in writing their business letters. (　　)

5) In many countries such as the U. S. business letters are often written in a communication style that looks like face-to-face chat. (　　)

6) Avoid using "you" voice when the purpose of writing is to point out your reader's mistakes. (　　)

7) Use "you" or "your" instead of "we" and "our", or "I" and "my" because "you" attitude shows your warmth and concern to your reader, while "I" or "we" attitude creates an impression of selfishness. (　　)

8) "Short delivery" means that the goods should be delivered as quickly as possible. (　　)

4. Translate the following phrases into Chinese.

1) business communication

2) information exchanges

3) voice mail

4) reach a deal

5) a reader-focused approach

6) a face-to-face talk

5. Make sentences with the following phrases.

1) appeal to

2) refer to

3) boil down to

4) free from

6. Fill in the blanks with words and phrases given below. Change the form when necessary.

correspondence	enhance	respond	eliminate	irrelevant	count
persuasive	convenience	refer to	punctual		

1) The newspaper welcomes ______ from readers on any subject.

2) She has been reliable and ______ in meeting her appointment.

3) The police has ______ two suspects from their investigation.

4) The professor delivered excellent lecture with ______ arguments.

5) The government ______ by banning all the rallies.

6) My opinion never ______ because I am the youngest child in the family.

7) This is a golden chance to ______ the reputation of the company.

8) The police did not ______ any particular names, although they said they had already arrested somebody.

9) Your speech is ______ to the topic.

10) You will find it very ______ to pay by credit cards when you purchase some items.

7. Translate the following sentences into Chinese.

1) Business letters here broadly refer to the correspondence that is transmitted for business purposes.

2) Effectively written business letters can help you reach a deal, improve customer satisfaction, promote the sale of your products, keep a good impression of your company and enhance your work efficiency.

3) In writing business correspondence avoids using ambiguous words, wordy sentences, jargon and clichés that may be confusing and misunderstood.

4) Conciseness does not mean writing exclusively in short sentences or omitting necessary detail. It means making every word count.

5) When writing a business letter, the tone most appealing to your reader is a tone that is friendly but efficient, a tone that makes your reader feel there's someone at the other end of the message who is taking notice and showing interest in his/her concerns.

6) Good sentence structure and correct usage of English grammar, spelling and words in your letter can leave a good impression of you as well as your company on your reader. Moreover, it improves readability of your letter and avoids ambiguity.

8. Translate the following letter into Chinese.

Dear Mr. Wang:

Thank you for your generous hospitality during our recent visit to Beijing. It added significantly to the pleasure of our visit.

My associates and I deeply appreciate the assistance which CBS Publishing Company accords The Foundation for Books to China. Obviously, the success of our labors depends upon our books reaching those who can use them. Hence, your labors are indispensable to our endeavors.

Beyond the pleasure of participating in a worthy endeavor, one of the great rewards of our Foundation is the friends that we make both far and near. We are delighted to include you in the ranks of our honored friends. We look forward to not only working with you over the years ahead, but also enjoying the pleasure of your companionship from time to time. I hope that we shall see you soon in California.

Sincerely,

Mark Johnson

9. Revise the following sentences for better effect.

1) If you fail to hand in your application in time you will not be considered as a candidate.

2) In order for us to handle your case properly, please give us all the relevant information.

3) We request that you fill in the form provided in our questionnaire.

4) We insist that you bring your résumé when you come for an interview.

5) We will be happy to provide you 10% discount if you make payment within a week.

6) We have biweekly direct cargo services sailing from Shanghai to San Francisco.

7) I can assure you that I'm the right person for the job with my excellent school record and one-year work experience in this field.

8) We offer only a small percentage of discounts as the goods are sold very quickly.

9) The schedule for the meeting has been put off till next week.

10) The rules and regulations must be observed by both parties.

11) You shouldn't load this kind of goods on deck.

12) You must not leave the office without shutting the windows properly.

13) It is impossible to fill your order this month.

14) You should have realized that wool sweaters cannot be washed in hot water.

15) Your machine cannot be repaired today.

10. Rewrite the following letter for clarity, conciseness and correctness.

Dear Mr. Fllini:

It was so good to meet you when you came here last month. I enjoy the chat with you very much. I hope that you had a safe journey back to Italy. I am sorry that I have not written to you before now but I have been rather ill and I have only just returned to the office.

I have now had a chance to think about the problem of low sales of Massari tractors. I feel that the biggest problem is price. At present, most of the business in India goes to Japanese manufacturers, who not only produce a high quality product, but who are much cheaper than Massari. However, Massari has a very good name and I am sure that a drop in price of 8% would be enough to attract many new sales. Would Massari be prepared to lower its prices by this much?

A second problem is publicity. Many landowners and farmers here do not know about the new Massari tractors. Our competitors often put large advertisements in agricultural magazines, which have fancy pictures that attract many readers and customers. Unfortunately, our low sales mean that we are unable to pay for any publicity. If Massari could pay for advertising, we would be prepared to arrange it.

These are some of our ideas. What is your idea? I look forward to hearing your opinions.

Yours sincerely,

Sujit Singh

Lesson Two

Selection of Media

1. Introduction

Market globalization requires business partners, buyers and sellers in international trade to work more closely and communicate more frequently. But they are usually located in different parts of the world, information exchanges between them often have to transcend national borders and time zones. Fortunately, advanced technology provides people with more medium selection to send and receive information quickly and conveniently over long distances. But it does not mean you may use whatever medium that comes handy. A good choice of the media will enhance communication efficiency.

Effective communication, which is more and more emphasized in today's business competition, includes choosing the medium that best adapts to the reader's needs and expectations while reaching the message sender's purpose with the lowest possible cost. A comparison of the most widely used media will give you a better idea in choosing the most efficient medium.

2. Communication media

(1) Letter

Letters here refer to those delivered by post office, are regarded as the most formal way of communication. They are also much more protective of the communicator's privacy, therefore, they are the best option for messages that are formal, private, and confidential, but do not need much feedback and are not very urgent. It's often used for sending letters of invitation, thanks, congratulations as well as documents that must be original, such as a contract. But letters take longer time and cost more money especially if they are heavy.

(2) Memo

Memo is the short form of memorandum, which is commonly used for interoffice communication such as company announcements, routine operating procedures and other informal documents. The communicators are usually company insiders and business partners known to each other, so the style can be less formal than letters.

Memos may be delivered by hand or by post office, or by e-mail.

(3) Fax

A fax is transmitted over a fax machine — a telecopy machine that creates a fax (a "hard copy" of a message) sent over phone lines. It can overcome the barrier of different time zones and can be easily kept in a file. The unique characteristic of a fax is that it can transmit the original message. It is, therefore, a convenient way to send messages that are handwritten or contain diagrams, tables and graphics or pictures. The drawback is that it lacks the privacy of a letter, and the quality can hardly be assured — the words may not be as clear as the original message and the pictures may be blurred.

In addition, you may send a letter, a memo or any paper document (such as an invoice, a draft contract) over fax machines.

(4) E-mail

E-mail is now the most widely and frequently used communication channel in the business community for it offers high speed, low cost and convenient access to both working staff inside a company and business counterparts outside the company without the restriction of office hours. It not only overcomes time-zone problems but also saves time in forwarding or distributing messages. It is especially effective to exchange messages that are time sensitive.

The style of e-mail messages can be quite flexible ranging from formal letters to informal memos and notes depending on the situation and the reader.

Installed with a special Microsoft program, e-mails can also be sent to the receiver's fax machine.

Since e-mail encourages greater collaboration and it has the advantage of nearly spontaneous response, it is often used for on-line discussion. In e-mail discussions, abbreviations are frequently used to save time and keystrokes, and smiley (symbols of facial expression) used to convey emotions. Nowadays more and more abbreviations are coined up for e-mail communication. However, for the consideration of your reader's understanding, it is advisable to use them sparingly, especially in important and formal messages. But it is necessary to understand as much as possible the frequently used abbreviations and smiley.

Though this medium is very convenient, it has its disadvantage. Security is low with e-mail communication. Never write an e-mail for highly confidential messages.

(5) Website

Website is the major support for today's flourishing e-commerce that links up suppliers and purchasers and allows them to share updated resources. The internet-based website has become an indispensable aid to business. It functions for many purposes covering desk research, information exchange, as well as shopping, banking, and even effecting payment.

The website's function of information supply and exchange is highly interactive and user-driven, web writers or composers should keep users' needs, preferences, and reading habits as the first priority.

A website can include photos, graphics and texts giving detailed information about companies, businesses, and product specifications, quantity, pricing, services, etc. But messages carried in a website are not given to a specific person. It is created on the cyberspace for the public and target readers. By breaking up, formatting, and sequencing the text passages into manageable chunks for online presentation, a website can tailor the information to different readers around the globe and provide methods for interactive communication through certain windows, or menus or e-mails in the website which allow readers to input their information. Meanwhile the hyperlinks also allow different and geographically dispersed readers to have maximum control as to what information they need and skip whatever they do not need. Readers can also download and print information and documents supplied in the website.

A website most facilitates readers' feedback, but it has little guarantee for privacy and is vulnerable to information loss in case of technical problems and infection of computer viruse.

(6) Telephone

Telephone is a convenient and fast oral medium. But it is often restricted to office hours, and it can be expensive for long-distance calls. Communicating over the phone, your attitude, emotion, confidence, and professionalism are conveyed by your voice, tone and way of speaking.

(7) Voice mail

Voice mail has become very common especially in developed countries because of their comparatively scarce and costly labor resources. As a matter of fact, some companies use voice mail for short memos and interoffice communication to save labor and paper work. Therefore you have to be prepared to leave a voice mail when you intend to make a phone call, as the receiver may not be available and may be replaced by a device to record your voice message.

(8) Teleconference

Teleconference allows several people at different places to communicate on line at the same time. They can talk with one another on a given topic. For instance, they can discuss the feasibility of a new proposal, and make decisions through consultation. In this way, they save the high cost (both in money expense and time) of traveling, and they work more efficiently.

(9) Videoconference

Videoconference uses multimedia operation which combines audio, video services with relevant graphic messages. It is more advanced than teleconference. People participate in a videoconference can not only hear each other's voice, but also see each other's facial expressions, written messages and graphics, which helps them to understand each other better. But the facilities are more expensive.

(10) Mobile phone

Mobile phone (or cell phone) is another convenient medium for business communication. It is used not only for making phone calls but also for sending text messages that are informal and short.

(11) Online dialogue program

The advance of Information Technology (IT) provides business people with more channels for online dialogue. Just take Microsoft Network (MSN) as an example, it allows people to initiate real-time multimedia interaction for either B-to-B or B-to-C communication. It can even integrate voice, data and video in transmitting message and exchanging information around the cyberspace through the internet.

3. Communication etiquette

(1) E-mail communication etiquette

E-mail is widely and cheaply available, but with overuse, it will cause information overload and result in "junk mail" being sent to a large number of people. Remember, there are people who get hundreds of e-mail messages a day, and they cannot possibly read them all. To avoid embarrassment and improve communication efficiency, follow the e-mail etiquette.

◇ Limit your purpose to sharing work-related information. Avoid personal message at work.

◇ Don't abuse the convenience of e-mail by sending unnecessary messages.

◇ Work offline to conserve network resources and cut the costs of internet connection charges.

◇ Know who your audience is, and who need the message you send.

◇ Double-check addressees to include everyone necessary.

◇ Know your audience culture before you begin composing.

◇ Use 24-hour time in international e-mail (18:00 rather than 6:00 p. m.), and indicate the appropriate time zone.

◇ Don't use the high priority feature, unless your message is truly urgent.

◇ Avoid sending work-related e-mail during holiday season unless it is very urgent.

◇ Use appropriate filters to screen out unimportant messages.

◇ Read e-mail in last-in, first out order: the last e-mail may summarize all previous issues.

(2) Telephone communication etiquette

For effective telephone conversation observe the following tips:

When making phone calls

◇ Be clear of your purpose, and get to the point of the call.

◇ Schedule the time of call in consideration of the time zone your receiver is in.

◇ Avoid distraction and interference, such as background noise. Call from a quiet location.

◇ Greet the person you are calling, and briefly introduce yourself, including your name, your organization, why you are calling, and ask, "Is this a good time to talk briefly or should I call you back?"

◇ Double check vital information to confirm you both agree on it.

◇ Close in a friendly, positive manner and thank the receiver for his/her time.

When receiving calls

◇ Answer promptly, and smile so as to sound friendly and positive.

◇ Identify yourself by announcing your own name, the company name, or the department.

◇ Focus on your caller's needs by asking "How may I help you?" If you know the caller's name, use it. Don't interrupt with pointless questions.

◇ Answer the caller's question promptly. If you can't, tell them what you can do for them.

◇ Repeat to confirm you have got complete and accurate information, such as the name, phone number, fax number, e-mail address or dates.

◇ Explain what you are doing if you have to put your caller on hold briefly or transfer the call. If you need more time, offer to call back.

Whether you make a call or answer a call always keep pen and paper at your finger tip to take notes.

(3) Voice mail communication etiquette

Just as important as how you communicate over the telephone is how you communicate using the voice mail. To leave an effective voice mail, try to do the following:

◇ Organize your thoughts and have a clear purpose. Make sure your main points are covered in the message. For instance, your name, phone number, main purpose, the time in which you are available.

◇ Avoid background noise. Prevent any bad connection or service interruption.

◇ Be brief and make your message simple. The time for recording is very short, usually no more than one minute.

◇ Be accurate. Make sure the data, time or date is correct. If speaking internationally, give your city and country code. Repeat the number when necessary.

◇ Keep your message current. Give the time at which you are calling.

◇ Respond promptly. Check your voice mail messages regularly and return all the necessary calls within 24 hours.

◇ Limit menu selections. When setting up the options of your telephone's answering recording, limit them to less than five, and always include one that reaches a live operator.

(4) Website communication etiquette

Presumably you created a website because you have something you want to share. To share it successfully, prevent some of the common website mistakes and build up a user-friendly website. Here's a guide to doing it.

◇ Don't distract your visitors with too much blinking text, scrolling text, animated GIF. Visitors may resent that you waste their time by forcing them to load animations and sound files against their will.

◇ Don't annoy your visitors with pop-up windows. They waste time and space.

◇ Avoid clutter. Don't stuff message on your page in a haphazard fashion, forcing visitors to pick out content like a jigsaw puzzle.

◇ Compress your image files. Graphics software can compress files, so they take up less space on your disk, and therefore take less time to load into your visitors' browsers. Get some graphics software and shrink those file sizes.

4. Considerations in media selection

The development of IT industry provides business people with more freedom in media selection. To make a wise choice, bear in mind the essential business communication etiquette in order to communicate effectively and internationally. From the communication media introduced above we can see that each of them has its advantages and limitations. Therefore, it's necessary for you to consider the following factors in choosing an appropriate medium:

◇ Formality

◇ Confidentiality

◇ Feedback

◇ Urgency

◇ Cost

◇ Reader's expectation

◇ Need for permanent record

If the message is to be formal, choose a letter rather than a fax, a memo rather than an e-mail.

If the message is confidential, send it by letter rather than memo or fax. If the message is short and simple, voice mail can be a good option.

If you need immediate feedback on something urgent and the addressee is geographically separated from you, the best medium can be e-mail, which provides high speed at low cost for sending messages over long distance and across time zones.

If you send a contract for your business counterpart to sign, send it in a letter or by express mail would be an expected or preferred medium from the recipient's perspective.

Although there is no hard rule as to which medium to use in each case, a wise choice of the most appropriate channel based on the above considerations is always advisable for effective communication.

Abbreviation for Internet Communication

2L8 too late	AFAIK as far as I know
AKA also known as	ASAP as soon as possible
BAK back at keyboard	BBL be back late
BCNU be seeing you	B4N bye for now
BRB be right back	BTW by the way
F2F face to face	FWIW for what it's worth
FYA for your amusement	FYI for your information
GFY good for you	GGBB gotta go bye bye
GL good luck	GMTA great minds think alike
G2G got to go	GTGB got to go bye
IDK I don't know	IM instant message
IMHO in my humble opinion	IMO in my opinion
INALB I'm not a lawyer but...	IOW in other words
IRL in real life	ITS I told you so
KIT keep in touch	LOL laughing out loud
LTL lets talk later	LTNC long time no chat

续表

LTNS long time no see	LU looking up
MAYB maybe	NM nothing much
NP no problem	NRN no reply necessary
NYO need your opinion	PLS please
PMFJI pardon me for jumping in	POV point of view
TIA thanks in advance	TMI too much info
TTYL talk to you later	TTYS talk to you soon
TU thank you	TX thanks
TY thank you	TYVM thank you very much
U you	U2 you too
UW you wish	WB welcome back

Smiley for Internet Communication

: -) smiley face	: -)) laugh
; -) wink (light sarcasm)	: - | indifference
8 -) big-eyed smiley	: - D shock or surprise
: - / perplexed	: - (sad
: - C real unhappy	: - P wry smile
; - } leer	; - (crying
: - e disappointment	: - @ scream
: - O yell	: - & tongue tied

New Words and Phrases

transcend [træn'send] *v.* to pass beyond the limits of 超越

emotions that transcend understanding 无法理解的情感

adapt (to) [ə'dæpt] *v.* to make suitable to or fit for 适合

a species that has adapted well to winter climes 很适应冬天气候的物种

confidential [kɔnfi'denʃəl] *a.* done or communicated in confidence; secret 秘密的，机密的

feedback ['fiːdbæk] *n.* information about certain actions, passed back to the person in charge, so that changes can be made if necessary 反馈，反应

The company welcomes feedbacks from people who use the goods it produces.

这家公司欢迎用户的反馈。

coin [kɔin] *v.* to invent (a word or phrase) 造(词或短语)

sparing [ˈspɛəriŋ] *a.* using little 少用的

sparingly *adv.* 有节制地;有限地

memo [ˈmeməu] *n.* memorandum 备忘录

interoffice [ˌintəˈrɔːfis] *a.* taking place between offices 各办公室之间的

an interoffice memo 各办公室间的备忘录

interoffice conferences 办公室会议

recipient [riˈsipiənt] *n.* one that receives 接受者

characteristic [ˌkæriktəˈristik] *n.* feature or trait 特性,特征

graphic [ˈgræfik] *a.* relating to or represented by a graph 用图表示的

drawback [ˈdrɔːbæk] *n.* shortcoming or flaw 缺点,缺陷

counterpart [ˈkauntəpɑːt] *n.* a person or thing that serves the same purpose or has the same position as another 相对物,对方

attachment [əˈtætʃmənt] *n.* a supplementary part; an accessory 附属物,附加装置

install [inˈstɔːl] *v.* to set in position and connect or adjust for use 安装

burden [ˈbəːdn] *n.* a source of great worry or stress 负担

flourishing [ˈflʌriʃiŋ] *a.* booming or thriving 繁茂的,繁荣的

link up associate with 和……联系在一起

indispensable [ˌindiˈspensəbl] *a.* not to be dispensed with, essential 不可缺少的;绝对必要的

cyberspace *n.* 网络空间,信息空间

chunk [tʃʌŋk] *n.* a thick mass or piece 厚块,大片

tailor to to make, alter or adapt for a particular end or purpose 为某一特定目的或目标而制作、修改或调整

a speech that was tailored to an audience of business leaders 适合商业领域领导人听的演讲

input [ˈinput] *v.* put in 输入

hyperlink *n.* & *v.* 超级链接

disperse [diˈspəːs] *v.* to drive off or scatter in different directions 使散开,驱散

facilitate [fəˈsiliteit] *v.* to make easy or easier 使容易

etiquette [ˈetiket] *n.* the practices and forms prescribed by social convention or by authority 礼节

filter [ˈfiltə] *v.* to pass through or as if through a filter 过滤,透过,渗透

browser [brauzə(r)] *n.* 浏览器

Notes

1. **business counterparts** 指和某公司有业务往来的那些公司
2. **ranging from formal letters to informal memos and notes** 范围包括正式书信和非正式备忘录以及便条

range from... to...: to vary within specified limits 在某一特定的范围内变化

e. g.: The age of the consumer of this product ranged from twenty to fifty. 该产品的消费者的年龄在20岁至50岁之间。

3. It is especially effective to exchange messages that are time sensitive. 它(e-mail)对实效性要求很高的信息非常有效。

4. the web is a highly interactive and user-driven medium 互联网是高度互动式的、以用户为主的传媒方式

5. Read e-mail in last-in, first-out order. 先读最后收到的邮件,后读最初发送的邮件。

6. Nowadays more and more abbreviations are *coined* up for e-mail communication. 现在人们为电子邮件沟通创造了越来越多的缩写词。

coin 创造;杜撰(新词)

7. tip (*used with on*) a helpful piece of advice 窍门,诀窍

e. g.: tips on cooking 有关烹调的窍门

I gave her a tip on removing ink from clothing. 我教她一个去除衣服上墨迹的窍门。

8. Don't use the *high priority feature*, unless your message is truly urgent. 除非你的信件十分紧急,否则不要使用"急件"标志。

9. Use appropriate filters to *screen out* unimportant messages. 使用适当的"过滤器",滤掉不重要的信件。

screen out: to separate or sift out 筛去,过滤

10. no more than one minute 不到一分钟

no more than... 不超过;仅仅

e. g.: I stayed there for no more than two days. 我仅在那里停留了两天。

He had no more than two dollars left in his pocket. 他口袋里只剩下两美元。

11. Limit menu selections. When setting up the options of your telephone's answering recording, limit *them* to less than five, and always include one that reaches a live operator. 限制菜单的选项。设定电话留言录音时,选项不要超过5个,并且其中一定要有一个选项接通电话接线员。

句中"them"指前面提到的"menu selections"(菜单的选项)。

12. videoconference a teleconference conducted via closed-circuit television 视频会议;电视会议

13. real-time multimedia interaction 实时多媒体互动交流

14. either B-to-B or B-to-C communication 公司对公司或者公司对客户之间的沟通

B-to-B: business to business

B-to-C: business to customer

15. Don't distract your visitors with too much blinking text, scrolling text, animated *GIF*. 不要用太多闪烁的或需要展开的文字以及动画图片,它们会分散观众的注意力。

GIF 可交换的图像文件

16. pop-up 忽然弹出的

17. Don't just throw a bunch of stuff up on your page in a haphazard fashion 不要把所有的内容都杂乱无章地堆积到网页上

18. jigsaw puzzle 拼图游戏

Exercises

1. Answer the following questions.

1) What are advantages and disadvantages of the media introduced in this section?

2) What is the common use of memo in business world?

3) What are main characteristics of website?

4) What factors does one have to consider in choosing an appropriate medium?

2. Discussion.

1) With the large amount of e-mail sent today, how to make sure they are not overused or abused in business field.

2) Do you think e-mail abbreviations should be used in business communication? Why?

3) Can e-mail and website put the traditional postal service out of business someday? Give your reasons.

3. Decide whether the following statements are true or false. Write "T" for true and "F" for false.

1) Letters are the best option for messages that are formal, private, confidential and very urgent. (　　)

2) Memos are usually used by company outsiders, such as business partners. (　　)

3) Faxes have the same advantages as that of a letter, and the quality is always reliable. (　　)

4) The biggest advantage of e-mail for information exchanges is that it can overcome time-zone problems. (　　)

5) Web writers should keep their needs, preferences, and composing skills as the first priority. (　　)

6) Some companies use voice mail for short memos and interoffice communication to save time and paper work. (　　)

7) If the message is confidential, send it by fax rather than memo or letter. (　　)

8) When you use e-mail, you should extend your purpose to share work-related information and personal message at work. (　　)

4. Choose the best answer to complete the following statements.

1) When you use voice-mail, make sure your main points are covered in the message including ______, etc.

A. your name　　B. your main purpose　　C. your phone number　　D. all of above

2) If the message is short and simple, ______ can be a good option.

A. fax　　B. memo　　C. letter　　D. voice-mail

3) If you need immediate feedback on something urgent and the addressee is geographically sep-

arated from you, the best medium can be ______, which provides high speed at low cost.

A. phone B. website C. e-mail D. fax

4) Telephone is a widely used communication channel because it is ______.

A. a fast and convenient oral medium B. not limited to office hour

C. cheap D. to avoid distraction

5) A website can include ______.

A. photos B. graphics C. texts D. all of above

6) Messages carried in a website are given to ______.

A. any specific person B. the public and target readers

C. other companies D. other buyers

7) Don't use the high priority feature, unless your message is truly urgent.

The underlined part of the sentence means:

A. "privacy" mark B. "urgency" mark C. "confidential" mark D. "attention" mark

8) It is always necessary to have pen and paper at hand when ______.

A. sending an e-mail B. sending a fax

C. answering a phone call D. scanning a website

5. Translate the following sentences into English.

1) 如今,商务沟通正朝着电子化方向发展,并且这种趋势发展得很迅速。

2) 电子商务不仅改变着传统的沟通方式,而且改变着工作环境本身。

3) 有了电子沟通,一个经理人员就可以在办公室以外的任何地方通过计算机发出信息。第二天早上,他的老板或者下属上班时就会在他们的计算机上看到它。

4) 传真可以克服不同时间区域的障碍。它的独一无二的特点就是可以传递原始文件。

5) 网络电子商务可以通过提供有关产品说明、数量和价格的信息加强客户服务。

6) 电子邮件的好处之一是当有人讲了一些你不感兴趣的事情,而你又不想回答时,你可以拒绝回复电子邮件,这要比不回答电话更容易。

7) 业务经理决定安装一个信息过滤装置来对付每天收到的大量的垃圾电子邮件。

8) 我公司产品的大多数消费者都是年轻人,年龄在 15 至 25 岁之间。

6. Translate the following sentences into Chinese.

1) Market globalization requires business partners, buyers and sellers in international trade to work more closely and communicate more frequently. But they are usually located in different parts of the world, information exchanges between them often have to transcend national borders and time zones.

2) Fortunately, advanced technology provides people with more selection of media to send and receive information quickly and conveniently over long distance. But it does not mean you may use whatever medium as you like.

3) A good choice of the media is necessary to enhance communication efficiency.

4) The style of e-mail messages can be quite flexible ranging from formal letters to informal memos and notes depending on the situation and the reader.

5) By breaking up, formatting, and sequencing the text passages for online reading, a website

should tailor the information to different readers around the globe and provide interactive communication through certain windows, or menus or e-mails provided in the website which allows readers to input their information.

6) A website can include photos, graphics and texts giving detailed information about companies, businesses, and product specifications, quantity, pricing, services, etc. But messages carried in a website are not given to a specific person. It is created on the cyberspace for the public and target readers.

7) Meanwhile the hyperlinks also allow different and geographically dispersed readers to have maximum control as to what information they need and skip whatever they do not need. Readers can also download and print information or documents supplied in the website.

8) Gone forever are the days when people depended solely on lined telephone, on writing letters to each other, or on sending telegraphs in case of emergencies to communicate with each other.

7. Apply your knowledge in the following business communication.

1) If you send the following messages to the receiver which media are you going to use? (Choose one medium you have learned from this lesson.)

2) Explain why you choose the medium for the message, and what the advantages are.

a. Receiver: Mike Johnson

Time: 18:00, September 15, 2010

Message: Many thanks indeed for all your cooperation in the installation of the equipment. The project has been progressing well. We are now at the final stage. If everything goes smoothly, the plant will go into production early next year. I'm sending you the enclosed documents and pictures, which show the final result of the plant.

b. Receiver: Mary Higgins

Time: 14:00, October 10, 2010

Message: I'm really sorry to have to bother you but James Hugo, a really important client, is visiting the company for three days in October, starting on 14th, to discuss a contract with us. Will you please book for Mr. Hugo a nice hotel room as soon as possible. Thank you very much.

c. Receiver: Frank Larson

Time: 12:00, December 12, 2010

Message: It's 9:30 on Wednesday morning. I'm at a conference in Milan now. Would you please send me as soon as possible the sales report for the first three quarters of this year? I'll leave Milan for Tokyo this weekend, and I'll be back to the company next Monday. See you soon.

Lesson Three

The Parts and Formats of Business Correspondence (Ⅰ)

1. Introduction

Your business correspondence can tell readers a lot about you and your company. A letter that is neat, easy to read, and present a professional image will leave a good impression on your reader. Therefore, almost all business correspondence is neatly typed except some short informal messages such as informal memos or notes. In today's global market place, your reader's first impression often comes from the appearance of your documents and the quality of the paper.

The appearance of a business letter in a hardcopy is given by

Paper quality The quality of the paper is judged by its weight and cotton content. Never use paper that is too flimsy.

Paper color White is the standard color for business purposes, although light colors such as gray and ivory are sometimes used. Memos can be made in papers of different color to distinguish them from that used for outsiders. Never use bright and dark colored paper for it makes reading difficult.

Paper size The size of papers varies slightly from country to country. In the United States, the standard paper size for business documents is 8.5 by 11 inches. Executives sometimes have heavier 7-by-10 inch paper on hand (with matching envelopes) for personal messages such as congratulations and recommendations.

Margins The document is to be centered in the page, leaving at least one-inch margins all around. You can use word-processing software to achieve the balance by defining the format.

2. Structure of business letters

Business correspondence has its special formats. The following are the most common parts and formats.

(1) The basic parts of business letters

Letterhead For letters to outsiders, many companies use letterhead stationery which is professionally printed at the top of the page, though some are printed at the bottom or even at the upper-left corner of the page. The letterhead includes the company's name and address. Other information that may be included is telephone number, fax number, website address, product lines, date of establishment, slogan and logo.

If letterhead stationery is not available, you can type the heading, which includes a return address, and leaves about a two-inch top margin.

Date line If you use letterhead stationery, place the date one to three blank lines beneath the letterhead. If without letterhead, place the date immediately below the return address.

The standard order of typing the date in the U. S. is month, day, year. For example:

September 12, 2010

While in Britain, the standard order is day, month, year. For example:

12 September, 2010

The day can be written or typed in either cardinal numbers (1, 2, 3, 4, etc.) or in ordinal numbers (1st, 2nd, 3rd, 4th, etc.).

Never use the short form of the month (e. g. Jan., Feb., Sept), or give the date in figures (e. g. 12/09/2005), which may cause confusion because in the U. S. this date would mean December 9, 2005, while in Britain it means 12 September, 2005.

Inside address The inside address gives the name and address of the recipient. It starts at least one line below the date line and contains any or all of the following:

The name of the recipient

The department name

Company name

Suite or room number

Street address

Post office box number

The name of the city and the country

If the receiver of the letter is in the U. S. the address also includes the name of the state which must be typed in capitalized two letter abbreviation followed by ZIP code. The same way is also used for the provinces and territories in Canadian address.

Precede the addressee's name with a courtesy title (such as Mr., Ms. or Dr.). If you do not know whether a person is a man or a woman, and you have no way to find out, omit the courtesy title and give the full name.

The person's job title can be placed on the same line of the person's name, or on the line below. Try to square the address as much as possible. If the title appears on the same line, place a comma between the name and the title. If it appears on the next line dispense with the comma.

Mr. Dick Eaton, President

Ms. Patricia T. Higgins Assistant Vice President

If the name of a specific person is unavailable, you may address the letter to the department, followed by the name of the company.

Customer Service Department Acme Construction Company

Director of Personnel International Trading Co. Ltd.

In order to avoid ambiguity, when you write letters to other countries, always include the name of the country, even if the city mentioned is the country's capital.

The following examples show all the information that may be included in the inside address.

> Dr. H. C. Armstrong
> Research and Development
> Commonwealth Mining Consortium
> The Shelton Building, Suite 391
> 353 Second St. SW
> Calgary, AB T2P
> Canada

> Mr. Thom Collins, President
> 164 Bay Road
> Liquorland
> Oklahoma City, OK 73125
> U. S. A.

Salutation The salutation is a polite greeting to the reader. Place it two lines below the inside address. The salutation should correspond to the first line of the inside address, that is, if the first line of your inside address is a name of a person, the salutation is "Dear + the name". The formality of the salutation depends on your relationship with the addressee. If in conversation you would say "Mary", the salutation in your letter should be "Dear Mary", otherwise, include a courtesy title and last name as "Dear Ms. Mary Jones". End the salutation with a colon, or a comma.

If the addressee is unknown, use "Dear Sirs", or "gentlemen". (Note that "Sirs" cannot be used alone without "Dear" and "gentlemen" cannot be used in singular form.), or "Dear Madam or Sir". If the addressee is a group, use "Ladies and Gentlemen". Or you may use a polite description, such as "Dear Friends", "Dear SPA supporters".

Body The body is the main part that conveys your message. It is generally single spaced with double space between paragraphs. There is no strict rule regarding the content of the letter, but it usually includes three parts:

1) The opening paragraph refers to any previous correspondence or introduces the purpose of the letter.

> I'm writing in reply to your letter of 16 January, in which you inquired about our KILL'EM fly spray.

2) The middle paragraph(s) supports the opening and/or provides additional information.

> Unfortunately, we have stopped producing this fly spray due to the fact that sales were rather disappointing. However, we are able to supply you with a maximum of 20 boxes from our stocks. If you would like to order these, please inform us before the end of the week.

3) The closing paragraph is short and serves as a request, suggestion, or look to the future.

I look forward to your reply.

Complimentary Close The complimentary close is a polite way to bring a letter to a close. It appears two lines below the last line of the body. Capitalize the first word and end with a comma.

The expression must match the salutation reflecting the relationship between the sender and the receiver of the letter. The most common complementary closings are:

Formal: "Yours truly," "Very truly yours," "Yours very truly," "Respectfully," "Respectfully yours," "Yours faithfully," (Used in Britain, but not used in the U. S.)

Informal: "Sincerely," "Sincerely yours," "Cordially," "Cordially yours,"

Personal: "Best wishes," "As always," "Regards," "Kindest regards," "Best regards,"

Signature The signature is the signing of the message sender's name. Type the name under the complimentary closing, leaving enough blank lines to sign your name. Never "sign" with a seal or stamp.

Sincerely yours, (*signature*) Harry Smith

You letterhead indicates that you are representing your company. However, if your letter is on plain paper and you want to emphasize that you are speaking legally for the company, you may type the company's name in capital letters below the complementary closing and place the title of the message sender on the same line with or below the typed name.

Very truly yours, ALVERS, INC. (*signature*) Harry Smith, Project Manager

(2) Additional Parts of Business Letters

Mailing or In-house Notation Letters that have a restricted readership or that must be handled in a special way should include mailing notations (e. g. "special delivery", "airmail", "registered mail", "certified mail") or in-house notations (e. g. "personal", "confidential"). Type them two lines below the date and in all capital letters.

CONFIDENTIAL

Reference Number Type the reference number below the letterhead in short form as "Our ref.:" for the sender's reference number, and "Your ref.:" for the recipient's. The purpose of this is to facilitate filing of the letter and link it with previous correspondence.

Subject Line The subject line tells recipients at a glance what the letter is about (and indicates where to file the letter for future reference). It is usually two lines below the salutation, forming part of the body. Some companies omit the word "Subject:", some replace it with "Re:" or "re:" (meaning "regarding"), and some underline the subject line. The following forms are commonly used:

SUBJECT: SALES CONTRACT NO. 2346 FOR 200MT OF SOYBEAN OIL

Subject: Sales Contract No. 2346 for 200 Metric Tons of Soybean Oil

Re: Sales Contract No. 2346 for 200 Metric Tons of Soybean Oil

SALES CONTRACT NO. 2346 FOR 200MT OF SOYBEAN OIL

Multiple-Page Letter Heading When typing a multiple-page letter, use letterhead for the first page. The following page or pages should have the same quality, size and color as the first page. The multiple-page heading bears the name of the recipient or his/her organization, the page number, and the date. The following styles are often used for multiple-page letters:

Ms. Katherine Black	Page 2	October 6, 2010

Ms. Katherine Black	-2-	October 6, 2010

Ms. Katherine Black Page 2 October 6, 2010

Reference Initials Use reference initials to identify the author of the letter and the typist.

Place initials at the left margin, a double space below the signature. When you type your own letter, don't use initials. When the signature block includes the writer's name, use only the typist's initials. Reference initials are usually given in the form of "author's initials/typist initials", or "author's initials: typist initials".

RS/sm

RS:sm

RS:SM

Enclosure Notation When you enclose anything in the envelope besides the letter, place an enclosure notation on the line below the reference initials. You can use any of the following styles:

Enclosure

Enc.

Enclosure: 1. Purchase Order No. 5657 2. Check No. 567

Copy Notation When you send a copy of the letter to a third person, place a notation directly below the enclosure notation or reference initials. The copy notation is indicated with "CC", or "cc" which is a holdover from the days of carbon copies. Many companies are now using "PC" (for photocopy).

PC: Margaret Ruth

CC: Margaret Ruth

cc: Margaret Ruth

Postscript Formal business letters seldom use "postscript" because it can appear as afterthoughts, indicating a lack of planning.

But studies show that postscripts are one of the first things people read and remember, especially when it is handwritten. It sometimes serves the purposes as a message that requires emphasis, or as a personal note.

When you use a postscript, place it two lines below your last notation. It may be preceded by "P. S.", but this is not strictly necessary.

Look at the following example to see where the different parts go in a business letter.

P. S. : You get 3% discount if you book the space within this month.

3. Format of business letters

The following are the most commonly used and accepted letter formats.

(1) Full Block Format

LETTERHEAD

Date

Addressee
Inside Address

Salutation:

Re: Full Block Format

This easy-to-type letter is becoming more and more popular and is widely used in many of today's modern offices.

It is a very efficient style because everything begins at the left margins, thereby eliminating the need for tabs.

But critics say it looks somewhat crowded and imbalanced.

Very truly yours,
(Signature)
Typed name

(2) Modified Block Format

LETTERHEAD

Date

Addressee
Inside Address

Salutation:

Re: Modified Block Format

Modified block style has traditionally been the most commonly used of all letter styles.

The most notable difference between this style and the full block is that the date and complimentary closing start at the center, or slightly to the right of center.

This letter style is appealing to the eye and is very popular.

Very truly yours,
(Signature)
Typed name

(3) Semi-block Format

LETTERHEAD

Date

Addressee
Inside Address

Salutation:

Re: Semi-block Format

The distinguishing features of this letter format are that the subject line is indented and all paragraphs are indented too.

It is important to remember that two tabs must be set: one for the date and complimentary closing and one for the indentation of the subject line and paragraphs.

This format may use more time to type than the previous two.

Very truly yours,
(Signature)
Typed name

4. Example letters

(1) A letter with the basic parts (Full block format)

12th June, 2010

Mrs. Lorry Mason
National Geographic Society
475 Kenwood St.
Duluth, MN55811
U. S. A.

Dear Mrs. Mason,
Thank you for your letter of 12 January, concerning your forthcoming visit to my company. I'll be glad to meet you at the time of your visit. Please confirm your flight number, so that my assistant, Helen Wei will be seeing you at the airport.

I look forward to seeing you.

Yours sincerely,
(Signature)
Jenny Chen

(2) A letter with basic parts and additional parts (semi-block format)

≡≡≡≡≡≡≡≡ ***TIANJIN TRADE FAIRS*** ≡≡≡≡≡≡≡≡

No. 56, Nanjing Rd., Tianjin 300045, China

Tel.: 86-22-23665783 Fax: 86-22-23665785

Our ref.: TF001

Your ref.:

November 20, 2010

CERTIFIED MAIL

Ms. Dawn Roberts

General Manager

Asian Food-Processing Equipment Co. Ltd.

100 King's Road

Hanoi, Vietnam

RE: THE THIRD TIANJIN AGRICULTURAL EQUIPMENT FAIR

Dear Ms. Roberts:

The Tianjin Agricultural Equipment Fair will take place from 4th to 12th April, 2010. This fair is an opportunity for both manufacturers and buyers from all over the world to seek business opportunities.

We are now accepting provisional bookings of space. Each year we receive more bookings than we can accommodate. So we advise you to book early if you want to take part in the fair. For representatives from overseas, we are able to arrange visas. (Please supply full passport details.)

Your company would find it worthwhile to have a stand at the fair. Price of the floor space is US $150 per sq. m. (min. $15M^2$) and payments should be made to a/c 2680805346, Bank of China, Tianjin Branch.

Should you require any further information, please contact us.

Yours faithfully,
TIANJIN TRADE FAIR
(Signature)
Anna Chen, Manager

ml
Enclosure: 10 free VIP tickets to the fair
cc: Eric Long, General Manager

P. S.: You get 3% discount if you book the space within this month.

5. Format of envelopes

The envelope should match the stationery in color and style. Most companies have the return address printed in the upper-left corner of the envelope, giving the same information as the letter-head. Otherwise you must type or write your return address the same way as your do for the inside address, usually in smaller typeface than the name and the address of the receiver. Name and address of the receiver is always single-spaced with all lines aligned on the left, and they should be in all capital letter, with no punctuation at the end of each line. The order in writing the address is from the smallest division to the largest, just opposite to the Chinese custom in writing addresses.

The in-house notation is placed three lines down the return address and is in all capital letters (as shown in example 3).

The stamp is put at the upper right corner of the envelope with mailing notation, if there are any, given in all capital letters below the stamp.

The format of the address on the envelope can be in blocked or indented style, but it is better to keep the same format with the inside address of the letter.

Example 3. Envelope (Block style)

Skyline Farm Machinery Manufacturing Company
56 Fuan Street, Tianjin, China
Tel. :0086 - 22 - 2336 5566

Stamp

REGISTERED

PERSONAL

MS. DAWN ROBERTS
ASIAN FOOD-PROCESSING CO. LTD.
100 KING'S RD
HANOI, VIETNAM

BY AIR

Example 4. Envelope (Indented style)

Linda Smith
12 King's Avenue
RECHMNOND
Surrey TW6 ISJ
Britain

Stamp

MR. GARRY MARSHALL
6345 GLENWOOD DRIVE
ALBUQUERQUE, NM 87001
U. S. A.

PERSONAL

PAR AVION

Example 5. Envelope (Mixed style)

Jack Sill
Central Business Consultants
Hyde Towers
Hong Kong

Stamp

Dr. Dawei Zhang
No. 305 Jinhui Building
Nanjing Rd. Heping Ward
Tianjin, China

Two-Letter Abbreviation of the USA States and Canada's Provinces and Territories

States of the USA

AL	Alabama	MT	Montana
AK	Alaska	NE	Nebraska
AZ	Arizona	NV	Nevada
AR	Arkansas	NH	New Hampshire
CA	California	NJ	New Jersey
CO	Colorado	NM	New Mexico
CT	Connecticut	NY	New York
DE	Delaware	NC	North Carolina
DC	District of Columbia	ND	North Dakota
FL	Florida	OH	Ohio
GA	Georgia	OK	Oklahoma
HI	Hawaii	OR	Oregon
ID	Idaho	PA	Pennsylvania
IL	Illinois	RI	Rhode Island
IN	Indiana	SC	South Carolina
IA	Iowa	SD	South Dakota
KS	Kansas	TN	Tennessee
KY	Kentucky	TX	Texas
LA	Louisiana	UT	Utah
ME	Maine	VT	Vermont
MD	Maryland	VA	Virginia
MA	Massachusetts	WA	Washington
MI	Michigan	WV	West Virginia
MN	Minnesota	WI	Wisconsin
MS	Mississippi	MO	Missouri
WY	Wyoming		

Provinces/Territories of Canada

AB	Alberta	NS	Nova Scotia
BC	British Columbia	ON	Ontario
MB	Manitoba	PE	Prince Edward Island
NB	New Brunswick	PQ	Quebec
NL	Newfoundland/Labrador	SK	Saskatchewan
NT	Northwest Territories	YT	Yukon Territory

New Words and Phrases

flimsy ['flimzi] *a.* lacking solidity or strength 易坏的；脆弱的

ivory ['aivəri] *n.* a pale or grayish yellow to yellowish white 象牙色

letterhead ['letəhed] *n.* the heading at the top of a sheet of letter paper, usually consisting of a name and an address 信头

margin [mɑːdʒin] *n.* the blank space bordering the written or printed area on a page 页边的空白

slogan ['sləugən] *n.* a phrase expressing the aims or nature of an enterprise or an organization; a motto 口号；标语

logo ['lɔgəu] *n.* symbol, or trademark designed for easy recognition 标志

recipient [ri'sipiənt] *n.* one that receives 接收者

precede [ˌpriː'siːd] *v.* to come, exist, or occur before in time 领先(于)；在……之前；先于

ambiguity [ˌæmbi'gjuːiti] *n.* doubtfulness; uncertainty 含糊；不明确

salutation [sælju:'teiʃən] *n.* a polite expression of greeting or goodwill 问候语

formality [fɔː'mæləti] *n.* an established form, rule, or custom, for the sake of procedure or decorum 礼节

notation [nəu'teiʃən] *n.* a brief note; an annotation 符号

holdover ['həuldˌəuvə(r)] *n.* one that is held over after an expired term of office 沿用

postscript ['pəustskript] *n.* a message appended at the end of a letter after the writer's signature 附言；后记

typeface ['taipfeis] *n.* the size or style of the letter or character 字体

dispense (**with**) [dis'pens] *v.* 1) to do without 省去

Machinery dispenses with much labor. 机器节省了大量劳力。

2) make unnecessary 不需；没有也行

This new office machine dispenses with the need for a secretary.

办公室有了这台新机器就不需要秘书了。

Notes

1. **hard copy**: a copy typed or written in paper (to distinguish from "electronic copy")
2. **cardinal numbers** 基数
3. **ordinal numbers** 序数
4. **in-house** 内部的
5. **body** (信件的)主体部分
6. **complementary closing** 结束祝词
7. **reference initial** (信件撰写人和/或打印人的)姓名首写字母
8. **block format** (or block style) 齐头格式
9. **indented format** (or indented style) 缩进格式
10. ***Memos* can be made in papers of different color to *distinguish* them *from* that used for**

outsiders. 为了与写给公司外部的便笺有所区别,备忘录可以用不同颜色的纸写。

memo (用于公司内部的)备忘录

to distinguish... from... 区分

e. g. : to distinguish right from wrong 区分正确与错误

11. personal messages such as congratulations and recommendations 诸如祝贺信和推荐信之类的个人信件

12. Try to square the address as much as possible. 尽量使地址两边对齐,组成一个方块。

13. If it appears on the next line *dispense with* the comma. 如果出现在下一行,省略逗号。

dispense with: to do without 省去,放弃

e. g. : We'll have to dispense with the luggage; we can't carry it. 我们必须放弃行李,我们无法拿了。

14. Name and address of the receiver is always single-spaced with all lines aligned on the left, and they should be in all capital letter, with no punctuation at the end of each line. 收信人的名字和地址需与左边边线对齐,单行间距,大写,且句尾无须点标点。

15. The copy notation is indicated with "CC", "Cc" or "cc" which is a holdover from the days of carbon copies. 抄送用"CC""Cc"或"cc"表示,它是过去使用的"carbon copy"的缩写,而现在我们依然沿用这种表示方法。

16. carbon copy 副本

17. provisional bookings 临时预订

18. a/c: (abbreviation for) account 账户

Exercises

1. Answer the following questions.

1) How can you improve the appearance of your business correspondence?

2) What are the differences between formal letters and informal letters? Give some examples for both?

3) How many points should be taken into consideration in order to write a formal business correspondence? And what are they?

4) Should a postscript be attached to a business correspondence? Why?

2. Choose the best answer to complete the following statements.

1) A letterhead includes ______.

A. name of the company B. address of the company

C. contact information D. all of the above

2) Most of the letterhead stationery is professionally printed with the letterhead at ______ of the page for letters to outsider.

A. the upper-left corner B. the bottom

C. the top D. the upper-right corner

3) The inside address contains all of the following information, except ______.

A. the date of typing of the message B. company name

C. the name of the city and the country D. the name of the state

4) The body of a letter usually includes the following parts, except ______.

A. the purpose of the letter

B. complementary closing

C. a request, suggestion, or look to the future

D. the middle paragraph

5) For a multiple-page letter, ______ should only be used on the first page?

A. letterhead B. paper of the same quality

C. paper of the same size D. paper of the same color

6) Most companies have the return address printed in the ______ corner of the envelope.

A. bottom-left B. upper-left C. bottom-right D. upper-right

7) The order in writing the address in English is ______.

A. from the smallest division to the largest

B. same as the Chinese custom in writing address

C. from largest division to the smallest

D. none of the above

8) Which of the following complementary closing is not acceptable in the US?

A. "Yours faithfully," B. "Yours truly,"

C. "Sincerely," D. "Best wishes,"

9) A mailing notation should be included in which of the following cases: ______.

A. the sender has something exciting mentioned in the letter

B. the exact address is unknown

C. the letter is confidential and only readable to someone intended

D. none of the above

10) What does the subject line tell the recipients?

A. What the letter is about. B. When the letter has been sent.

C. Who wrote the letter. D. Who typed the letter.

3. Decide whether the following statements are true or false. Write "T" for true, and "F" for false.

1) If you use letterhead stationery, place the date immediately below the return address. ( )

2) If the city mentioned in the letter is the country's capital, it will not be necessary to give the country's name. ( )

3) The salutation should correspond with the form of address in a conversation. ( )

4) If you have no idea about the addressee, the salutation can be written as "lady and gentleman". ( )

5) "Re" or "re" means "return". ( )

6) Almost all business documents are typed or printed nowadays in order to be neat and professional. (　　)

7) A letter will always be more effective with a postscript. (　　)

8) "Enc" is the abbreviation for "Enclosure" which shows that there is something enclosed in the envelope. (　　)

9) In-house notation is placed three lines down the return address and is in either capital letters or small letters. (　　)

10) The format of return address on the envelope is always better to keep the same style with the inside address of the letter. (　　)

4. Translate the following massage into English and write it in an appropriate letter format.

写信人:张少华

职务:出口部经理

所在公司:天津纺织品进出口公司

地址: 中国 天津市 幸福路 86 号

邮编:300012

收信人:Johns 先生

职务:总经理

所在公司:K & D COMPANY LTD.

地址:890 harrison Street, Suite 203, Oak Park, CA60369, USA

事由:中国纺织品展览会

日期:2010 年 10 月 16 日

信的内容:如您所知,中国纺织品展览会将于 10 月 14 日至 30 日期间在伦敦国家展览厅举行。如果您或您的一位同事希望参观这个有趣的展览会,请告诉我,以便给您送上入场券。

由于在整个展览会期间我在馆内未设办公室,请提前通知我您打算光临的日期和大概时间,以便安排接待您。

Lesson Four

The Parts and Formats of Business Correspondence (II)

Besides letters introduced in the previous lesson, there are other types of business correspondence. This lesson introduces memos, faxes, e-mails and websites as they are very common in today's business communication.

1. Interoffice memorandum

An interoffice memorandum or memo in short is mainly composed of the following parts:

(1) The parts of a memo

Heading Many companies have preprinted memo forms, which include the title MEMO or INTEROFFICE MEMORANDOM or INTEROFFICE CORRESPONDENCE (all in capital letters) centered at the top of the page or aligned with the left margin.

Below the title, the following words are printed: *To*, *From*, *Date*, and *Subject* for the sender of the message to fill in such information as the name of the recipient, the name of the sender, the date of writing, and the main idea of the message. Sometimes more information such as department, telephone number is given.

Example 1

INTEROFFICE MEMO

TO:
FROM:
DATE:
SUBJECT:

Example 2

MEMO

To:	Date: ______________
From: ______________	Subject: ______________

Example 3

MEMORANDUM	
TO: ________________	
DEPT: ________________	FROM: ________________
DATE: ________________	TELEPHONE: ________________
SUBJECT: ____________	PAGE: ________________

The above pieces of information can be arranged in any order. The word *SUBJECT* can also be presented as *Re*.

When using plain paper without printed heading, leave at least a 1-inch margin at the top, the bottom and the sides for the message.

The body The body of a memo contains the message sent between company insiders or people working in the organization. It is usually direct and concise.

Start the body of the memo three lines below the heading. Align the left margin with the portion of the heading, and set the right margin so that it is equal to the left.

Addressees When sending a memo to a long list of people, include the notation *See distribution list* or *See below* in the *TO*: blank at the heading; then list the names at the end of the memo. Arrange the list alphabetically, except when high-ranking officials deserve more prominent placement. You can also address memos to a group of people. For instance: *TO : All Sales Representatives*, *TO : New Product Team.*

Courtesy Title You need not use courtesy titles anywhere in a memo. First initial and last name, or first name, or even initials alone are often sufficient. However, use a courtesy title if you would use one in a face-to-face encounter with the person.

Subject The subject line of a memo should be short and clear, helping busy recipient quickly find out what your memo is about.

Second Page If the memo carries over to a second page, head the second page just as you do in the second page of a letter.

Writer's Initials Unlike a letter, a memo does not require a complimentary close or a signature, because your name is already prominent at the heading. However you may initial or sign your name at the bottom of the memo, particularly if the memo deals with money or confidential matters.

Other Elements Treat reference initials, enclosure notations, and copy notations just as you would in a letter.

When delivered by post office, address the envelope the same way as you do with a letter. With hand delivery or interoffice mail use a special envelope that bears the recipient's name, department number or room number. If a regular envelope is used, write or type *Interoffice Mail* at the place where the stamp normally goes.

(2) The format of a memo

BRAXTON & TEAQUE CONSULTING

MEMO

To: All department managers **Date:** July 17, 2010

From: Tom Robinson **Subject:** Memo writing

Memos are internal correspondences within an organization. As the background of the information exchanged is known to the message senders and receivers, memos are usually brief and direct.

Because senders and recipients are colleagues known to each other, courtesy titles are mostly omitted in memos. Sometimes the writer just use given name to address the recipient.

Memos may be delivered by hand, by the post office (when the recipient works at a different location), or through interoffice mail.

2. Fax

Fax is the short form of facsimile. As Fax can transmit letters, memos, notes and other business documents, its format depends on what kind of message (letter or memo) you send and what result (formal or informal) you want to reach.

(1) The basic parts of a fax

Heading Preprinted Fax forms with the title FAX MESSAGE or FACSIMILE (either in all capital letters or just capitalize the first letter) at the top of the page are often used.

Below the title, the heading of a fax message gives similar information as that in a memo except you have to provide your fax number, though fax machines can provide the sender's fax number automatically.

Body The space under the heading is for the body. When sending an informal message, the signature can be spared.

(2) The format of a fax message

BRAXTON & TEAQUE CONSULTING

Fax Message

From: Pat Woods **Date:** August 10, 2010

To: Katherine Long **Fax number:** 02 - 663 256

Allegro Microsystem Inc.

Subject: The visit to your company

Katherine:

I'll visit your company on the 15th of next month. Could you please give me the following information:

1. The work schedule of your company
2. The location of your Export Dept
3. The latest model of your products

Please fax me back

Thanks.

3. E-mail

(1) E-mail account

To send an e-mail message you must, first of all, have an e-mail account and your recipient's e-mail address, which contains the following parts:

llchang@ tjufe. edu. cn

① ② ③ ④

①The symbol of the user's name

②The name of the place where the user has an e-mail account

③The top-level domain

④Country code

(2) The parts of an e-mail

All e-mail messages include two major parts: the header and the body. Salutation, complimentary close and signature are additional parts.

Header The e-mail header depends on the computer program you use. Some programs have a shorter header, while others have a longer header with more details. But most headers contain similar information as follows.

To: Contains the recipient's e-mail address.

From: Contains the sender's e-mail address.

Date: Contains the time you send your message.

Subject: Contains the main idea of the message or a key word, so that your reader can get the gist of your message at a glance.

Cc: Allows you to send copies of a message to more than one person at a time. It also allows everyone on the distribution list to see who else received the same message.

Bcc: Stands for *blind copy*. It allows you to send copies to people without the other recipients knowing.

Attachments: Contains the name(s) of the file(s) you attach to your e-mail message.

Body The space below the header is for the body of your message, which may include salutation and complementary closing.

Even though it is not strictly required for e-mails, start your message with a salutation as a greeting and end it with a complimentary close. This personalizes your message. However, e-mail salutation and closing can be less formal than those introduced in writing letters, depending on your relation with your recipient and the occasion. The following are a few examples of salutations with their matching complementary closings.

Salutation	Complementary closing
Hi Linda,	Best regards,
Hello, everyone,	See you later,
Hi,	Best wishes,
Recipient's name,	Thanks,

Leave one line space above and below your greeting to set it off from the rest of your message. You may end your greeting with a colon (formal), or a comma (conversational), depending on the level of formality you want.

Your message begins one blank line space below your greeting, and double space between paragraphs.

Include a complementary closing one blank line below your message.

Signature Start your signature one blank line space below the complementary closing. You may type your name or use an electronic signature file. An electronic signature file can create free advertising on every message you send and differentiate you from the crowd. Look at the following example of e-signature file.

Frank Leslie

fleslie@ sybervant. com

www. sybervant. com

508 – 226 – 2386

(3) The format of an e-mail message

The format of an e-mail message depends on your recipient and your purpose. You may choose to have your e-mail resemble a formal letter or to keep it as simple as an interoffice memo.

An example of e-mail message

To: jmark@ worldnetatt. net

From: hmiddleton@ hermanmiller. com

Subject: Message writing information

Cc. :

Bcc. :

Attached:

Dear Ms Julian Hamilton,

Writing an e-mail message is simpler as you don't have to type the date and inside address. You don't even have to mention the previous letter as you can involve the previous message in your e-mail.

But if you wish the recipient to contact you in other ways provide your contact information at the end of the message as is shown in this letter.

If you need any further information contact me with the following address.

Sincerely yours,

Helen Middleton
Human Resource Manager
hmiddleton@ hermankiller. com
www. hermanmiller. com
888 – 443 – 585 (USA and Canada only)

Herman Miller. Inc.
866 East Main Ave.
P. O. Box 302
Zeeland, MI 49464 – 0302
U. S. A.

4. Website

A website involves verbal and artistic design which reflects the characteristics and nature of an organization. The following are basic points of a reader-friendly website.

(1) Advanced organizers

Advanced organizers or "top-level summaries" are introductory lists created as the first level of a web page with hyperlinks to the secondry level. They provide a synopsis or quick overview of the information and allow the reader to see whether the document contains the information they need.

(2) Scannable text

Users primarily scan web pages for the information they need, therefore, a web site contains scannable text.

A scannable text is usually created by:

◇ Highlighted keywords (Variation of font, style, color and hypertext links)

◇ Sub-headings

◇ Bulleted lists and tables

◇ One idea per paragraph. Provide the right amount of information

◇ Short paragraphs with plenty of space. Avoid small font sizes (below 12 points)

◇ Webpage that fits on one screen

(3) Pictures and graphics

People's eyes are drawn to graphics and text more than to text alone. A website uses a combination of graphics and words to catch audience's attention. However, pictures and graphics may use more time to download, do not include too many of them.

(4) Contact information

A website includes complete and up-to-date names, addresses, and phone numbers, etc. for readers to contact you.

(5) An example of a website text

The following example gives you a glimpse of how to break down a text for a hypertext environment.

1) The top-level summery

Welcome to New Horizon Power Company's Website

Company　Product　Training　FAQ's

Click the underlined words to get the secondary level text.

2) The secondary level text

Company

New Horizon Power Company Ltd. is an unlisted public company, incorporated in 1987 to design, manufacture, sell and install renewable energy equipment based on solar, wind, hydro and biomass energy sources.

The company is one of the largest and most experienced Renewable Energy companies in China, with a workforce of experienced and dedicated staff.

Based on the East coast of China, the company's headquarters are unique in the eastern hemisphere.

Product

▲ Solar Panels & Accessories

▲ Wind & Hydro Turbines

Training

▲ Designer's Course

▲ Overseas Training

▲ Solar Energy Course

▲ 12 or 24 Volt power systems

FAQ

▲ Estimating your power demands

▲ How to reduce generator fuel bills

▲ Remote area power system

▲ AMP and Watt hour calculator and solar design tool

You can get the third-level text by clicking the ▲, which gives more details.

In addition to a word text, you can integrate informational pictures or graphics with the text.

New Words and Phrases

preprinted [ˈpriːˈprintid] *a.* printed beforehand 预先印好的

align [əˈlaind] *v.* to arrange in a line 排列

supervisor [ˈsjuːpəvaizə] *n.* one who supervises 主管人

alphabetically [ˌælfəˈbetikəli] *adv.* in the arrangement of the customary order of the letters of a language 按字母顺序地

deserve [diˈzəːv] *v.* to be worthy of 应受,值得

prominent [ˈprɔminənt] *a.* immediately noticeable; conspicuous 显著的

sufficient [səˈfiʃənt] *a.* being as much as is needed 足够的

encounter [inˈkauntə] *v.* a meeting, especially one that is unexpected, or brief 会面

facsimile [fækˈsimili] *n.* a method of transmitting images or printed matter by electronic means; fax 传真

domain [dəˈmein, dəuˈmein] *n.* a sphere of activity, concern, or function; a field 域名

header [ˈhedə] *n.* printed information, such as a title, date, or page number, positioned in the top margin of a page 标头

attachment [əˈtætʃmənt] *n.* a supplementary part; an accessory 附件

synopsis [siˈnɔpsis] *n.* a brief outline; an abstract or a summary 大纲

scannable [ˈskænəbl] *a.* being able to be scanned 可浏览的

graphic [ˈgræfik] *n.* of or relating to pictorial representation 图片

log [lɔg] *v.* to enter into a computer the information required to begin a session 登陆

Notes

1. **Start the body of the memo three spaces below the heading. *Align* the left margin *with* the portion of the heading, and set the right margin so that it is equal to the left.**
   便笺的正文应写于标题下空三行处,正文与标题左边对齐,然后再定好右边边距的位置,以保证整个信文左右边距相等。
   to align (with): to arrange in a line 使成一条直线
   e.g.: aligned the car with the curb 使汽车沿路边排成一条直线
2. **Single space the paragraphs in block style, double space between each paragraph. Indenting paragraphs is optional. If the memo is very short, you may double-space it.**

在齐头式的便笺中，使用单行距，段落之间用双行距。也可选择缩近式。如果便笺内容很短，也可使用双行距。

3. Arrange the list alphabetically, except when high-ranking officials deserve more *prominent placement.* 按字母顺序排列收信人姓名，如果其中包括重要人物，应将其姓名排在靠前的位置。

prominent placement （放在）显要位置

4. If regular envelope is used, write or type "Interoffice Mail" at the place where the stamp normally goes. 如果使用普通信封，在贴邮票的位置注明"公司内部便笺"的字样。

5. Leave one line space above and below your greeting to *set* it *off* from the rest of your message. 在问候语的上下各空一行，使它和正文隔开。

set sth. off 把（某物）分开

e. g.: features setting him off from the crowd 使他与人群分开的特征

6. An electronic signature file can create free advertising on every message you send and *differentiate* you *from* the crowd. 电子签名既可以为你发出的每一封信做免费广告，又可以使你的信件与众不同。

differentiate *v.* 区别；区分

e. g.: Can you differentiate an e-mail message from a fax message? 你能区别电子邮件与传真信件吗？

How to differentiate between the two pictures? 如何区分这两张图片？

7. A website involves verbal and artistic design which reflects the characteristic and nature of an organization. 一个公司的网站可以用语言文字和富有艺术特色的设计来体现公司的特点和性质。

8. Users primarily scan web pages for the information they need, therefore, it is best to design a web site with scannable text. 用户访问网站主要是有目的地搜寻他们所需要的信息，因此，网站中的内容应能够浏览。

scannable text 可浏览的文本

9. sub-heading 副标题

10. Bulleted lists and tables 标有符号的列表和表格

11. In addition to a word text, you can *integrate* informational pictures or graphics *with* the text. 除了文本文件，你还可以附上传递信息的照片和图片，使它们与文本相结合。

integrate... with... : to make into a whole by bringing all parts together 使成一体；使结合

e. g.: to integrate oneself with the mass 与群众打成一片

to integrate theory into practice 把理论与实践相结合

12. FAQ Frequently Asked Questions 常见问题

Exercises

1. Answers the following questions.

1) What are the main features of letters, memos, faxes, emails and websites in terms of format?

2) What are the similarities and differences among letters, memos, faxes and emails in massage writing?

3) How do you address your readers when your memo is to be sent to more than 10 persons?

2. Choose the best answer to complete the following statements.

1) A memo is unlike a letter in which of the following points?

A. It is to be typed. B. It may have an enclosure notation.

C. The date of writing is needed. D. A complementary close is not needed.

2) Memos can not be sent in which of the following way: ______.

A. hand B. telephone C. post office D. interoffice mail

3) An E-mail address must include the following parts, except ______.

A. the symbol of the user's name

B. the name of the place where the user has an e-mail account

C. the user's real name

D. the top-level domain

4) An Email header includes the following points, except ______.

A. the post code

B. the recipient's and the sender's e-mail address

C. the time you send your message

D. the main idea of the message

5) In writing memos, you can address your reader in which of the following ways?

A. Dear Madam or sir

B. Dear Sir

C. Gentlemen

D. First name

6) Which of the following media gives the best result if your message involves many colorful photos and you don't have any specific reader?

A. E-mail B. Website C. Letter D. Fax

7) In which of the following media the message needs to be up dated regularly?

A. Letters B. Faxes C. E-mails D. Website

8) Scannable text can be produced by ______.

A. highlighted keywords D. bulleted lists

C. short paragraphs B. all of the above

3. Decide whether the following statements are true or false. Write "T" for true, and "F" for false.

1) Preprinted memo forms are available in many companies. (   )

2) Memos are usually less formal than letters. (　　)

3) When a memo is sent to a group of people, you can arrange the names in alphabetical order. (　　)

4) A memo usually requires a complimentary close or a signature. (　　)

5) The heading of a fax message gives exactly the same information as that of a memo. (　　)

6) In most cases, a fax number is needed in the heading of a fax message. (　　)

7) An e-mail message can be as formal as a letters. (　　)

8) Senders and recipient of memos usually know each other. (　　)

9) The subject line is to give the main idea of the message. (　　)

10) "Cc" in an e-mail means the message is sent to more than one reader. (　　)

4. Translate the following sentences into Chinese.

1) If you need any further information contact me with the following address.

2) The subject line of a memo should be short and clear, helping busy colleagues quickly find out what your memo is about.

3) If the memo carries over to a second page, head the second page just as you do in the second page of a letter.

4) You may choose to have your e-mail resemble a formal letter or to keep it as simple as an interoffice memo.

5) People's eyes are drawn to graphics and text more than to text alone.

6) A website involves verbal and artistic design which reflects the characteristics and nature of an organization.

7) New Horizon Power Company Ltd. is a listed company, incorporated in 1987 to design, manufacture, sell and install renewable energy equipment.

8) The company is a renewable energy company in China, with a workforce of experienced and dedicated staff.

5. Arrange the following messages into a proper form of business correspondence. You may rearrange or add some parts to the messages if necessary.

1) On behalf of the entire group at Miller Life Insurance Company, I want to congratulate you on being awarded Sales Representative of the Year. It's very inspiring to all of your co-workers to know of your excellent performance and fine record. If you can spare the time, I'd like to take you to lunch to celebrate. I'll give you a call next week.

2) I should much appreciate to have the opportunity of meeting you personally on my forthcoming visit to Beijing. We are running into considerable difficulties over our government import licenses and I should like to discuss the situation with you without delay. My secretary will telephone you on Wednesday, December 14th, to see whether arrangement can be made for a meeting.

Lesson Five

Résumé

1. Introduction

One of the major documents needed for preliminary application for employment or a professional position is a résumé.

A résumé is a structured, written summary of your education, work experience, relevant skills, etc. for the job for which you have applied.

When writing a resume provide the following information:

◇ **Name, address and contact information** Include telephone number, e-mail, or URL if you have one.

◇ **Career objective** Indicate the position for which you are applying for.

◇ **Education** Provide such information as the university you attended, you major, the main courses you studied, the degrees earned. You may also include off-campus training, relevant seminars or workshops you have attended.

◇ **Work experience** State the work and jobs you have done. You may also mention your part-time jobs and intern positions.

◇ **Skills or areas of knowledge** Indicate your skill and ability that are needed in your intended career, e. g. computer skills, foreign language skills.

◇ **Activities** Describe activities in which you participated to demonstrate your abilities of communication, leadership, cooperation, teamwork, etc. which are related to the job and position you apply for.

◇ **Honors and achievements** Indicate any awards, honors, achievements, and accomplishments you have had.

Some people especially professionals, write a Curriculum Vitae (abbreviated as CV) instead of a résumé. A CV is slightly different from a résumé in that it usually gives more details including not only educational backgrounds and work experience, but also teaching and/or research experience, publications, presentations, affiliations, etc.

2. Writing strategy

(1) Give a concise and convincing "Career Objective".

Since most employers read this part fully, write it in a concise and convincing way in your résumé so that your prospective employer will have a clear idea about what qualification should be expected from you.

(2) Highlight your strength and facts that support your career objective.

If you are still studying in college or you have just recently graduated without much work experience, education may be your strongest selling point. Make sure to put the emphasis on your education. In addition to listing the university (or universities) you attended, you may include information about

◇ degrees earned
◇ grade point average
◇ majors and minors
◇ date of program completion

If you have worked in a certain field for more than a year, your work experience may be your strongest qualification. Give more emphasis on your work experience rather than on education, esp. the job(s) which is(are) related to your target field and position.

(3) Emphasize your achievements by giving the specific effects and results

Employers are less interested in titles and duties and more interested in previous accomplishments. Give your achievement in a specific and concrete way. Use more action verbs (such as implement, develop, expand, run, organize, design, improve) rather than adjectives (such as good, excellent, great, wonderful).

3. Communication for results

(1) Quantify your achievements in terms of percentages, amount of money to make your accomplishments more concrete.

Instead of writing	Write
Work efficiently in budget management	Implemented cost-cutting measures that reduced expenses of the company by 15%
In charge of overseas marketing	Expanded our market share by 10%
Responsible for developing a new filing system	Developed a new filing system that reduced paperwork by 50%
Work as Director in Department of Claims and Adjustment.	Handled all customer complaints and resolved all product order discrepancies.
Designed a new ad at the prime time on TV	Designed a new ad that increased sales by 10 percent
Worked for fund raising for cancer research	Raised 2,500 yuan in 15 days for cancer research

(2) Use short, parallel phrases and sentence segments.

In order to save your reader's time, use short, parallel phrases and sentence fragments starting with impressive action verbs instead of weak statements and whole sentences. **e. g.** :

Instead of writing	Write
I'm in charge of after-sales service and my work improved customer satisfaction.	Promoted customer satisfaction through personal interaction

续表

Instead of writing	Write
I'd like to work for customer-service in a market-oriented company.	Contribute to strong customer-service focused on a creative, marketing-oriented setting
I worked in the company to plan investment strategies and recommend specific investments.	Planed investment strategies; Recommended specific investments

(3) Provide reference

Many employers need reference for further proof as to the applicant's qualification, characteristics, integrity, skills, etc. State in your résumé that reference is available upon request. Or better give the name and contact information of a reference at the end of the résumé.

(4) Be truthful and accurate

Make sure you have not included any misleading or false information on your résumé. Chances are your "inaccuracies" will eventually be discovered and you'll lose all credibility with your prospective employer.

4. Formats and examples of a résumé

Résumé writing usually follows the three styles given below:

(1) Chronological résumé The most often used style, emphasizing what, when, and for whom you did the job or jobs. Education and work experience is presented in reverse chronological order, with the current one first. Dates are prominent. Employers often prefer this style.

An example of a chronological résumé

David Zhang

E-mail: dzhang@ tjufe. edu. cn

Present Work Address:	**Permanent Address:**
Department of International Trade	7 Hubei Road
Tianjin University of Finance & Economics	Heping District 300555
25 Zhujiang Road, Hexi District 300222	Tianjin, China
86 - 22 - 28175555	86 - 22 - 23356666

OBJECTIVE

Management position requiring knowledge of international trade and English

EDUCATIONAL HIGHLIGHTS

Major Courses in Business:

- Business and Professional Communication
- Marketing

◆ Human Resource Management
◆ Advertising Principles
◆ Human Relations

Major Courses in Office Administration:

◆ Word processing skills in Microsoft Word
◆ Office management
◆ Business Correspondence in English

EDUCATION

Date	Diploma Received	University
2008 ~ 2010	Master Degree of Business Administration	Tianjin University of Finance & Economics, Tianjin, China
2002 ~ 2006	Bachelor of Arts	Tianjin University of Finance & Economics. Tianjin, China

MAJOR ACHIEVEMENTS

2002 ~ 2006	Graduated with GPA of 85
2002 ~ 2006	Awarded 100% scholarship for excellent work

WORK EXPERIENCES

Date	Position	Achievement
2007 ~ 2010	Assistant Manager	Export Department of SINOCHEM Tianjin, China
2006	Intern	Asian Fabric Imports & Exports Corp. Tianjin, China

MAJOR ACHIVEMENTS

Date	Achievement
2006 ~ 2010	Participated in a team to penetrate into a new market and increased the market share in Europe by 10%
2006	Handled customer complaints and adjustments and enhanced their degree of satisfaction

REFERENCE

Available upon request.

(2) **Functional résumé** Highlight achievements and work skills, with dates playing a less prominent role. This style is normally used for experienced job seekers who have a variety of experiences, or who have been unemployed for a long period of time, or have jumped jobs too frequently.

An example of a functional résumé

Jennifer Lee

550 Blue Sky Road

Shanghai, China

Home (022) 25558678; Work (022) 23332866.

jlee@ netmail. com

OBJECTIVE

A marketing position with an opportunity for eventual managerial status

ACHIEVEMENTS

Selling/Retailing

- Launched the sales of electric appliance for spring 2010 and increased the turnover rate by 10%
- Designed floor plan and shelf display for World Trade Fair of Electric Appliance
- Published and promoted 35-page marketing website

Public Communication

- Composed business news articles as an intern and authored editorial articles as a freelance columnist for the *Business Weekly*
- Drafted professional fund-raising letters for the Hope Project and raised RMB 12,000, which helped 20 young people realize their dream to go to college

Management

- Trained part-time employees in cash register operation and customer service

WORK EXPERIENCE

- Sales representative, at Sports Equipment Center, in 2008-Present
- Sales clerk, at Electric Appliance Manufacturing Corp., in 2005-2007
- Assistant manager, at Electric Appliance Manufacturing Corp. during off-campus work experience program, in 2004

EDUCATION

- Major: Bachelor of Arts in Information Science, Shanghai University of Commerce,
  Shanghai, China, June 2000 – June 2004

- Minor: English for Special Purpose, Shanghai University of Commerce, Shanghai,

  China, June 2003 – 2004

Computer Skill

- Microsoft Word, Excel, Access, PowerPoint
- HTML web design

Honor

- Top sales representatives in 2010
- First Prize in English speech context in 2007

Reference

Christie Chen, cc358@ yahoo. com

(3) **Electronic résumé** A computer friendly form that can be scanned, stored, updated, and extracted accurately by computer. In an electronic résumé, the "Objective" is usually replaced by Keyword Summary.

An example of an electronic résumé

Susan Hanning

1355 Edna Street Napa, CA94558

(415)555 –5760 (Office) (415)555 –5799 (Residence)

KEYWORD SUMMARY

Sales supervision. Fabric import. Customer relations. Customer complaints. Files & records. Correspondence. Microsoft Word, Powerpoint, and Excel, keyboarding, 55 wpm. Fluent in English

EXPERIENCE

Fabric Imports Napa, California

Salesperson July 2005 – Present

- Awarded top salesperson for the last three years
- Strengthened customer relations with Spanish-speaking accounts
- Generated 10 new key accounts
- Ordered stock, promoted warehouses sales, and designed showroom fabric displays

Richland College Dallas, Texas

Secretary Jan 2002 – July 2005

- Personal secretary to Dean of Instruction
- Supervised office management
- Maintained daily calendar for the Dean
- Developed less complicated procedure for handling student complaints
- Composed letters and memos and answered e-mail messages

Jack-in-the-Box Dallas, Texas
Fountain Clerk (Part-time) Feb 2000 – Dec 2001

- Took orders from drive-through window
- Prepared fountain items such as carbonated drinks and ice-cream orders
- Cleaned counters and tables
- Created best-selling new shake flavor

EDUCATION

Richland College Dallas, Texas

- received associate of Arts Degree in Business May 2001

PROFESSIONAL AFFILIATIONS

Napa Sales Club. Chamber of Commerce

A hard copy of this document is available upon request.

(4) **An Example of a CV curriculum vitae** (CV) usually gives more in formation on academic and professional work.

JOSEPH RABEN

CURRENT STATUS

Director, Paradigm Press, Inc.
Editor, Computers and the Humanities
Director, SCOPE

EDUCATION

Ph. D., Indiana University, 1964
M. A., Indiana University, 1959
B. A., University of Wisconsin, 1954

PROFESSIONAL EXPERIENCE

International Summer School of Linguistics, University of Pisa, 1985, 1987
Summer School for Computers and the Humanities, University of Illinois, 1970
Instructor-Professor, Queens College, CUNY, 1969 ~ 2001
Instructor, Princeton University, 1965 ~ 1967
Teaching fellow, Indiana University, 1965 ~ 1967
Graduate assistant, Indiana University, 1963 ~ 1965
Graduate assistant, New York University, 1962 ~ 1963

U. S. Army, editor of translations, GHQ Tokyo, 1960 ~ 1961

RADIO LECTURE SERIES

"Poetry and Politics", 26 lectures, 1983

"The American Novel", 39 lectures, 1977

PUBLICATIONS

Books edited:

(with Shigeharu Sugita) *Toward a Computer Ethnology*, Osaka

Osaka Ethnological Museum 2005

Data Bases in the Humanities and Social Sciences, Amsterdam

North Holland, 1996

Computer-Aided Research in the Humanities, New York and Oxford

Pergamon Press, 1992

Articles in:

Review of English Studies *Data Processor*

Keats-Shelley Journal *Scholarly Publishing* (3)

Journal of English and Germanic Philology

Educational Record *Language*

Philological Quarterly *Transaction/Society*

Computer and People *Science*

HONORS

Listed in (1) *Who's Who in the East*, *Contemporary Authors*

(2) *Directory of American Scholars*, Vol. 4. English, Drama & Linguistics

All-University Fellowship, Indiana University, 1965

Legislative Scholarship, University of Wisconsin, 1959

GRANTS

National Science Foundation $80,000

Carnegie Corporation $60,000

Andrew W. Mellon Foundation $58,000

IBM $50,000

US Steel Foundation $12,000

PROFESSIOANL ACTIVITIES

Program committees

International Conference on Computers and the Humanities,

North Carolina State University, 1998

Society for Scholarly Publishing, Washington D. C., 1995

National Educational Computing Conference, Norfolk VA, 1995
International Conference on Computational Linguistics, Stockholm, 1990

Session chairmanship

National Educational Computing Conference, Kansas City, 1997
Conference on Computers in the Undergraduate Curricula, Atlanta, 1987
Fall Joint Computer Conference, Anaheim CA, 1982

Funded studies

Acceptability of Electronic Publishing for Tenure and Promotion 1995
Feasibility of a Central Editorial Facility 1993

GUEST SPEAKING INVITATIONS

Clark University
University at Pisa
William College
University of Pennsylvania
State University of Pennsylvania
University of Montreal

PERSONAL

Telephone: (307) 5678 - 0907
E-mail: jraben@paradin.com
Address: Route 1, Laramie, WY82070, U.S.A.

5. Telephone conversation for interview announcement

Mary Larson, a job applicant, receives a phone call for a job interview from Jane Moore.

Moore: Hello, this is Jane Moore from ABC Company. May I speak to Ms Larson, please?

Larson: Mary Larson speaking.

Moore: Good morning, Ms. Larson. We have received your résumé, and we are impressed enough to arrange an interview for you to meet Mr. Smith White, the Vice President on Friday morning at 10:30. Does it suit your schedule?

Larson: Yes, it suits me fine. So I'll meet with Mr. Smith White, the Vice President at his office on Friday morning at 10:30, is that right?

Moore: That's right. Mr. Smith's office is in Room 203, on the 2nd floor of the Office Building.

Larson: Please wait a minute. Let me write it down. Room 203, on the 2nd floor of the Office Building. Thank you.

Moore: You are welcome.

Larson: By the way, Ms. Moore, could you let me know some of the critical areas we will discuss during the interview?

Moore: I guess it will be on your skills and expectations.

Larson: I see. Thank you very much for your help.

Moore: My pleasure. Bye-bye and good luck!

Larson: Thank you, bye!

New Words and Phrases

résumé [ˈrezju(ː)mei] *n.* a brief account of one's education, qualifications, and previous occupations 履历表；简历

preliminary [priˈliminəri] *n.* 1) something that precedes, prepares for, or introduces the main matter, action, or business 开端,初步

Training is a necessary preliminary to employment. 培训是就业时不可缺少的第一步。

a. 2) prior to the main matter, action, or business; introductory 预备的，初步的

a preliminary investigation 初步调查

URL Uniform Resource Locator 用于 Internet 服务程序上，指定信息位置

Curriculum Vitae [kəˈrikjuləmˈvaitiː] *n.* a brief account of one's career; résumé (Latin = course of life) 履历表，简历

convincing [kənˈvinsiŋ] *a.* serving to convince 令人确信的

chronological [ˌkrɔnəˈlɔdʒikəl] *a.* arranging in the order of time of occurrence 按时间发生顺序排列的

intern [inˈtəːn] *n.* a recent graduate undergoing supervised practical training 实习生

I work as an intern. 我做实习生。

reverse [riˈvəːs] *a.* turned backward in position, direction, or order 相反的

highlight [ˈhailait] *n.* 1) an especially significant or interesting detail or event 最重要的或最有趣的细节或事件，精华

Visiting your company is the highlight of my trip. 拜访贵公司是此行的重点。

v. 2) to make prominent; emphasize 强调

to highlight this part by using a different color 用不同的颜色强化这一部分

fountain clerk one who sells drinks in a bar or restaurant 冷饮销售员

reference [ˈrefərəns] *n.* 1) a piece of written information about a person's qualifications, character, and ability, etc. especially when the person is looking for employment 推荐信，介绍信

2) a person who is in a position to recommend another or to vouch for his or her fitness for a job 介绍人，证明人

When you look for a job, good references will help you. 找工作时,好的介绍信(或介绍人)会帮你大忙。

ethnology [ˌeθˈnɔlədʒi] *n.* 1) cultural anthropology 人类文化学

2) the branch of anthropology that deals with the origin, distribution, and characteristics of the races of humankind 人种学

fellowship [ˈfeləuʃip] *n.*   the financial grant made to a fellow in a college or university 学院或大学中给予研究员的财政资助

humanities [ˌhjuːˈmænətis] *n.*   studies such as literature, languages, history 人文学科

Notes

1. **prime time** （电视台广播的）黄金时间
2. **Work experience is presented *in reverse chronological order*...**
   in reverse chronological order: arranging in the opposite direction of time of occurrence 按逆时间顺序排列
3. **An Associate of Arts degree** usually abbreviated as "AA", is intended for students to complete the first two years of a baccalaureate (*Ame.* 学士学位) degrees (BA or BS) An Associate of Arts degree is awarded after the successful completion of a program of 60 ~ 64 semester credits. 授予完成大学本科两年课程的学生的学位(文科一般需修满 60 ~ 64 个学分)
4. **off-campus training** 校外培训
5. **workshop**: an educational seminar or series of meetings emphasizing interaction and exchange of information among a usually small number of participants 研习会,讨论会
   e. g. : a creative writing workshop 创造性写作研讨会
6. **chronological résumé** 按时间发生顺序编写的履历
7. **functional résumé** 按工作经验编写的履历
8. **electronic résumé** 电子版履历
9. **Jack-in-the-Box**: a chain fast-food restaurant in the US 一美国连锁快餐店
10. **carbonated drinks** 碳酸饮料
11. **teaching fellow** 特聘教师
12. **graduate assistant** 研究生助教
13. **Who's Who in the East, Contemporary Authors** 东方现代作家名人录
14. **Session chairmanship** 会议主席
15. **Fall Joint Computer Conference** 秋季联合计算机会议
16. **National Science Foundation** (NSF): An independent federal agency created by Congress in 1950 to promote the progress of science, to advance the national health, prosperity, and welfare and to secure the national defense with an annual budget of about $5.5 billion, it supports basic research conducted by America's colleges and universities in many fields such as mathematics, computer science and the social sciences. （美国）国家科学基金会
17. **Carnegie Corporation**: Carnegie Corporation of New York was created by Andrew Carnegie in 1911 to promote "the advancement and diffusion of knowledge and understanding." Under Carnegie's will, grants must benefit the people of the United States. 卡内基公司
18. **Andrew W. Mellon Foundation**: The Andrew W. Mellon Fellowships in Humanistic Studies supported exceptionally promising students pursuing doctoral programs in the humanities

since 1983. 安德鲁·梅隆基金会

19. **IBM**: the world largest computer company in the world founded by Bill Gates 美国国际商用机器公司

20. **US Steel Foundation**: United States Steel Foundation, a nonprofit membership corporation, was founded in Delaware in 1953 to provide support in a planned and balanced manner for educational, scientific, charitable, civic, cultural and health needs on behalf of United States Steel Corporation. 美国钢铁基金会

Useful Expressions

For educational background:

1. Major in economics (or economics major)
2. Major in Business Administration, have especial interested in "Marketing"
3. Bachelor of Arts, Business Administration
4. Major in Physics and minor in Practical Mathematics
5. Graduated from Tianjin Normal University in 1990
6. Received Bachelor of Arts degree in English Literature and then a MBA degree

For work experience:

1. Proven leadership skills involving managing, developing and motivating teams to achieve their objectives
2. Good at analytical, design and problem solving skills. Dedicated to maintaining high quality standards
3. Seek a position as a Distribution Manager that utilizes my 7 years of distribution and logistics management experience
4. Implemented a warehouse management software system, trained users, and developed procedures to integrate the computerized system
5. Led cross-functional team integrating the distribution system with a new database merchandising system
6. Managed the complete project including bidding, design, scheduling, purchasing, subcontracting, and customer service
7. Reduced Distribution Center expenses by more than $1.5 million, a 30% reduction, over a 2-year period while maintaining productivity levels, service quality, and inventory accuracy

Phrases related to education.

educational background	教育程度	curriculum	课程
major	主修	minor	辅修
educational highlights	重点课程	specialized courses	专业课
required course (compulsory)	必修课	selective course (optional)	选修课
special training	特别培训	full-time regular school	全日制正规学校
part-time jobs	业余工作	summer jobs	暑期工作
vacation jobs	假期工作	refresher course	进修课程

extracurricular activities	课外活动	physical activities	体育活动
recreational activities	娱乐活动	academic activities	学术活动
social activities	社会活动	rewards	奖励
scholarship	奖学金	excellent League member	优秀团员
excellent leader	优秀干部	student council	学生会
off-job training	脱产培训	in-job training	在职培训
educational system	学制	academic year	学年
semester	学期(美)	term	学期(英)
supervisor	论文导师	marks	分数
fail	不及格	pass	及格
post doctorate	博士后	doctor (Ph. D)	博士
master	硕士	bachelor	学士
graduate student	研究生	undergraduate	本科生
government-supported student	公费生	commoner	自费生
extern	走读生	intern	实习生
prize fellow	奖学金生	boarder	寄宿生
graduate	毕业生	foreign student	留学生
auditor	旁听生(美)	guest student	旁听生(英)
academic degree	学位	academic title	职称

Phrases related to schools and departments:

School of Liberal Arts	文学院
School of Science and Technology	理工学院
Department of Chinese Language and Literature	中国语言文学系
Department of Western Languages and Literature	西方语言文学系
Department of Oriental Languages and Literature	东方语言文学系
Department of Sociology	社会学系
Department of Political Economy	政治经济系
Department of Economics	经济系
Department of Journalism	新闻系
Department of Physical Education	体育系
Department of Architecture and Civil Engineering	建筑工程系
Department of Hydraulic Engineering	水利工程系
Department of Chemical Engineering Mechanics	化工机械系
Department of Precision Instrument	精密仪器系

Phrases related to work and position:

occupational history	工作经历	public relations (PR)	公关
assistant manager	经理助理	accountant	会计
second job	第二职业	auditor	审计员
human resource (HR)	人力资源	financial analyst	金融分析师

area manager	地区经理	financial manager	财务经理
logistic supervisor	后勤主管	senior engineer	高级工程师
researcher	研究员	market research	市场调研

Research & Development (R&D) 研究和发展(简称:研发)

Chief Executive Office(CEO) 执行总裁,首席执行官

Chief Financial Office(CFO) 财务总监

Exercises

1. Answer the following questions.

1) What information does a résumé generally included?

2) What are the differences between a résumé and a CV?

3) What styles does a résumé writing usually follow? What style do you prefer? And why?

2. Choose the best answer to complete the following statements.

1) When you write your résumé in reverse chronological order, ______.

A. you state your most recent work experience first

B. you state the first job you had first

C. you state your most successful job first

D. you state the highest position you have had

2) You may include your intern position in ______.

A. your education B. your work experience

C. your skill D. your achievements

3) A professional with a lot of academic experience and publication would rather write ______ in employment application.

A. a request B. a résumé C. a CV D. an introduction

4) A functional résumé ______.

A. is usually written by people with little work experience

B. is usually written by people with little education

C. is usually written by people who have changed their jobs very often

D. is usually written by people who don't have much achievements

5) The advantage of an electronic résumé is that ______.

A. it can be scanned B. it can be updated

C. it is computer-friendly D. all of the above

6) An employment applicant who is seeking "A marketing position with an opportunity for eventual management status" wishes to work as ______.

A. a sales clerk B. a marketing personnel

C. a manager D. a shop owner

7) A résumé that highlights work skills.

The underlined part of the sentence means ______.

A. emphasizes B. puts light on

C. gives work skill at the beginning D. gives work skill at the end

8) "I need a résumé in hard copy" means ______.

A. the résumé must be typed

B. the résumé must be filed

C. the résumé must be hand written

D. the résumé must be typed or written in a piece of paper

3. Decide whether the following statements are true or false. Write "T" for true, and "F" for false.

1) There is no difference between a résumé and a CV. ( )

2) Chronological résumé usually highlights achievements and work skills, with dates playing a less prominent role. ( )

3) Electronic résumé is a computer friendly form that can be scanned, stored, updated, and extracted accurately by computer. ( )

4) A functional résumé highlight your work experience. ( )

5) A job hunter just graduated from university without much work experience would rather use chronological résumé focused on education. ( )

6) It's necessary to provide all skills you have in your résumé. ( )

7) A reference is a statement about an applicant's qualifications, character, and dependability. ( )

8) "I graduate with a GPA of 90." GPA here means Grade Points Average. ( )

9) A résumé usually contains more in-depth details about your experience and activities. ( )

10) Specifics about what you've already done are not helpful, since employers are more interested in what you might be capable of doing in the future. ( )

4. Translate the following sentence segments into English.

1) 负责计算机程序设计的初级职务

2) 高级管理人员的行政助理,将用上速记和打字技能

3) 谋求能够发挥我在生物学方面的学识,并有晋升前途的职位

4) 能够运用我的创造性写作的才能的职位

5) 负责人力资源管理的职务

6) 外贸部门的职位,有机会晋升到该部门的经理职务

7) 行政秘书的职务,注重交际技巧和与人为善的态度

8) 工程部门设计工程师的职位

9) 谋求一家中型公司的计算机程序员职位

10) 担任跨国公司的推销员,可以随时到国外担任短期或长期工作。

5. Translate the following sentence segments into Chinese.

1) An administrative position which will bring my initiative and creativity into full play

2) An executive assistant position utilizing my interest and experience in office administration

3) Trouble shooting and repairing electric equipments

4) A position requiring analytical skills in the financial or investment field

5) To begin as an accounting trainee and eventually become a manager

6) A position as data-processing manager that will enable me to use my knowledge of computer systems

7) MBA and advanced scientific degree in Biotechnology

8) I am a person of integrity and team player

6. Change the following sentences into phrases and sentence segments, adapting them to a résumé.

1) I developed and conducted formal classes for groups of 50 to 500 people. And I often gave lectures, used audiovisual aids, hands-on exercises, and extensive question-and-answer in my sessions.

2) In my work I monitored job performance and gave on-the-spot training.

3) I have written sales and fund-raising letters for a variety of products and I have organizing experiences for sales campaign.

4) I launched advertising campaign for Five Star pencils. In the campaign I presented the pencils in a fresh way to consumers and increased sale by 20%.

5) I set short-term goals to achieve manager's long-term goals, and motivated employees to reach them. I ordered parts for repair shop and sales department. I assigned daily duties to store employees.

6) I analyzed available data to determine opponents' size, strength, capabilities, and plans. I received six months' intensive training in collecting, analyzing, and reporting data from multiple sources. I analyzed protocol, content, and electronic signature of radio signals to determine size, activity, type, and location of broadcasting unit.

7. Write a résumé with the information given below and arrange it in an appropriate format:

Campus address	Activities and skills
Permanent address	Awards and prizes received
Contact information	Characteristics and personalities
Job objective	Reference
Education and work experience	

8. Make a telephone conversation in pairs with two students sitting back to back, one gives the other, a job applicant eager for an interview, an interview announcement.

Lesson Six

Application Letter

1. Introduction

An application letter is a letter that accompanies your résumé as a cover to inform the reader of your reason and purpose for sending the résumé. It is, therefore, also known as "cover letter".

There are two kinds of application letters:

1) **Solicited application letter** is a letter written in response to an announced job opening. If you send a solicited application letter, you know what qualifications the organization is seeking from the ad. But you may have many competitors competing for the same job or position because they have seen the ad too. So you must give more emphasis on your qualifications to catch the reader's attention.

2) **Unsolicited application letter** is a letter sent to an organization that has not announced an opening. In sending an unsolicited application letter, you stand a better chance of getting individualized attention since there are fewer or no competitors. You must know the needs of the employer and focus on the needs.

Both solicited and unsolicited letters present your qualifications similarly. The only difference is in the opening paragraph. In a solicited letter you should state how or from which source you learned about the job openings, while in an unsolicited letter you should start with emphatic sentences to capture the reader's attention and interest.

An application letter can be a hard copy, or an electronic one. If you want to accompany an electronic résumé, you should prepare an electronic application letter. The contents are the same with a hard copy application letter, except the signature. Give your electronic contact information such as your e-mail address and/or your URL at the end of your letter. Tell what word-processing program your résumé is saved in. Never use all capital letters in typing your application letter.

2. Writing strategy

To write an effective application letter, you must bear in mind the following points:

◇ Address the letter to a specific individual by name and title whenever possible. Such information is usually available in the company's website. Or you may ask the company's receptionist. Writing to a particular person in charge will insure that you get an early response.

◇ State your reason for writing and the position you are applying for.

◇ For a solicited application letter state how you found the job listing in the opening paragraph.

◇ For an unsolicited application letter catch the reader's interest, and create a bridge between the attention-getter and your qualifications.

◇ Select the highlights and your qualifications that are relevant to the job for which you are applying. Do not reiterate all the information in your résumé.

◇ Emphasize the contribution you can make to the company.

◇ Keep the letter short, but not too short. If the letter is too short with only a few sentences, it may create a negative impression that you lack interest in the job or you have very little to say about yourself. The appropriate length is usually one full page.

◇ Give your contact information.

◇ Mention your résumé is enclosed or attached.

3. Communication for results

(1) Use strong words

Remember that an employer may receive hundreds of application letters after listing a job vacancy. To catch their interest and attention, you must use strong words to impress them, otherwise they may not read on for the rest of the letter.

Strong words are action words or verbs as the under lined words given below.

Instead of writing	**Write**
I am writing to apply for the job of Sales Clerk, which was advertised in the Jan. 7th Tianjin Evening.	In the Jan. 7th Tianjin Evening, your ad mentioned "proven skills". I believe I have what you are looking for in a Sales Clerk.
I'm skilled at taking short hand and I'd like to apply for the position of secretary in your export division.	When you need a secretary in your export division who can take shorthand at 120 words a minute in English and Chinese, please call me.
I completed three college courses in business communication, earning an A in each course, and have worked for the past year at Imperial Construction.	Using the skills gained from my study in college, I developed a system of letter collection for Imperial Construction, which increased work efficiency.

(2) Focus on your reader's interests

State how you can contribute to the company or organization you apply to, instead of what you want and how you will benefit from it.

Instead of writing	Write
I am looking for a position which gives me a chance to advance quickly.	My experience in sales promotion would help me market Apple computers to schools and families.

4. Example letters

(1) An unsolicited application letter

123 Huawei Road
Nankai District
200033
Tianjin, China
October 21, 2010

Ms. Lora Wagner
Director of Administration
Maxwell Inc.
Tianjin Branch
Tianjin, China

Dear Ms. Lora Wagner:

When you are ready to hire an administrative assistant who is accurate and enthusiastic, who is bilingual and experienced in computer software used in office work, please consider me for the job.

I recently completed a four year study as an English major and computer minor in Tianjin Foreign Language Institute. I have excellent school record with straight As for Spoken and Written English, and good knowledge in marketing and business communication.

In addition, I can use a variety of computer software to speed up office work, such as writing letters and reports, keeping files, etc. This has been proved during my internship in a trading company.

I learned from your website that you have a service network with operations in the US and many countries in Europe. I believe my fluency in both spoken and written English, and my intercultural communication skill will be invaluable for my contribution to Maxwell Inc.

I would appreciate an interview with you. I'll phone you next Monday morning to arrange a meeting at your convenience.

Sincerely,
(*Signature*)

David Zhang

Encl. A résumé

(2) An unsolicited electronic application letter

To: Mr. Deng Ping, Director of Human Resource <dp@ yahoo. com>
From: Lingling Wang <llwang@ yahoo. com>
Subject: Application
Cc:
Bcc:
Attached: C:\jobhunt\résumé\scan

Dear Mr. Deng:

My education as finance major and my work experience as an editor for the school paper make me an ideal candidate for a journalist of Financial Times.

I'm going to graduate this summer with a Bachelor Degree of Arts. Over the past 3 years I have been working in my spare time as an editor and photographer for the school paper which is published weekly and has 5,000 readers on campus.

Besides a good record for my academic work, I have good oral and written communication skills both in Chinese and English, for which I have been granted full scholarship.

I'm outgoing and I love traveling and meeting new people. Moreover, I can work independently as well as cooperatively.

I wish to have an opportunity to discuss my qualifications with you. Please contact me at 022 - 23889999 after 3:00 p. m., or e-mail me at llwang@ yahoo. com.

Sincerely,
Linlin Wang
llwang@ yahoo. com
www. abcd/mmm/students/ktre/ptel. com

(3) A solicited application letter

Xinxing Road
Heping District 300056
Tianjin, China
June 16, 2010

Ms. Patricia White, Director of Human Resource
Tianjin Tourist Agency
456 Bright View Rd. 30066
Tianjin, China

Dear Ms. White:

Your ad in China Daily on June 15, 2010 for a tourist guide caught my eye. My work experience and four-year university study of English and French, as well as intercultural communication would allow me to serve your new tourist agency well.

While attending college full-time, I was a tourist guide in a company similar to yours during my vacations. With the knowledge and skills I learned, I guided tourists from different countries, traveling to many historical and scenic spots in China and Southeastern Asia.

The "qualifications" mentioned in your ad are just my strength — I can work both independently and cooperatively in a multi-cultural team; I have strong communication skills in both English and Chinese, and I can accept frequent travel within and outside China.

My personal attributes and competency could be best explained if I am given an interview. Please contact me at 022 -28171431, or hwl@ yahoo. com.

Sincerely,
(*Signature*)
Wanly Huang

Encl. Résumé

(4) A solicited electronic application letter

To: Mr. Jackson <lj@ yahoo. com>

From: Maria Anoka <manoka@ tufe. edu. cn>

Subject: Application for job 389

Cc:

Bcc:

Attached: C:\jobhunt\résumé\scan

Dear Mr. Jackson,

I'm interested in the Accounting position announced on Motorola Website (job389).

I will receive a B. S. in Accountancy in July this year.

During my four years of study, I've learned the management of fixed assets, risk management and inter/intra-company communication. I can analyze financial statement and compare them to past statements to identify trends and recommend ways to reduce costs and run the business even more efficiently.

I can use Excel to create computer graphics to provide the clear, reliable accounting data that Motorola needs to continue growing each year. Visit my web page to see the design of the graphics I made for a project of ABC company.

My three years of experience at ABC Company has given me the opportunity to work with customers of large-and-medium-sized enterprises and show responsibility. I developed a procedure for working out financial reports which saved so much time that I was asked to teach it to the other employees in my department.

Attached is a scannable résumé in Microsoft Word 2005. I'd like to come to your company for an interview on any Tuesday or Thursday afternoon.

Maria Anoka

manoka@ tufe. edu. cn

www. tcgh/business/students/ manoka/report. com

5. Telephone conversation

Huang leaves a voice mail to a tourist agency for a job application.

Recording of the answering machine: Tianjin Tourist Agency. Dial 1 for Service Department; dial 2 for travel schedule; dial 3 for Administration Department; dial 4 for Human Resource Department; dial 5 for an operator.

Huang dials 4

Ms. White's answering machine: Patricia White's office. Sorry, I'm not available now. Please leave a message.

Huang: Good afternoon, Ms. White. This is Huang Heping calling for a job application at 18:00 o'clock on Monday, June 20th.

I'm 26 years old, with an MBA degree from Hong Kong University. I have good communication skills and fast learning ability. My work experience in customer service, in English and Chinese translation, and my passion for multinational culture facilitate me to assist your honorable tourist agency to achieve goals. I'm looking forward to an interview. Please call me at 022 – 28171431. Thank you, Ms. White, and have a good day!

New Words and Phrases

enthusiastic [inˌθjuːziˈæstik] *a.* having enthusiasm 热心的，热情的，热烈的

be enthusiastic for (*or* about) sth. 对某事热心

become enthusiastic over a research project 热衷于一项研究项目

candidate [ˈkændideit] *n.* a person who seeks to gain a certain position 应聘人，候选人

bilingual [baiˈliŋgwəl] *a.* able to use two languages 能讲两国语言的

bilingual education 双语教育

scholarship [ˈskɔləʃip] *n.* a grant of financial aid awarded to a student 奖学金

competency [ˈkɔmpitənsi] *n.* capability and qualification in certain field 资格，能力

vacancy [ˈveikənsi] *n.* 1) a place or a position which is vacant or unoccupied 空缺，空职

fill (up) a vacancy by recruiting 通过招聘填补空缺

2) an empty or unoccupied space 空白

This will help to fill a vacancy in our knowledge. 这有助于弥补我们知识上的空白。

Notes

1. application letter 求职信

2. solicited application letter 招聘求职信（根据用人单位的招聘信息而发出的求职信）

3. unsolicited application letter 非招聘求职信（毛遂自荐，本人主动发出的求职信）

4. straight A 全部成绩都是 A（优秀）

In universities in US and many other western countries, grades are given in the following standard:

A means "excellent", which is equivalent to 90 points or above in 100 points system

B means "good", which is equivalent to 80 points or above

C means "medium", which is equivalent to 70 points or above

D means "pass", which is equivalent to 60 points or above

F means "failure", which is below 60 points

5. Bachelor Degree of Arts (B. A.) 文学学士学位

6. B. S.: Bachelor of Science 理学学士

Relevant expressions:

Bachelor of Arts (B. A.) 文学学士

Master of Arts (M. A.) 文学硕士

Doctor of Literature (Litt. D.) 文学博士

Bachelor Degree of Science 理学学士学位

Bachelor of Science (B. S.) 理学学士

Master of Science (M. S.) 理学硕士

Doctor of Philosophy (Ph. D.) 哲学博士

The specific field of your study can be given after the degree. **e. g.**:

Ph. D. in Applied Management and Decision Sciences 应用管理和决策学博士

Ph. D. in Education (*or* Doctor of Education) 教育学博士

Ph. D. in Public Health 公共卫生学博士

Ph. D. in Health Services 保健社会学博士

Ph. D. in Human Services 公共事业学博士

Ph. D. in Public Policy and Administration 国家政策和管理学博士

Doctorate of Management in Organizational Leadership 组织领导管理学博士学位

Doctor of Business Administration 企业管理学博士

Doctor of Education in Educational Leadership 教育管理学博士

Doctor of Health Administration 卫生管理学博士

7. fixed assets 固定资产

Useful Expressions

1. Dr. Saul Wilder, a consultant to your firm and my Organizational Management professor, has informed me that Aerosol Monitoring and Analysis is looking for someone with excellent communications skills, organizational experience, and leadership background for a management position.
2. In reply to your advertisement in today's (newspaper), I respectfully offer my services for the development and prosperity of ABC Company.
3. In response to your advertisement in (name of the newspaper) of January 15, I wish to apply for the position of (secretary, accountant, clerk, salesman, etc).
4. I am writing to inquire whether you will need the services of a young man with three years of vocational training and some part-time work experience. I would like to fill in any vacancy as one of your office staff during the summer vacation period.
5. I can write shorthand with 120 words per minute, and typewriting 55 words in English.
6. I believe that my enclosed résumé will demonstrate that I have the characteristics and experience you seek. In addition, I'd like to mention how my work experience last summer makes me a particularly strong candidate for the position.
7. I feel confident that I can meet your special requirements for "a good command of English", because I graduated from the English Language Department of ______ University with excellent record in English.
8. Please find enclosed an outline of my education and business training, credentials for my

English and computer skills, and two letters of recommendation.

9. Please contact me at (317) 555 – 0118 any morning before 11:00 a. m., or leave a message.

10. I'm looking forward to have an opportunity to discuss my qualifications with you.

Exercises

1. Answer questions.

1) What is the difference between a solicited application letter and an unsolicited application letter?

2) How to write an opening paragraph for a solicited letter and an unsolicited one?

3) What is the proper length of an application letter?

2. Questions for discussion.

What information should a complete application letter include?

3. Decide whether the following statements are true or false. Write "T" for true, and "F" for false in the brackets.

1) Never submit a résumé through e-mail; it is considered too informal. (   )

2) Application letters should be addressed to a specific person, not to the company in general. (   )

3) To ask for an interview in an application letter is too forward and bold to be appropriate. (   )

4) Unsolicited letters are organized in the same way as solicited letters, but are addressed to different readers. (   )

5) An application letter must not only reveal your experience, but also show how that experience can benefit a specific organization. (   )

6) In a solicited letter it is unnecessary to state the exact job title because employers already know what they are looking for. (   )

7) "You" attitude is not necessary in an application letter because employers understand that you must focus on yourself. (   )

8) Mentioning all the specifics given in your résumé is not helpful, since employers can read them in the attached résumé. (   )

9) Emphasizing what you can benefit from the position is necessary in application letters. (   )

10) Electronic contact information is to be given instead of a signature for e-mail application letter. (   )

4. Choose the best expression from each of the following groups of sentences of A B C and D for an application letter.

1) A. Because I have taken such a huge number of technical courses, my writing skills are not well developed, only slightly better than most people's.

B. Technical courses have enabled me to understand your products so that I could explain them to customers.

C. My writing skills are not as good as my technical skills.

D. My technical skills are much better than my writing skills, but I can still put a sentence together effectively.

2) A. My professor is willing to verify the written recommendation over the phone.

B. You can verify the recommendation by calling Professor Jackson.

C. Professor Jackson would love to discuss this recommendation over the phone.

D. Professor Jackson can provide more specific information about my coursework and qualifications.

3) A. I anxiously await a phone call from you so that we can meet to discuss job opportunities.

B. I can't wait to hear from you.

C. Any time that you want to call and have me for an interview, I am available.

D. I look forward to talking to you about how my qualifications could meet the corporate needs.

4) A. As president of the Environmental Protection Club, I spoke to community groups and wrote bulletins. This experience would help me to speak and write effectively as a sales representative for Motorola.

B. I was president of the Environmental Protection Club; I spoke and wrote for the club a lot; I could speak and write for your company.

C. I spoke to community groups and wrote bulletins when I was president of the Environmental Protection Group. I am qualified to do the same things for Monsanto.

D. My duties as president of the Environmental Protection Club included speaking to community groups and writing bulletins. These skills are essential to the management responsibilities of the position your company is seeking to fill.

5. Choose the best answer to complete the following statements.

1) You can write ______ when you know that the company is hiring.

A. a solicited application letter　　B. an unsolicited application letter

C. an electronic application letter　　D. any one of the above

2) When you want to work for an organization that has not announced openings, you should write ______.

A. a solicited application letter　　B. an unsolicited application letter

C. an electronic application letter　　D. any one of the above

3) You should start your letter by catching the interest of your prospective employer when ______.

A. writing a solicited application letter　　B. writing an unsolicited application letter

C. writing an electronic application letter　　D. writing any one of the above letters

4) In writing electronic application letters, avoid using ______ which makes reading difficult.

A. all capital letters　　B. capital and small letters

C. black ink　　D. blue ink

6. Translate the following phrases and make sentences with them.

1)恳请准予面试

2)随信附上我的履历表

3)附寄成绩单一份

4)申请这个职位

5)从基层做起

6)在大学主修会计

7)填补贵公司空缺

8)推荐信

7. Filling in the blanks with the words and phrases given below.

opportunity	contact	leadership	experience	candidate
demonstrate	position	informed	consultant	effectively

Dear Ms. Rennick:

Dr. Saul Wilder, a 1)____ to your firm and my Organizational Management professor, has 2)____ me that Aerosol Monitoring and Analysis is looking for someone with excellent communications skills, organizational experience, and 3)____ background for a management 4)____. I believe that my enclosed résumé will 5)____ that I have the characteristics and experience you seek. In addition, I'd like to mention how my work experience last summer makes me a particularly strong 6)____ for the position.

As a promoter for Kentech Training at the 1997 Paris Air Show, I discussed Kentech's products with marketers and sales personnel from around the world. I also carry out research and wrote reports on new product development and compiled information on aircraft industry trends. The knowledge of the aircraft industry I gained from this position would help me analyze how Aerosol products can meet the needs of regular and prospective clients, and the valuable 7)____ I gained in promotion, sales, and marketing would help me use that information 8)____.

I would welcome the 9)____ to discuss these and other qualifications with you. Please 10)____ me at (317) 555 -0118 any morning before 11:00 a. m., or leave a message. I look forward to meeting with you to discuss the ways my skills may best serve Aerosol Monitoring and Analysis.

Sincerely yours,

John Smith

8. Translate the following sentences into English.

1)应5月2日贵公司在中国日报上的广告,本人愿应聘市场调研员职位。

2)本人熟练的英文和法文一定能在贵公司的谈判和翻译中派上用场。

3)本人在商界供职10年,迄今一直担任人事部主任。

4)求学中,我曾获得奖学金及演讲比赛冠军。

5)本人毕业于香港大学,并在加州大学获得文学硕士学位。

6)随信附上我的履历表和我的英文老师的推荐函。

7)我在大学期间从课堂上和工作中得到广告知识和工作经验。

8)我希望得到面试的机会以便更详细地说一说我的能力。

9)本人对公司办公业务非常熟悉。如有机会为贵公司服务,会为公司作出贡献。

10)如贵公司有意面试,本人每天上午11:00至晚上10:00随时待命。

9. Suppose you are looking for job and have read the flowing ads in a certain paper write a letter of application in appropriate format.

1)**English Translator**

Location:Shanghai

Job Requirements:

- At least one year of work experience as an English translator
- Good English, both written and spoken
- Good Chinese, both written and spoken

2)**Helpdesk**

Location:Beijing, Guangzhou

Job Responsibilities: Deliver professional IT technical service to HP customers via telephone or software such as net meeting.

Job Requirements:

- Good language skills and the ability to undertake service and daily communications with customers
- Related computer science education background or related IT support experience
- Could use English/Chinese/Japanese verbal, written and listening skills to perform tasks
- At least one - year of helpdesk work experience, or IT work in an MNC Company

(MNC:Multinational Corporation)

10. Suppose you were the applicant of the following job seeking ads, adapt each of them to an effective voice mail within 30 seconds.

1)A Chinese lady, 26, with an MS degree in Investment, Finance, 2 years overseas experience, with one year as a team leader in the high tech industry and more than a year in the finance industry as a financial analyst, possesses excellent verbal and written skills and confident and sensitive communication skills, fluent in English, Japanese and Chinese. I'm Keenly seeking a career in the Business Development and Finance area.

2)An ambitious gentleman, 25, with a Bachelor degree, over 3 year in Libya, North Africa in construction project marketing. Good understanding of both Chinese and foreign backgrounds. I have strong communication capabilities, especially in multinational environment. I'm able to help joint venture or foreign company to expand business into China's market.

3)A Chinese gentleman, who is a recent graduate of the University of science and Technology. Obtained MS in advanced computer science with Information and Communication Technology (ICT) management, also gained knowledge in finance and economics from the China Centre for Economics Research (CCER), Beijing University. A good understanding and skills in IT products, as well as IT market and IT related businesses, qualified for roles that require combined knowledge in IT and management, such as IT/business, consultant/analyst.

4) A 22 year-old lady, a fresh graduate in Finance and Accounting from Nankai University, Tianjin I have a strong finance and accounting background, very enthusiastic and keen to learn on the job, able to handle multiple tasks and work under pressure I'm a team player with top communication skills. A positive outlook and enjoying challenges and two of my personality traits. I am looking for finance related jobs in banks or consulting firms.

5) A 30 year old Chinese, English interpreter, with over five years of translating experience, familiar with construction engineering, business negotiations, small and medium international meeting or forum interpretation, looking for business English related full-time or part-time jobs, such as international project assistant.

Lesson Seven

Establishing Business Relations

1. Introduction

In order to enlarge market share and promote sales, business companies have to establish relations with new customers besides keeping existing ones. The following are the major sources where information about potential customers is available.

◇ Website	◇ Trade fairs
◇ Trade directory	◇ Banks
◇ Advertisements	◇ Chamber of Commerce
◇ Friends and business partners	◇ Commercial Counselor's Office

Information from the last three sources is usually more reliable but is subject to certain fees and charges.

In choosing a customer or partner in foreign countries, some research is often needed to have a better knowledge about the country or region in such aspects as:

◇ Business policy and customs practice
◇ Political and economic stability
◇ Diplomatic relation with your own country
◇ Culture and interests of potential buyers
◇ Geographic conditions (such as ports, shipping lines)
◇ Natural environment (such as climate)

Besides extending your desire to target companies to establish business relations, you may also introduce your own company and products to the public through appropriate media, such as website, brochure to solicit business and attract potential customers and partners.

2. Writing strategy

In writing a letter for building up business relations, you should:

1) Mention the source from which you get the information.

2) State your purpose in writing—your wish to build up business relations with the firm in question.

3) Briefly introduce your business and main scope of products. If there are any detailed product catalogues and relevant information, include them as attachment or enclosure or refer your readers to your website.

4) Offer credit references if possible.

5) Express your hope of receiving a reply from the recipient.

In replying to such letters, you should:

1) Mention the date in which you have received the letter. This can be omitted in an e-mail message as the date is automatically given.

2) Express your thanks to your reader for the proposal.

3) Provide information requested.

4) State clearly if you accept the proposal or not.

5) Give a reason if you decline it, and end your letter with a positive note for future business.

In composing an e-mail message replying to a proposal or request for information, include the previous message of request in your e-mail, so that you don't need to mention it in your letter, and your reader will know why you are writing the message. (See example letter 5)

3. Communication for results

Letters for establishing business relations often involve introduction of the firm. When giving such introductions:

1) Make it brief and focused on information most attractive and important to your recipient. Leave long and not very important details in your company's website or introductory brochures.

2) Use superlative degree of adjectives such as "best", "largest" sparingly as they may sound bragging and boasting. If you must use these words support them with facts and figures.

Instead of writing	Write
We are one of the largest companies in the world with a long history.	Founded in 1891 our company has 157,000 employees world wide and 35,000 in the head quarter.
The company is financially strong with large profits.	The company's sales revenue hit US $18 billion and net profit reached US $102 million in 2006.

4. Example letters

(1) An introduction of the company and products

SOUTH CHINA SILK PRODUCT CO. LTD.

Nanjing, China Tel: 86 - 25 - 4356 7788

Ms. Renee Easton

General Manager

Universal Channel Corp.

5 Rock Street

Rockbridge, IL62081

U. S. A.

September 7, 2010

Dear Ms Easton:

We noted your name and address in the U. S. Business Directory. We are writing with a desire to enter into direct business relations with you.

South China Silk Product Co. Ltd. is one of the leading manufacturers of silk products in China, with the headquarter based in Nanjing, China.

The company has 30 years of business experience in this field. Its products range from the traditional embroidered silk blouse to the latest fashion, some of which have been displayed in the latest fashion show in Paris, and are well received by customers at home and abroad. They even attracted many celebrities and dignitaries including the former British Prime Minister Madam Thatcher.

We have a reliable and committed work team of 2000 employees. In our business practice, we strive for a win-win result with our customers based on the principle of equality and mutual benefits.

For further details about our company and our products please visit our website at www.scspc.com. And for our financial standing, you can get reliable information from Bank of China, Nanjing Branch.

You are cordially invited to visit our company at your convenience, and we await your favorable reply.

Sincerely yours,

SOUTH CHINA SILK PRODUCT CO. LTD.

(Signature)

Larry Chang, Director

(2) A positive reply from an importer

Universal Channel Corp.

5 Rock Street, Rockbridge, IL#62081

Tel: 858 - 8905 - 3366

Mr. LARRY CHANG
South China Silk Product Co. Ltd.
31 Hubei Rd.
Nanjing, China

September 14, 2010

Dear Mr. Larry Chang:

We learned from your letter of September 7, 2006 that you are interested in establishing business relations with us for the sale of silk products.

Your desire coincides with ours. I believe a friendly trade relation will benefit both sides.

Presently we are interested in Art. No. 36 displayed on your website. Please send us your samples and pricelist, as well as information about terms of payment and time of delivery.

Your prompt reply is highly appreciated.

Sincerely,
(Signature)
Renee Easton

(3) Seeking new customers

RAINBOW PHARMACEUTICAL MEDICINE CO.

176 Jianguo Str., Anhui, China Tel.: 0553 – 4545 8350 E-mail: temc@ergo.com

March 15, 2010

Mr. Paul Williams
Ferozson Medicine Ltd.
3766 Woodhill Avenue
Greenwood, DE19970
U. S. A.

Dear Mr. Williams:

Your company has been introduced to us by Messrs. Green & Co. Ltd., Illinois, as a major importer of Chinese Herb Medicine. As a producer and exporter of this item with 20 years of experience, we hope to enter into business relations with you.

Our products are sold to many countries and enjoy a good reputation on the world market. You will find our company an ideal partner providing first-class commodity and after-sale service.

For details of our products, please check the catalogue enclosed.

Please inform us of your specific interest, so that we can send you our samples and quotation by air.

We appreciate your favorable reply.

Yours sincerely,
(Signature)
Liu Wei-min
Manager

Enclosure: 1

(4) A negative reply to the exporter's proposal

Ferozson Medicine Ltd.

3766 Woodhill Avenue, Greenwood, DE19970
Tel.: 858 2690 4356 Fax: 858 2690 4357

March 20, 2010

Mr. Liu Wei-min
176 Jianguo Street
Anhui, China

Dear Mr. Liu Wei-min:

Thank you for your letter of March 15, 2005, introducing your company and informing us of the business opportunity.

Presently, our orders for the first half of the year have already been filled. However, we will contact you when we need to place an order.

Sincerely,
(Signature)
Paul Williams

(5) E-mail from an exporter requesting the introduction of new customers

TO: Maurice Lang <mlong@ m&t. com>
FROM: Katy Foster <kfoster@ goha. com>
DATE: May 9, 2010
SUBJECT: Seeking customers in Germany
CC: Susan Lee, General Manager
BCC:

Dear Mr. Lang:

We are very grateful for your cooperation over the past years.

Now we are eager to enlarge our market of electronic products in the western area of Germany. But we don't have any relation in that area.

Therefore, I'm writing to you with the hope that you would be kind enough to recommend some most capable and reliable importers in the area, who are interested in our electronic products.

We appreciate you for your recommendation.

Sincerely,
HERMAN MILLER, INC.

Reply from the receiver

To: Katy Foster <kfoster@ goha. com>
From: Maurice Lang <mlong@ m&t. com>
Subject: Wholesaler /Distributor in Germany
Attached: Financial Report of Tech-gate Ltd.

Dear Ms. Foster:

The following company is known in our country as a major distributor and wholesaler in electronic products.

Tech-gate Ltd.
Schiller Street145
33668DORTMUND
GERMANY

We don't have direct contact with the firm, but their business operation seems to be sound according to its financial report published for the past two years.

I hope the above information is of help to you.

Encl.: A financial report

Yours sincerely,

Maurice Lang

(6) An online company introduction

3M COMPANY

Who We Are

3M is a diversified technology company with a worldwide presence in the following markets: consumer and office products; display and graphics; electronic communications; health care; transportation; and safety, security and protection services. What makes us so diverse is our ability to apply our technologies — often in combination — to an endless array of customer needs.

Our Values

◇ Provide investors an attractive return through sustained, quality growth.

◇ Satisfy customers with superior quality, value and service.

◇ Respect our social and physical environment.

◇ Be a company employees are proud to be part of.

3M At a Glance

◇ Worldwide sales: US $21.2 billion

◇ International sales: US $12.9 billion (61 percent of company's total)

◇ Companies in more than 60 countries

◇ 3M products sold in nearly 200 countries

◇ More than 69,000 employees

3M Businesses

3M serves customers through six business segments, which increase speed and efficiency by sharing technological, manufacturing, marketing and other resources.

These six businesses are:

◇ Consumer and Office Business

◇ Display and Graphics Business

◇ Electro and Communications Business

◇ Health Care Business

◇ Industrial and Transportation Business

◇ Safety, Security and Protection Services Business

(Note: "◇" is hyperlink which can be clicked for further detailed information.)

5. Telephone conversation

Mr. Liu Weimin calls Mr. Paul Williams through an operator.

Operator: Ferozson Medicine Ltd. how may I help you?

Liu: I'd like to speak to Paul Williams, please.

Operator: Yes, one moment please.

Liu: Thank you.

Operator: Sorry, he is on another line, would you hold?

Liu: No, thanks, I'll call back later.

A few minutes later, Liu calls again.

Liu: Good morning, Operator, is Mr. Williams available now?

Operator: Yes, just a moment. I'll put you through.

Liu: Good morning, Mr. Williams. This is Liu Weimin from Rainbow Pharmaceutical. We have introduced some new products on the markets, and the prices of our products have been adjusted. I would like to send you our latest catalogue and a few samples of our new products. I think you'll be interested. Now, I'd like to confirm the address of your company. Is your postcode 19970?

Williams: That's right. And please address your parcel to Ms. Lisa Faulkner, the new secretary.

Liu: Could you spell the name, please?

Williams: Yes, that's L-I-S-A for Lisa, and F-A-U-L-K-N-E-R for Faulkner.

Liu: Okay, L-I-S-A for Lisa, and F-A-U-L-K-N-E-R for Faulkner.

Williams: Right.

Liu: Thank you very much. Goodbye.

Williams: Goodbye.

New Words and Phrases

enclosure [in'kləuʒə] *n.* a supplement to a business letter 附件

catalogue ['kætəlɔg] *n.* a printed list of goods with necessary descriptions 产品目录

synonym: brochure, pamphlet, illustrative leaflet

celebrity [si'lebriti] *n.* 1) a famous person 名人

a celebrity fundraising dinner 一次社会名流筹措资金的晚宴

2) renown; fame

celebrity exercise books 人人皆知的练习书

dignitary ['dignitəri] *n.* a person of high rank or position 高官

standing ['stændiŋ] *n.* status; reputation 信誉

distributor [dis'tribjutə] *n.* one that markets or sells merchandise, especially a wholesaler 经销商，批发商

wholesaler ['həuseilə] *n.* a businessman who sells goods in large quantities 批发商

dealings [ˈdiːliŋz] *n.* transactions or relations with others, usually in business 交易,商业往来

Our business dealings with this firm have been going on well.

我们和这家公司的商业往来进展顺利。

We've never had any dealings with them since then.

从那以后我们再也没有和这家公司做过交易。

diverse [daiˈvəːs] *v.* different; various 不同的, 各种各样的

many diverse designs 各种不同的设计

diversify [daiˈvəːsifai] *v.* to make different or various in form or quality; vary 使不同, 使多样化

Our factory's products diversified several years ago. 几年前我们工厂就开始使产品多样化了。

diversified [daiˈvəːsifaid] *a.* vary in form or style 多样化的, 形形色色的, 分散经营的

a company with diversified technology 技术多元化的公司

return [riˈtəːn] *n.* profit 盈利;利润

sustain [səsˈtein] *v.* to keep over a long period 持续一段时间

He owes his success to sustained hard work. 他把他的成功归功于长期艰苦劳动。

He couldn't sustain his interest in the job. 他对这工作的兴趣不会维持很久。

Notes

1. trade directory 企业名录

2. Chamber of Commerce 商会

3. Commercial Counselor's Office 商务参赞处

4. Credit reference 资信证明人

5. pricelist 价目表,价目单

6. terms of payment 支付方式;付款条件

7. time of delivery 装船期,交货期

8. quotation 报价

9. Art. No. short form of "Article Number" 货号

10. place an order 订货

11. Chinese herb medicine 中草药

12. We are writing with a desire to *enter into direct business relations with* you. 为了与贵公司建立贸易联系,特致函联系。

Similar expressions: enter into business / trade relations/ relationship with 或 establish business relations with 与……建立业务联系

13. We are sure you will be interested and *find a ready market* when you place an order with our company. 我们相信你们会感兴趣的,并且如果你方从我公司订货一定能畅销。

find a ready market (in...) 打开……的市场,畅销

14. You will find our company an ideal partner providing first-class commodity and af-

ter-sale service. 贵方会发现我公司是理想的合作伙伴,提供一流产品和售后服务。

15. **Therefore, I'm writing to you with the hope that you would *be kind enough to* recommend some most capable and reliable importers in the area, who are interested in our electronic products.** 兹致函,希望能推荐一些在这一地区最有能力、最可靠并对我们的电子产品感兴趣的进口商。

    to be kind enough to ... 用于表示礼貌和客气

    e. g. : Will you be kind enough to do me a favor? 能帮我个忙吗?

16. **We don't have direct contact with the firm, but their business operation seems to be sound according to its *financial report* published for the past two years.** 我们和这家公司没有直接联系,但从它们过去两年发布的财务报告来看,它们的经营状况似乎还是不错的。

    financial report 财务报告

Useful Expressions

1. Having had your name and address from the Commercial Counselor's Office of the Embassy of the People's Republic of China in Britain, we take this opportunity to write to you and see if we can establish business relations by starting some practical transactions.
2. Our products are sold on many countries and enjoy good reputation on the world market. We are willing to enter into business relations with your firm on the basis of equality, mutual benefit and exchange of needed goods.
3. In compliance with your request, we are sending you a catalogue by air together with a range of pamphlets for your reference.
4. We write to you with a view to building up business relations with your firm.
5. With a view to expanding our business at your end, we are writing to you in the hope that we can build up business relations with your firm.
6. As this item falls within the business scope of our corporation, we shall be pleased to enter into business relations with you at an early date.
7. The enclosed catalogue will give you some general idea of our lines of arts and crafts.
8. We have received with pleasure your letter of September 20, from which we learned that you are willing to import Chinese Black Tea from us.
9. Your letter addressed to our Head Office has been passed on to us for attention and reply.
10. Our bankers are the Hong Kong & Shanghai Banking Corporation in Hong Kong, and they can provide you with the information about our business and finances.

Exercises

1. Answer questions.

1) From where can a business person obtain the names and addresses of the firms that may be potential partners and customers?
2) What are the most important factors to be considered in building up business relation with a

new customer?

3) What information should be contained in the first letter sent to your prospective clients for the purpose of setting up business relations?

4) What's the function of including the previous message of request at the beginning of your e-mail reply?

2. Choose the best answer to complete the following statements.

1) We have been informed that you are ______ the market ______ textiles.

A. at, of B. at, for C. in, for D. in, of

2) We always adhere ______ the principle of equality and mutual benefit.

A. on B. to C. in D. at

3) We are sending you the samples ______ requested.

A. be B. are C. as D. for

4) We take pleasure in enclosing a copy of your latest catalogue ______ for in your letter dated December 11.

A. ask B. asks C. asked D. asking

5) We owe your name and address ______ the Chamber of Commerce of Shanghai.

A. to B. for C. with D. by

6) Our products enjoy ______ in the world market.

A. most popular B. great popularity C. good seller D. selling fast

7) In ______ with your request, we sent you three samples this morning of our computer disk.

A. comply B. complied C. compliance D. complying

8) We shall ______ a reply.

A. appreciate your giving B. appreciate you to give

C. appreciate you for giving D. appreciate for your giving

9) We ______ herewith two copies of our illustrated catalogue for your consideration.

A. include B. enclose C. inquire D. exclude

10) We avail ourselves ______ this opportunity to approach you in an attempt to establish business relations with you.

A. by B. to C. on D. of

3. Decide whether the following statements are true or false. Write "T" for true, and "F" for false in the brackets.

1) Business firms can enlarge their market share through building up business relations with new customers. ( )

2) A website is a more reliable source of information about potential customers. ( )

3) Cash payment is needed for any inquiry about new business opportunities. ( )

4) Chambers of Commerce is not obliged to give any replies to inquiries about any business firms. ( )

5) Consideration of a country's political and economic stability is necessary in choosing customers in the country. ( )

6) A detailed introduction of your own business should be given at the very beginning in writing a letter to establish business relations. (　　)

7) A reply to such letters as proposing to set up business relations should never be sent by e-mail. (　　)

8) A self-introduction is always needed in writing a reply. (　　)

4. Translate the terms and expressions from Chinese into English and use them in making sentences.

1)企业名录　　2)财务信誉

3)商会　　4)售后服务

5)建立贸易联系　　6)属于……的经营范围

7)主要出口商　　8)试订货

5. Translate the terms and expressions from English into Chinese and use them in making sentences.

1) find a ready market　　2) Commercial Counselor's Office

3) under separate cover　　4) trade fairs

5) in the market for　　6) take the opportunity to

6. Fill in the blanks with the words and phrases given below, and change the form when necessary.

offer	under	upon receipt of	enter	through
enjoy	acquaint	in the market for	learn	fall/ come

We 1) ______ from the Chamber of Commerce that you are 2) ______ tablecloths. Since this article 3) ______ within the scope of our business activities, we take this opportunity to express our wish to 4) ______ into business relations with you.

Good Luck brand tablecloths are known for their good quality and fine workmanship. They have enjoyed great popularity in the US market. We are sure that 5) ______ our joint efforts they will 6) ______ fast sale in your market.

In order to 7) ______ you with our products, we are airmailing to you 8) ______ separate cover several brochures together with a pricelist. 9) ______ your specific inquiry, we shall send you our 10) ______ without delay.

7. Translate the following sentences from Chinese into English.

1)贵公司已由英国伦敦商会推荐给我公司。

2)兹介绍,本公司是中国纺织品的主要出口商之一,经营此项业务已有多年经验,我方愿同贵公司建立贸易关系。

3)感谢你9月10日的来信,希望就如下问题商讨开展业务的可能性。

4)随函附上一本产品目录及价目单,以便使你方了解我方现有出口商品。

5)你们寄给我驻巴基斯坦参赞处的信已转给我们办理,因为该项商品的出口由我公司专营。

6)据悉您是中国绿茶的潜在客户,而中国绿茶正属于我们经营范围之内。

7)承蒙贵国商会介绍,我们得知贵公司的名称及地址。

8)我们的产品销往许多国家,在世界市场上享有盛誉。

9)我公司于 1966 年开始其快餐(snack food)业务,在 40 多个国家都有分公司,是世界上最大的跨国快餐公司之一。

10)这家公司是本地区主要儿童用品零售商,专营玩具、儿童服饰及婴儿用品。

8. Translate the following sentences from English into Chinese.

1) We've come to know your name and address from the Commercial Counselor's Office of the Chinese Embassy in London.

2) We are willing to enter into business relations with your firm on the basis of equality, mutual benefit and exchange of needed goods.

3) Your company has been kindly recommended to us by Mr. John Smith as one of the main importers of furniture in your area.

4) Through the courtesy of the Oriental Industry Ltd., we have the name of your firm and have learned that you are interested in establishing business relations with our company for the purpose of importing chinaware.

5) We specialize in exporting light industrial goods in the Far East, but we have no trade contact with your company. We address this letter to you with the desire of entering into direct business relations with you.

6) We are importers of quality clothing materials, and have large annual requirements for our markets in Europe.

7) We are very well connected with all the major dealers of light industrial products, and feel sure we can find ready market here for your goods if they moderately priced.

8) Our bankers are the Hong Kong & Shanghai Banking Corporation in Hong Kong, and they can provide you with the information about our business and finances.

9. Translate the following passage of company introduction into Chinese.

John Deere

In 1837, John Deere founded the company that would come to bear his name. Incorporated as Deere Company in 1868, it has grown from a one-man blacksmith shop into a corporation that today does business around the world and employs approximately 47,000 people. It is one of the oldest industrial companies in the United States.

The company continues to be guided, as it has been since its beginning, by the core values exhibited by its founder: integrity, quality, commitment and innovation.

10. Rewrite the following letter for conciseness.

Dear Sirs:

Having had your name and address from the Commercial Councilor's Office of our Embassy in Pakistan, we avail ourselves of this opportunity to write to you and see if we can establish business relations with you.

We are a state-owned corporation specializing in the export of table-cloths, and are in a position to accept orders against customers' samples specifying design, specifications and packaging requirements. We are also prepared to accept orders for goods with customers' own trade marks or brand names.

In order to give you a rough idea of our various table-cloths, we are airmailing you under separate cover a copy of our latest catalogue for your reference. If you find any of the items interesting, please let us know as soon as possible. We shall be glad to send you quotations and samples upon receipt of your concrete enquiries.

We await your early reply.

11. Suppose you have just received a letter from one of your customers as given below, write a letter of reply for the opportunity of establishing business relations with the firm mentioned.

Dear Sir:

One of our major clients, Shelly Cotton Ltd., is looking for some large textile manufacturers for the purpose of establishing relations. We recommended your firm to them.

Shelly Cotton Ltd. has been our client for 30 years, showing satisfactory results in its business dealings.

For your reference, we have enclosed some particulars about the firm. We ask that this information be held in confidence. If you are interested, contact the firm with the following address:

Shelly Cotton Ltd.

59 Furget Rue

Paris 39887

France

We are ready to offer any additional information upon request concerning this firm, and are looking forward to your reply.

Sincerely,

the Chamber of Commerce, London

12. Make a telephone conversation in pairs with two students sitting back to back, one is calling the other, a potential customer, to confirm the address of the receiving company and the name of the receiver before sending certain mails.

Lesson Eight
Status Inquiry

1. Introduction

In today's global marketplace, millions of companies and business people are involved in all kinds of business. When you log onto the website "www. ebay. com", you will find numerous companies introducing themselves and their products and services. But not all of them are reliable and trustworthy. Developing business relations with the right partnerships is critical to the success of your business. In order to minimize risk exposure and identify new business opportunities, it is of utmost importance to inquire into the status of your potential customers as well as customers you are going to do business for the first time in order to learn exactly who you are dealing with before signing contracts and accepting credit applications.

In addition to new customers, it is advisable to conduct regular status inquiry to current customers of small business in today's highly competitive and risky world market, especially under the following circumstances:

◇ Your record about the customer is out-dated.

◇ Your customer suddenly changes his/her usual way of doing business.

◇ You and your customer have an opportunity to work on a big project.

◇ Your customer's order has a sudden surge or drop.

Getting a complete picture of the financial health of your customers depends on fresh, accurate and objective data, which can be obtained from:

◇ Commercial Counselor's Office

◇ Chamber of Commerce

◇ Banks

◇ Enquiry Agencies

The inquiry can be made by either the seller or the buyer regarding:

◇ The credit history of the business owner

◇ The public records of the business

◇ The international profile of the business

Inquiry into the above details can help you manage risk, reduce liability and avoid fraud. As such information is considered top secret by a company, it is to be handled with confidence. Most banks are reluctant to provide it directly to unknown traders. Therefore, when checking on a bank reference you have to make an inquiry to the relevant bank through your own bank.

Some banks and inquiry agencies provide credit inquiry forms that can be obtained directly from the banks or downloaded from their websites. When you need such information, just fill in the form with the information required, such as the name and address of your company and the company to which the inquiry is to be made, the contact numbers, the amount of credit, the media through which you expect the return mail to be sent to you and other particular information related to the inquired firm.

2. Writing strategy

In writing a letter of status inquiry, such words as *Confidential* or *Private and Confidential* are to be typed one blank line space below the inside address. These words are also typed on the envelope if the letter is to be delivered by post.

Include in your letter the full name and address of the company you want to inquire into and inform your reader of the specific information you need.

Considering the confidential nature of such information, always end your message with a promise to keep the information provided in confidence.

3. Communication for results

Business letters should be written with courtesy, especially when you are making a request or asking a favor.

Instead of writing	Write
Determine for us whether this firm is suitable for our credit.	Would you please help us determine whether this firm is suitable for our credit.
Do you understand what I mean?	Have I made myself clear?

4. Example letters

(1) A credit inquiry from an exporter

FAR EAST TRADING CORP.

Tianjin, China

December 20, 2010

Information Service Dept.
Bank of China
Tianjin, China

<u>Private & Confidential</u>

Dear Sirs:

A purchase order from James Smith & Co. at 23 Granville Court, Los Angeles,

CA690909, U. S. A for $7,500 worth of merchandise listed Citibank, California as a credit reference.

We would appreciate it if you could approach this bank and provide us information on the credit history of James Smith & Co. Key facts would include how long the owner, Donna Gard, has had an account with the City Bank, and whether she has any outstanding debts. We will keep any information you send us confidential.

A postage paid envelope is enclosed for your convenience.

Sincerely,

FAR EAST TRADING CORP.

David Anderson

David Anderson

Export Manager

(2) A favorable reply from the bank

BANK OF CHINA

Tianjin, China

December 28, 2010

Mr. David Anderson

Export Manager

Far East Trading Corp.

Tianjin, China

Private & Confidential

Dear Mr. Anderson:

With reference to your letter dated December 20, 2005, we'd like to give you the information we have received from the City Bank, California about James Smith & Co. at 23 Granville Court, Los Angeles, CA690909, U. S. A.

James Smith & Co. was a private company founded in 1995, and it has been keeping an account with the City Bank ever since.

The company has kept a fairly good credit record, and it doesn't have any outstanding debts up to now.

Considering its financial capacity, we think a credit not exceeding US $ 8,000 would be safe in your business transaction.

The above information is given as confidential and without any responsibility on our part.

Yours truly,
Bank of China, Tianjin

(3) A credit inquiry from a consulting agency

AAA BUSINESS CONSULTING AGENCY
Tianjin, China

6 October, 2010

Chamber of Commerce
Libya Embassy
Beijing, China

Confidential

Dear Sir:

We have received a letter of inquiry from one of our clients, asking the financial standing and business integrity of

Kasu Tradinging Corp.
10 – 15 Grand Square
Katalulu 106
Libya

We should be obliged if you could provide us with relevant information concerning the above company, so that we'll be able to respond to our client.

You can rest assured that any information you give us will be treated with strict confidence. And any expense you have for this matter will be paid by us upon receiving your bills.

We look forward to your prompt reply.

Yours truly,

AAA BUSINESS CONSULTING AGENCY

(4) An unfavorable reply from the Chamber of Commerce

LIBYA CHAMBER OF COMMERCE

Beijing, China

22 October, 2010

AAA Business Consulting Agency
Tianjin, China

Private and Confidential

Dear Sir:

The information we have received regarding your inquiry of 6 October, 2005 are as follows:

Kasu Trading Corp. is a family-run business established in 1988. Its main business line is importing and distributing machinery and electronic products. In 1999, the company was running at a loss and its credit record is getting from bad to worse since then. Now it is running in debt of more than US $ 1,2000 due to the local bank by the end of this year.

Therefore we advise you to inform your client to act with caution in their business dealings with Kasu Trading Corp.

The above information is given to you as most confidential.

Yours sincerely,

LIBYA CHAMBER OF COMMERCE

(5) An inquiry made through an online application for credit report

GRAYDIAN INTERNATIONAL

Business Credit Information Provider

For our reliable and up to date credit report please submit your inquiry by filling in the form below.

Report Type: *Express mail*
Subject Name: *CARDINAL INDUSTRIAL CORP. LTD.*
Subject Address: *7176 NE 21st St. WA26789 U. S. A.*
Subject Phone: *098 3565 4789*
Your Name: *YOULIANG ZHANG*
Company Name: *SHANGHAI FOREIGN TRADING CORP.*
Phone: *86 021 6677 7766*
Fax: *86 021 6677 7777*
Email: *ylz1998@ sftc. com*
Your Country of Residence: *CHINA*
Other Comments: *Please inform us with the subject's business profile, owner profile and financial status*

Submit

(6) Reply to the online credit report application

GRAYDIAN INTERNATIONAL

Business Credit Information Provider

I. Company Profile:

Name of the company: CARDINAL INDUSTRIAL CORP. LTD.
Ownership: Private
Main business: Manufacturing and distribution
Working staff: 150 people
Credit rating: C +
Time of establishment: 1982
Registered capital: US $ 10,000,000
Total asset: US $ 80,000,000 (up to December 31, 2006)
Annual turnover rate: US $ 16,000,000 (in the year of 2006)
Annual profit: US $ 4,000,000 (in the year of 2006)

II. Business Owner Profile

Judicial person: Harry Jones

Position: General Manager

Nationality: American

Education: Master of Engineering from University of Ohio, graduated in 1979

III. Bank with Current Account

National Bank of America

Currency: US Dollar

HSBC Bank in Shanghai

Currency: RMB

IV. Main Markets

60% of its products are distributed domestically, and 40% are sold in Southeast Asia.

V. Recommendation

This company has a fairly good state of operation and strict administrative system.

Its annual business turnover is a little above average level, but its pressure of loan and debts to be paid back within 5 years are a bit heavy. We recommend you to adopt payment by L/C within 30 days in your business transaction with this company.

VI. Warning

All information provided herewith is for your reference in your decision-making without any legal obligation of Graydian International. According to international practice, any information we have supplied are highly confidential and not to be disclosed to a third party.

VII. Enclosure

A balance sheet of Cardinal Industrial Corp. Ltd. for 2009

5. Telephone conversation

Mr. Wang wants to talk to Mary Lin. Linda Carlos, Mary's secretary, answers the phone.

Carlos: Mary Lin's office. This is Linda.

Wang: Hello, Linda, This is David Wang.

Carlos: Hi, Mr. Wang. What can I help you with?

Wang: I need to talk with Ms. Lin.

Carlos: Certainly. Hold on. I'll put you through.

Wang: Thanks.

Carlos:	Sorry, Mr. Wang, Ms. Lin is at a meeting now. Could you leave a message?
Wang:	Yes, tell her that my new office in Tianjin has been set up. It is closer to the manufacturer and the port. Transportation expenses will be significantly reduced for your next order.
Carlos:	That's good news. Congratulations.
Wang:	Thanks. The phone number for the new office is 86 – 20 – 12345678, and the fax is 86 – 20 – 12345679.
Carlos:	Yes, your phone number for the new office is 86 – 20 – 12345678, and the fax is 86 – 20 – 12345679.
Wang:	Right. Thanks, Linda. Bye.

New Words and Phrases

status [ˈsteitəs] *n.* a state of affairs; situation 状况，地位

We have to make an inquiry because the company's financial status is unknown.

我们必须作调查，因为公司的财务状况不清。

inquiry [inˈkwaiəri] *n.* (*or* enquiry) act of requesting information 咨询，查询，调查

inquire [inˈkwaiə] *v.* 询问；查明

We write to inquire about the financial status of the company.

我们来函询问该公司的财务状况。

status inquiry 资信调查，信用调查

exposure [ikˈspəuʒə] *n.* 1) risk, danger 风险 2) the act or an instance of exposing 暴露

profile [ˈprəufail] *n.* 1) an outline of an object or a person 轮廓

2) exposure to public notice 形象

regarding [riˈgɑːdiŋ] *prep.* in reference to; with respect to, concerning 关于

We don't have any information regarding this matter. 我们没有任何有关这个事情的消息。

integrity [inˈtegriti] *n.* adherence to a strict moral or ethical code 正直，诚实，完整

standing [ˈstændiŋ] *n.* status with respect to rank, reputation, or position in society or a profession 信誉；声望；地位

turnover rate *n.* 营业额，销售额

outstanding [autˈstændiŋ] *a.* not settled or resolved 未完成的；仍然存在的；未解决的

e. g.: outstanding debts 有待偿还的债务

a long outstanding problem 长期悬而未决的问题

exceed [ikˈsiːd] *v.* surpass 超过

post [pəust] *n.* a delivery of mail 邮寄

credit inquiry forms *n.* 资信调查表

confidential [ˈkɔnfiˈdenʃəl] *a.* secret 机密的

confidence [ˈkɔnfidəns] *n.* a secret 机密

The information is given to you in strict confidence. 提供给你的信息要严格保密。

distribute [disˈtribjuːt] *v.* to supply (goods) to retailers 分销

Notes

1. enquiry agencies 信用调查机构，咨询机构

2. minimize risk exposure 把风险降至最低

exposure *n.* （often used with *prep.* "to"）

（1）风险

e. g.：exposure to exchange risk 汇兑风险

exposure to loss 遭损风险

（2）暴露

e. g.：Exposure to the cold wind left the trees leafless. 暴露于寒风中的树木光秃秃的。

3. financial standing 财务状况，信用状况

4. the international profile of the business 企业（或公司）的国际运营状况

5. When taking up a bank reference you have to make an inquiry to the relevant bank through your own bank. 如果（对方提供的）资信证明人是银行，你必须通过自己的银行向有关银行咨询。

6. These words are also typed on the envelope if the letter is to be *delivered by post*. 如果信件由邮局发送，这些字也要打在信封上。

to deliver by post 邮寄

7. When you need such information, just fill in the form with the information required, such as the name and address of your company and the company to which the inquiry has been made, the contact numbers, the amount of *credit*, as well as the media you expect the return mail to be sent to you. 如果你需要这些信息，只需将所要求的信息填入表格，例如你公司和你要咨询的公司的名称、地址、联络号码、赊账金额以及你希望对方回信的方式。

credit：an arrangement for deferred payment of a loan or purchase 赊欠

e. g.：a store that offers credit 提供赊账的商店

I bought my stereo on credit. 我赊购了一台音响。

8. family-run *a.* 家族经营的，家族管理的

Other types business company：state-run（or state-owned），joint venture，private

9. ... it has been keeping an *account* with the Citibank ever since. ……该公司一直都在花旗银行有账户。

account *n.*

（1）a formal contractual relationship established to provide for regular banking or business services 账户

e. g.：We have opened an account with the Bank of England. 我们在英国银行开了账户。

（2）statement of money paid or received 账户，账目

e. g.：Accounts are settled at the end of each year. 每年年底结账。

Any payment for this project will be on our account. 该项目的所有付款记入我方账

户。

(3) a customer having a business or credit relationship with a firm 客户

e. g.: Our salespeople visit their accounts regularly. 我们的推销员定期拜访他们的客户。

10. Citibank （美国）花旗银行

11. We believe a credit not *exceeding* US $ 8,000 would be safe. 我们认为不超过8 000美元的信贷是安全的。

exceeding: *a.* surpassing in amount or degree 超过

e. g.: Payment exceeding US $ 5,000 is to be effected by L/C. 付款超过5 000美元须用信用证支付。

12. A postage paid envelope is enclosed for your convenience. 为了您的方便，附上一个贴好邮票的信封。

13. with (*or* in): reference to 关于

e. g.: He spoke with reference to the new project. 他讲了关于新项目的事情。

14. from bad to worse 每况愈下

15. ... the company was running at a loss. ……该公司亏损了。

16. Report Type 报告邮递方式

The "Report Type" usually offers three choices for different speeds and prices:

(1) "Regular mail" 普通邮件 It usually takes 10 – 12 days.

(2) "Express mail" 特快专递 It usually takes a week.

(3) "Super flash" 紧急邮件 It usually takes 3 days.

17. ownership 所有权

18. private 私有的，用以区别"state-owned"国有的

19. credit rating 信用等级

20. registered capital 注册资金

21. total asset 总资产

22. Judicial person (*or* legal person) 法人

23. Business Owner Profile 公司所有人简介

24. Bank with Current Account 往来账目开户行

25. HSBC: short form of Hong Kong and Shanghai Bank of China 汇丰银行

Useful Expressions

1. San Jones has applied to us for an agency and given your name as a reference. We should be glad if you could inform us of their credit standing and ability to conduct business.
2. We refer you to our bank, the Bank of China, for a statement about our financial standing.
3. We would be most grateful for any information you can give us about Mr. Goger's credit worthiness and reputation that will help us in making a decision about his application. Your comments will be treated as strictly confidential.
4. Messrs. Smith & Co. has given us your name as a reference. We would appreciate your ad-

vising us whether that company is of good repute and should be allowed credit up to that amount.

5. As we have not had any dealings with you before, we wish to know the names of the banks with which you have accounts.
6. The firm under inquiry is operating under sound and experienced management and enjoys a high reputation in the business circles for their punctuality in meeting obligations.
7. We regret our inability to give you any information concerning the firm as we have had only small transaction with them.
8. The above information is given only for your reference and without any responsibility on our part.
9. As far as our information goes the firm is punctually meeting its commitments and a credit in the sum you mentioned would seem to be safe.
10. As there are signs of instability in operation and turnover rate of the corporation due to the transition of ownership we advice you to act with caution in your business dealings with the firm.

Exercises

1. Answer the following questions.

1) Why is it very important to inquire into the business status of the company with which you are going to enter into business relations?

2) Who will make the status inquiry, the seller or the buyer? Why?

3) What will a company inquire about the status of its future partner?

4) From where can a company obtain the information about the status of its future partner?

5) What should be typed one blank line space below the inside addresses?

2. Questions for discussion.

1) What are the benefits and risks in developing business relations with other business partners?

2) What writing strategies do you think should be adopted in writing a status inquiry?

3. Choose the best answer for each of the statement.

1) Which of the following is not necessary to be inquired of in a status inquiry?

A. the prospective company's reputation

B. the prospective company's management

C. the prospective company's financial standing

D. the prospective company's geographical location

2) Reliable information of a company's integrity may be obtained from ______.

A. president of the company　　B. working staff of the company

C. Chamber of Commerce　　D. website

3) Information of status inquiry should be <u>handled with confidence.</u> The underlined part of the sentence means ______.

A. treated as secret　　B. dealt with care

C. considered trustworthy D. acknowledged as a special favor

4) "Reference" in this lesson means ______.

A. a book where information can be found

B. correspondence between business partners

C. relevant authorities to be consulted for approval

D. a person or institution who provides written testimony

5) When the reference provided is a bank, the inquiry should be made ______.

A. by any buyer who decides to do business with the firm

B. by someone who is knowledgeable in business practice

C. through the local authority

D. through the local bank

6) Which of the following is an appropriate ending for a letter of status inquiry?

A. Stating your wish to do business

B. Expressing your thanks to your reader

C. Promising to keep the given information as a secret

D. Introducing your company

7) Could you tell us if the company has any outstanding debt?

The underlined part of the sentence means ______.

A. prominent B. tremendous C. not yet settled D. paid

8) If you receive an unfavorable reply to your inquiry, you'd better ______.

A. be very careful in doing business with the firm

B. make another inquiry to a different agency

C. go to the firm and see for yourself

D. do business in large quantity

4. Decide whether the following statements are true or false. Write "T" for true, and "F" for false in the brackets provided.

1) Owing to the geographic distance between the buyer and the seller and the differences in legal systems, trade practice and customs, doing international business often involves more risks. ( )

2) Before starting a concrete transaction, the seller and the buyer needn't make an investigation into the other party's credit if they are new to each other. ( )

3) It is much more important for the seller to know the buyer's credit than vice versa. ( )

4) The seller can inquire into the financial standing of the buyer through his bank only. ( )

5) The seller may ask his own bank or consult an inquiry agency, or ask references provided by the buyer for the buyer's financial standing. ( )

6) Generally, in the first transaction, the buyer would provide his own bank and some trading partners as the credit references for the seller to make inquiry. ( )

7) In writing credit inquiry letters, be sure that the questions raised are specific and easy to answer. ( )

8) The letter giving credit information should be factual and fair. ( )

5. Translate the terms and expressions from Chinese into English.

1) 资信调查 2) 信用证明

3) 经营范围 4) 商会

5) 营业额

6. Translate the terms and expressions from English into Chinese.

1) the financial standing 2) inquiry agency

3) maximum credit 4) in strict confidence

5) reputation for meeting obligations

7. Make sentences with the following words and expression.

1) with reference to 2) concerning

3) from bad to worse 4) exposure

5) on one's part 6) act with caution

7) integrity

8. Filling in the blanks with the words and phrases given below.

appreciate	confidential	information	enclosing	reply
Credit	reference	order	evaluate	helpful

Dear Sirs,

We have received a purchase 1)____ from P&T in your territory. As this order is going to require huge capital injection, the 2)____ of the said company then becomes a very important issue with Lighthouse International.

The said company located in LKPM Building, has given your name as a 3)____. We are sure you can understand how 4)____ it will be if you can supply us with accurate and detailed information about this company. You information will enable us to 5)____ them for risk management.

We 6)____ your kindness in providing us with the 7)____ needed, and we will certainly keep everything strictly 8)____. We are 9)____ a 10)____ envelope for your convenience.

We thank you for your help.

Very truly yours,

(signature)

Eugenio Cima

Controller

9. Translate the following sentences into Chinese.

1) In order to minimize risk exposure, it is of utmost importance to inquire into the business status of the company with which you are going to enter into business relations.

2) When check on a bank reference you have to make an inquiry to the relevant bank through you own bank.

3) We would appreciate it if you could approach this bank and provide us information on the

credit history of James Smith & Co.

4) Key facts would include how long the owner, Donna Gard, has had an account with the City Bank, and whether she has any outstanding debts.

5) The company has kept a fairly good credit record, and it doesn't have any outstanding debts up to now.

6) We have received a letter of inquiry from one of our clients, asking the financial standing and business integrity of VLD Ltd.

7) We advise you to inform your client to act with caution in business dealings with Kasu Trading Corp.

8) The above information is passed on to you for your personal reference only and without any responsibility on our part.

9) For your information, we have for the past one year had a few transactions with this firm for semiconductor radios on L/C basis.

10) We believe that they owe their reputable position among the local wholesalers in our district to their steady and sincere way of conducting business.

10. Translate the following sentences into English.

1)请提供可做资信证明的公司或银行名称。

2)有关我方的资信状况,您可以向您所在的城市的任何一家商业银行咨询。

3)最近上述客户向我公司申请贷款,并提供贵公司作为资信证明人。

4)有关我公司之信誉状况,请向中国银行查询。

5)如能提供有关该公司信誉及财务状况的信息,我方将不胜感激。

6)如贵方能够提供你们掌握的任何有关材料,我方将十分感谢。

7)请告知该公司是否拥有可靠的信用,并说明向该公司提供多少信贷为安全。

8)我方保证对贵行提供的任何情况予以绝对保密。

9)兹附上写好地址的回函信封,并表示感谢。

10)公司声望很高,值得信任。他们资金雄厚,偿债及时。您完全可以放心地给予他们信贷。

11. Write a letter with the information given below.

You've received a request to be a reference for Spencer-Crane Company, and you're required to provide some information about their creditworthiness and reputation. However, your experience with them has been unsatisfactory because they often delay in payment. So, you have to write an unfavorable reply to the request for their credit information.

12. Make a telephone conversation in pairs with two students sitting back to back. One is calling someone who happened to be unavailable at the moment, so he/she leaves a message, and the other student takes the message.

Lesson Nine
Product Inquiry and Reply

1. Introduction

Inquiry about the prices and products is usually the first step in a business transaction. It is often made by buyers to sellers requesting information about certain commodities they intend to purchase. As far as the content is concerned, enquiries are of two types: general and specific. The former is sent to acquire some general information about products, such as asking for price lists, samples, catalogues, terms of payment. The latter expresses a definite wish to purchase a specific product if conditions are met, and it requires more detailed information such as price terms, quantity, port of shipment, packing.

An inquiry should be written directly and clearly. Some companies have preprinted inquiry forms which simplify the work; you need only to fill in the form with the necessary information. Some companies provide an online inquiry system that enables distant buyers to send their inquiries easily and quickly.

2. Writing strategy

If it is a first inquiry (inquiry made to a new firm for the first time), start your letter by telling your recipient from which source you got the name of the company and its products. Meanwhile, you can give a brief introduction of your own business.

In writing the letter, you may give the name of the product in the subject line so that your reader will get the main idea of your letter immediately. Then, state your interest in the product you intend to buy, and ask for information about the product and purchase, which mainly includes some or all of the following, depending on if it is a general or specific inquiry.

◇ Pricelist	◇ Discounts
◇ Catalogue	◇ Terms of payment
◇ Sample	◇ Time of delivery
◇ Product specifications	◇ Port of shipment
◇ Quotation	◇ Insurance
◇ Packing	◇ After-sales service

On receiving a letter of inquiry, reply as early as possible. Otherwise, the inquirer may turn to other suppliers and you would lose a potential customer and business opportunity.

In writing a reply to such an inquiry, you may:

(1) Express your thanks to the inquirer for his or her interest in your products.

(2) Answer the questions asked and provide other relevant and necessary information.

(3) State briefly to first inquirers the strengths and advantages of your products.

(4) If you are unable to supply the products required, give a reason or explanation. Always end your letter positively by offering a substitute product and providing relevant information to your inquirer, or expressing your willingness to do business with the inquiring firm in future.

3. Communication for results

On inquiring about prices do not use such negative words as "low", "cheap", because it creates bad image and is hard for your reader to accept.

Instead of writing	Write
Please provide us the cheapest quotation.	Please provide us the best quotation.
Please give us the lowest price.	Please give us the most favorable price.

4. Example letters

(1) A first inquiry

LETTERHEAD

Dear Sir:

Re: Coconut and Olive Oil

We have learned at www. ebay. com that you are a broker for various kinds of food ingredients in South America.

We are a major importer and distributor for food and oil products in China. Our market has a great potential for moderately priced edible oil, especially the kind mentioned in the caption.

We are now considering placing an order with you for your coconut oil and olive oil. Would you please send us detailed information concerning the prices, discounts, commission, terms of payment, delivery schedule, and packing, together with the catalogue and samples for the above products.

We look forward to your early reply.

Yours sincerely,

(Signature)

Gary Zhang

Manager

(2) Reply to the first inquiry

FAX MESSAGE

To: Mr. Gary Zhang
From: Bob Frost, Manager
Subject: Coconut and Olive Oil

Date: October 20, 2010
Attachment: 1
Pages: 1/1

Dear Mr. Gary Zhang:

We welcome your inquiry and would like to provide you with our most favorable terms for the goods in the subject.

A catalogue of the full range of our goods and quotations is attached. You will see detailed information about Coconut and Olive Oil on page 3 of the catalogue. The samples have been sent to you by air, and will reach you within next week.

Other relevant information is given below:

Quality

Our products are of superior quality thanks to our good crop as well as our highly sophisticated equipment and processing technique. This is apparent from the color and taste of our samples.

Packing

The oil is packed in glass bottles, with 2 gallons in each bottle packed in a paper box, 8 boxes in a carton reinforced by hook iron.

Payment

We accept payment by irrevocable and confirmed L/C.

Discount

We offer 2% discount for purchase of 1,000 gallons of each product.

Delivery

Our time of delivery is within 30 days after receipt of your covering L/C.

We are looking forward to receiving your order.

Sincerely,

Bob Frost

(3) An e-mail message of a specific inquiry

TO: ykuang@starhouse.com.cn
FROM: cathylee@eaglewing.com
SUBJECT: Our interest in your briefcases & handbags
ATTACHED:

Dear Ms. Kuang:

During the Chinese Export Commodity Fair held in October, 2010, we had the pleasure of visiting your booth and are impressed by your briefcases and hand bags made in a variety of artificial leathers.

We are considering placing an order with you. Please send us as soon as possible your most favorable prices CIF Singapore for the following items:

Art. No.	**color**
W035	white
W036	red
W037	black
W038	lavender
W039	brown

In your reply, please inform us of the terms of payment and the discount you offer for purchase of no less than 500 of each Article Number listed above.

Your prompt reply is appreciated.

Yours sincerely,

Ms. Cathy Lee, Import Manager
cathylee@eaglewing.com
www.eaglewingcommerce.com
Phone: 508 - 366 - 3956
Fax: 508 - 366 - 3958

(4) Reply to the specific inquiry

STARHOUSE CO. LTD.

TO: Ms. Cathy Lee, Manager
FROM: Kuang Yu-ling, Manager
SUBJECT: Supply of briefcases & handbags
DATE: October 2, 2010
ATTACHED: Quotation

Dear Ms Lee:

Thank you for your interest in our briefcases and handbags. I'm attaching a quotation with terms and conditions given below.

Price: As listed in the quotation
Payment: L/C at sight
Discount: 3% for 500 pieces of each item
Packing: In paper box lined with polythene sheets
Delivery: November 30 ~ December 2

Presently, our stock is fully ordered, and our workers are working overtime in order to meet the increasing demand. If you would like your order to be shipped in November/December, please place your order no later than October 31.

We are looking forward to your order.

Sincerely,
Kuang Yu-Ling

(5) An importer's Request for a Proforma Invoice

K&D CO. LTD.

TO: Kuang Yu-ling, Manager
FROM: Cathy Lee, Manager
SUBJECT: Order of briefcases & handbags

ATTACHED:
DATE: October 29, 2010

Dear Ms. Kuang:

We have received with thanks your sample and pricelist for the leather shoes. We found the quality and styles satisfactory, and the prices acceptable too.

Our clients asked us to obtain from you a Proforma Invoice for 2000 pairs of leather shoes with the following specification and quantities:

Dobo Brand Men's Shoes 500 pairs
Dobo Brand Women's Shoes 500 pairs
Alice Brand Girl's Shoes 500 pairs

Would you please send us your Proforma Invoice as soon as possible for the above commodities with prices based on CIF Lagos, Nigeria, so that our clients will be able to apply for an import license.

We thank you for your good cooperation.

Sincerely,
(Signature)
Cathy Lee

(6) Reply to the request for a Proforma Invoice

STARHOUSE CO. LTD.

TO: Cathy Lee, Manager
FROM: Kuang Yu-ling, Manager
SUBJECT: Order of briefcases & handbags
ATTACHED: Proforma Invoice
DATE: October 29, 2010

Dear Ms. Lee:

In compliance with your request, we are sending you the enclosed Proforma Invoice. Please note that our prices remain valid for 2 weeks.

For your information, there is a large demand for our leather shoes and our supply is running short. Please order without delay.

We look forward to receiving your order at an early date.

Best regards,
STARHOUSE CO. LTD.

(7) A proforma invoice form

TIANJIN INDUSTRIAL & TRADING CO., LTD.

TIANJIN, CHINA

PROFORMA INVOICE

To Messrs: No:
Time of shipment: Date:
Port of shipment:
Terms of payment:
Insurance:
Validity:

ITEM NO.	DESCRIPTION	QUANTITY	UNIT PRICE	TOTAL AMMOUNT

TOTAL AMOUNT:

5. Telephone conversation

Jack White is calling Dan Moore for the arrangement of a visit.

Secretary: Dan Moore's office.

White: Is Dan in?

Secretary: May I tell him who's calling?

White: Yes, this is Jack White from ABC Industrial Ltd.

Secretary: Just a minute, please, Mr. White.

White: Thank you.

Moore: Hello, Jack.

White: Hello, Dan.

Moore: Haven't heard from you for quite some time. How can I help you?

White: I'm going to Europe next week, and I'd like to visit your company during the trip. I wonder if I could meet you sometime between Tuesday and Friday.

Moore: Well, let me check my schedule. How about Wednesday morning?

White: Perfect. Then, I'll meet you on Wednesday morning around 10 o'clock. Is that okay?

Moore: It suits me fine.

White: I'll talk with you about the contract between us, which will end in about two months. Meanwhile, I'll bring you the samples of our latest products.

Moore: Fine, I'll be seeing you then and we'll discuss about the possibility of an extension of the contract.

White: Great. I'm looking forward to seeing you.

Moore: So do I. Bye-bye, and have a nice day.

New Words and Phrases

sample ['sæmpl] *n.* a part that is representative of a whole 样品

terms of payment 支付条款

quotation [kwəu'teiʃən] *n.* statement of the price of a certain product 报价单

This quotation applies only to the deal under negotiation. 这个报价仅用于本谈判中的交易。

We asked the American firm for a quotation for 10,000 tons of wheat.

我们要求该美国公司报 10 000 吨小麦的价格。

packing ['pækiŋ] *n.* the act or process of one that packs 包装

specification [ˌspesifi'keiʃn] *n.* a detailed statement prescribing materials, dimensions, and quality of goods to be sold or manufactured 规格,说明

discount ['diskaunt] *n.* a deduction from the stated price 折扣

We give ten percent discount for cash. 如用现金付款,我们可打九折。

Right now, jeans are sold at a discount. 目前牛仔裤正在打折销售。

offer [ˈɔfə] *n.* the bid of price 发盘

commission [kəˈmiʃən] *n.* a percentage paid to the agent from the profits of goods sold 佣金

His salary is low, but he gets 20% commission. 他的薪水低,但他可得到20%佣金。

substitute [ˈsʌbstitjuːt] *n.* one that takes the place of another 替代品 *v.* replace 替代

broker [ˈbrəukə] *n.* one that acts as an agent for others 经纪人,中间商

caption [ˈkæpʃən] *n.* a title, short explanation, or description 标题

carton [ˈkɑːtən] *n.* containers made from cardboard 硬纸盒,纸板箱

irrevocable [iˈrevəkəbl] *a.* impossible to retract or revoke 不可撤销的

confirmed [kənˈfəːmd] *a.* 保兑的

booth [buːθ] *n.* a small stand for the display and sale of goods 展位

polythene [ˈpɔliθiːn] *n.* 聚乙烯

proforma invoice 形式发票

enclose [inˈkləuz] *v.* put sth. in an envelope attached to a letter 随信附寄

valid [ˈvælid] *a.* effective or binding 有效的

license [ˈlaisəns] *n.* proof of permission granted in the form of a document 许可证

acceptance [əkˈseptəns] *n.* 1) compliance by one party with the terms and conditions of another's offer 接受,认可 2) a formal indication by a debtor of willingness to pay 承兑

Notes

1. general inquiry 一般性询盘

2. specific inquiry 具体询盘

3. Chinese Export Commodity Fair 中国出口商品交易会

The Chinese Export Commodity Fair, abbreviated as CECF, is the greatest trade show in China. It is a biannual event held in spring and autumn in Guangzhou, capital of south China's Guangdong Province with the attendance of representatives from domestic and overseas enterprises and companies.

4. L/C (letter of credit) 信用证 **L/C at sight** 即期信用证

Letter of credit, often called documentary credit, is a document issued by a bank promising to pay a specified amount of money to an exporter. It is the most common mechanism for financing international trade.

5. Proforma invoice 形式发票

Proforma invoice is an invoice sent for form's sake. Unlike an ordinary invoice or commercial invoice, it is not issued to confirm certain amount of money paid by the buyer for the goods he/she purchased. It is issued before the buyer's payment for the goods mainly for the following purposes:

(1) to serve as a formal quotation or as a price reference;

(2) to enable the buyer to make the necessary preliminary arrangements, such as obtaining an import license for the goods he would like to order;

(3) to inform the buyer of the amount payable for the goods to be shipped.

A proforma invoice is not necessarily involved in every transaction.

6. We *had the pleasure of visiting* your booth. 我们有幸参观了你们的展台。

have the pleasure of doing sth. 有幸做……（客套用语）

e. g.： May we have the pleasure of your presence? 敬请光临。

7. In cartons *lined with* polythene sheets. 用聚乙烯薄膜做内衬的纸板箱。

be lined with: to cover the inner surface of 用……作内衬

e. g.： a coat lined with fur 用毛皮作里子的大衣

8. We are the major importer and distributor in our area for the captioned products and wish to *place a large order with* you. 我们是本地区标题货物的主要进口商，希望向你方大量订货。

place a large order with sb. 向……大量订货

Similar expressions: place a trial order 试订购; place a repeated order 再订购

9. A catalogue of the full arrangement of our goods and quotations is attached. 附上我方全部产品的目录和报价。

10. The oil is packed in glass bottles, with 2 gallons in each bottle packed in a paper box, 8 boxes in a carton reinforced with hoop iron. 产品油使用玻璃瓶包装，每瓶两加仑，外加纸盒，8 盒装一纸板箱，用铁带捆扎。

11. Our time of delivery is within 30 days after receipt of your covering L/C. 收到你方相关信用证后30日内装运。

12. *In compliance with* your request, we are sending you the enclosed Proforma Invoice. 应你方来信中的要求，我方随信寄去形式发票。

in compliance with 顺从；遵照

13. The prices given in the quotation for the above goods are valid for two weeks. 以上产品报价两周内有效。

Similar expressions: The prices remained good for 3 days.

The prices are open for 3 days.

Useful Expressions

1. As requested, we are sending you herewith our proforma invoice No. 779 in quadruplicate for 3,000 meters of cables, model DD65 and DD66.
2. We are thinking of placing an order for your "Rainbow" brand colored TV. We would be very grateful if you could make us an offer for 1,000 units with details about payment and shipment.
3. Please inform us the quantity that can be supplied from stock.
4. We regret to say that we have run out of stock now. But we'll get in touch with you as soon as the next supply comes in.
5. These items you just mentioned are most popularly received on overseas markets.
6. Do you make machines according to the buyer's samples and specifications?
7. The price varies somewhat in different seasons.

8. After comparing our price with that of other manufacturers, you will no doubt find the price given in our proforma invoice very favorable to you.

9. From the attached quotation you will find that the price indicated therein is CIF Lagos, inclusive of 5% discount.

10. In order to enable you to apply for the necessary import license, we are sending you the proforma invoice No. 123 in triplicate. Please note that we'll inform you if there is any change in price.

Exercises

1. Answer the following questions.

1) What is the main difference between a general inquiry and a specific inquiry?

2) What information should be given in an inquiry?

3) Why is it necessary to reply soon to an inquiry?

4) What information do you supply to a first inquirer?

5) What can you do if you don't have the product inquired about?

6) What are the major functions of a "proforma invoice"?

2. Choose the best answer to complete the following statements.

1) When a(n) ______ is made, a foreign trade transaction is concluded.

A. offer B. counter-offer C. acceptance D. inquiry

2) When making an inquiry, it is improper to include in your letter ______.

A. the way of payment for the goods B. the bargaining over the prices
C. the product name D. the packing of the goods

3) It is strongly advisable that when replying to an inquiry, the seller start his letter by ______.

A. directly informing about the prices
B. providing details of the product
C. telling honestly that the product is out of stock
D. thanking the inquirer for his interest

4) We are pleased to inform you that we ______ in Chinese silk garments and would take this opportunity to send our quotation.

A. specialize B. interested C. supply D. sell

5) Which of the following is NOT necessarily included in an inquiry?

A. Product name. B. Price. C. Terms of payment. D. Terms of arbitration.

6) "We are sorry to say the goods required by you are ______."
Which of the following does NOT fit in the blank?

A. running short B. in sufficient supply
C. not available D. out of stock

7) When receiving an inquiry, you should ______.

A. reply within a reasonably short time B. tell the sender you are not interested
C. reply at any time within a week D. ignore it

8) "The prices given in the quotation for the above goods are valid for two weeks."

Which of the following CAN replace the underlined word?

A. remaining B. lawful C. good D. null

3. Decide whether the following statements are true or false. Write "T" for true, and "F" for false.

1) The recipient of an inquiry can recommend a substitute product in the reply if the required goods are not in supply. ( )

2) The quotation can stay good as long as the inquirer wish. ( )

3) The proforma invoice is issued by the inquirer to the inquired. ( )

4) A proforma invoice is indispensable in all business transaction. ( )

5) An inquiry is not important for it's only the first step in a business transaction. ( )

6) Detailed information concerning the product and sales terms such as insurance and commodity inspection should always be covered in a reply to an inquiry. ( )

7) The inquired must give enough attention to an inquiry, or else he may lose a prospective buyer. ( )

8) A delayed reply to an inquiry may turn a customer away. ( )

4. Translate the following terms into Chinese, and then explain them in English.

1) general inquiry
2) specific inquiry
3) inquiry form
4) online inquiry
5) proforma invoice

5. Translate the following phrases into English.

1)售后服务
2)食物调料
3)食用油
4)全部产品系列
5)人造皮革
6)替代产品
7)进口许可证
8)保兑的不可撤销信用证
9)营业日/工作日
10)最优惠交易条件

6. Filling in the blanks with the words and phrases given below.

interested	quotation	specifications	place	exporter
sight	inquiry	reference	discount	enter

(1)

Dear Mr. Wu:

The local chamber of commerce informed us that you are the major ______ of high quality sweaters.

As we mainly deal in Chinese textiles in Australia, we are especially ______ in your products and are looking for a possible business relationship with you. Could you be kind enough to send us your ______ on FOB basis as well as to indicate other terms like payment, delivery, quantity discount and product ______. If your prices are favorable, we'd like to ______ a large order with you.

We look forward to your prompt reply.

Yours sincerely,

Peter Anderson

(2)

Dear Mr. Anderson:

We have received your ______ of 12th August and thank you for your desire to ______ into business relations with us. Enclosed please find a copy of our summer catalogue and price list as you requested.

As you can see from the catalogue, you have a wide selection of sweaters that will appeal to your customers of all ages. And we are sending you by separate post some samples for your ______.

As our usual practice, we grant a 2.5% quantity ______ on an order exceeding 200 items. Payment is to be made by confirmed, irrevocable L/C at ______.

As our products are well received in European and North American markets, it would be to your advantage to try out a shipment.

We look forward to your order.

Yours faithfully,

Wu Bin

7. Translate the following sentences into English.

1)你公司10月23日来函已收到,很高兴你方对我公司的丝绸制品感兴趣。现按你方要求附寄报价单及目录。

2)对于超过100件的订单我方将给予5%的折扣。

3)请在报价单中注明产品的具体型号及其他有关信息,并请速寄样品。

4)我方以信用证方式结款。在收到即期信用证后20天之内装运。

5)如果你方价格比其他竞争对手的优惠,我们将向你们订货。

6)这是本季目录,你看了可以对我们的产品有一个大概的了解。

7)为了便于我方提出报价,能否请你谈谈你方所需的数量。

8)请及时通知我方下列货物的最新价格。

8. Translate the following sentences into Chinese.

1) Please quote us your most favorable price CIF London, stating the earliest date of shipment and the discount you will allow.

2) Thank you for your letter of May 15 inquiring about our air conditioners. But we regret to have to tell you that the items requested are not available for the time being.

3) As demand for this product is quite large, it's difficult to meet the time of delivery as requested. But if you place your order not later than the end of this week, we could ensure shipment not later than April 15.

4) If you can supply goods of the following specifications and quality required, we may place regular orders for large quantities.

5) In compliance with your letter of July 4, we are sending you a quotation sheet with detailed information about the products and other relevant terms and conditions as well.

6) Here is our CIF New York price list. Please note that all the prices in the list remain valid till the end of this month.

7) We are likely to place a large order with you if the price is favorable.

8) Thank you for your inquiry, and enclosed please find our current catalogue and price list quoting CIF Shanghai.

9. Revise the following letter for better results.

Dear Sirs,

We are importers in Canada. We want to inform you that our customers are interested in your footwear. The designs and qualities are very attractive and the market for your products will be big. So we want to ask you for the lowest quotation of all your products. And other information like time of delivery and terms of payment are also needed. And it will be very helpful if you could send samples of the materials which make the products.

Please reply soon.

Sincerely,

Paul Howard

10. Write a reply to the following letter.

Dear Sir:

Your name has been given to us by the London Chamber of Commerce as a leading producer of shoes in a variety of pure hide.

Will you please send us a copy of your catalogue, together with details of your prices and terms of payment? We should find it most helpful if you could also supply samples of the various skins in which the products are made.

We are distributors of leather products here in our country and believe that there will be a promising market for good quality and moderately priced shoes in this area. If your products are up to the standard, we will place large orders with you.

We also hope you will be able to state the discount you allow for orders of over 1,000 pairs of the leather shoes.

We look forward to hearing from you.

Sincerely,

David Shaw

11. Make a telephone conversation in pairs with two students sitting back to back, making an arrangement for a visit.

Lesson Ten
Offer, Counter-Offer and Order

1. Introduction

An "offer" is the terms and conditions given by the seller in response to an inquiry made by the buyer for acceptance in order to conclude a deal. If, in some special case, the terms and conditions are offered by the buyer, it is called a "bid".

In a business transaction an offer can be a "firm offer" or a "non-firm offer".

A firm offer is a written offer that is not to be withdrawn, revoked, or amended during the validity, which is a specified period of time. If the offer is accepted by both parties during the period, it will be an enforceable contract. Otherwise, the offer expires.

In a non-firm offer the terms and conditions can be changed, or amended. For this reason, the phrase "*subject to our final confirmation*" is always included in a non-firm offer. A non-firm offer often plays the role as a quotation.

A non-firm offer allows sellers to have more time and flexibility in choosing business opportunities and making decisions on prices so that it is more favorable to them in a changeable market. However, a non-firm offer will eventually be made into a firm offer in order to be effective in a transaction.

When the receiver disagrees with the offer sent to him or her and makes some changes, the changed one is called a "counter-offer", while the original one, when expired, will be replaced by the counter-offer. If it is amended again, another counter-offer is made until an acceptable one is worked out. This final and accepted offer is firm and legally binding to both parties. It is not uncommon for a business negotiation to go through several rounds of offer and counter-offer before an agreement is reached.

If buyers agree with the term of an offer, they usually place an order — a formal request to the seller for the purchase of certain goods at a specified quantity. On receiving an order, if the seller agrees with the terms and is in a position to supply the required goods, he will give the buyer an acceptance, a formal statement indicating his accent. According to commercial law, an order is not binding on either party until it is accepted. Then a sales confirmation or purchase confirmation can be worked out by both parties on the basis of the terms and conditions provided in the order.

2. Writing strategy

In response to an inquiry, an offer may be sent, in which the following are usually covered:

◇ An expression of thanks for the inquiry

◇ Details of the goods, prices, discount, and terms of payment

◇ Terms of price which indicate what the price cover, followed by the named place of delivery or destination (e. g. FOB Shanghai)

◇ The time of shipment, and/or date of delivery

◇ The time period in which the offer is valid

If the offer is rejected, a letter of rejection is to be written, which should include:

◇ An expression of thanks for the offer

◇ Reason for inability to accept the offer

◇ A counter-offer if necessary, or

◇ A wish of other business opportunities in future

3. Communication for results

When giving your argument for a disputed assertion, provide specific support for your view.

Instead of saying	Say
I'm sure you'll agree that our offer is quite reasonable.	Our offer was made based on the consideration of the world market and the quality of our product.
It is well-known that our soybeans are of high quality.	Our soybeans are produced with choice seeds in pollutant-free environment.

4. Example letters

(1) A firm offer made in reply to buyer's inquiry

Dear Mr. Faulkner:

Thank you for your letter dated November 12, inquiring about our Unshelled Peanuts, for shipment to Odense.

As requested, we are making you the following offer, subject to your reply reaching us by November 20, Beijing time.

Specification: Unshelled Peanuts, 2006 crop
Quantity: 100 metric tons, 3% more or less
Origin: Shandong, China
Price: At RMB 5,500 per metric ton, CIFC2% Odense
Terms of payment: L/C at sight
Shipment: Per steamer during January/ February, 2007 with transshipment at Copenhagen
Port of shipment: Qingdao, China
Port of destination: Odense, Denmark

Inspection: By China Commodity Inspection Bureau, to be made three days before shipment

Insurance: By China People's Insurance Company covering All Risks and War Risk for 110% of the total invoice Value.

Since no steamer is available from here to Odense, transshipment is to be made in Copenhagen. The additional cost for the transshipment is included in the quoted price.

We are looking forward to your order.

Yours truly,
KK FOOD, OIL & CEREAL IMP. & EXP. CORP.
(Signature)
Liu Xing, Export Manager

(2) A counter-offer from the importer

Dear Mr. Liu Xing:

Thank you very much for your reply to our inquiry. We have studied your offer with our clients and we have to say your price is too high to be acceptable.

We would have placed a regular order with large quantities with you but such a high price makes it impossible for us to do so, as it would leave us with little profits. In order to conclude the deal we suggest you reduce the price by 10%.

We are a big dealer of agricultural products in our area. Cooperation between us will benefit you not only in making export profits, but also in expansion of your market.

We are obliged for your careful consideration of our suggestion.

Sincerely,
(Signature)
David Faulkner

(3) Seller rejects the counter-offer

Dear Mr. Faulkner:

Thank you for your letter of November 14th. We are surprised to learn that you think our price "too high to be acceptable". Our offer was made based on the consideration of the world market and the quality of our product.

The price of peanuts is on the rise this year because of reduced output caused by severe drought in the major peanut producing area in the Northeast of China and poor agricultural climate in the Southeast of America.

In addition, the Unshelled Peanuts we supply are produced with choice seeds in pollutant-free environment.

Presently, we have received many orders from other buyers at the price we offer you, and our stock is running low. We, therefore, can not accommodate your request to reduce our price.

Please order now for the limited stock of high quality products.

Yours truly,
KK FOOD, OIL & CEREAL IMP. & EXP. CORP.
(Signature)
Liu Xing, Export Manager

(4) A letter declining an order and offering a substitute

Dear Ms. Lucinda:

Snow White Brand Cashmere Sweater

We thank you for your order on October 5 for 2,000 Lotus Brand Sweaters.

However, we no longer carry Lotus line of sweaters. Our new Snow White line has replaced the Lotus that you asked about. Snow White Brand features a wider range of colors and sizes, and is more contemporary in style.

We have enclosed the pricelist of Snow White line products and airmailed you samples and a catalogue for your reconsideration.

As for our terms of payment, we insist on confirmed, irrevocable letter of credit available by draft at sight, reaching us one month before shipment, valid for negotiation in China till the 21st day after the prescribed time of shipment.

We look forward to your reply.

Sincerely,
(Signature)
Jack Williams
Manager

(5) Sending a firm offer to an old customer by e-mail

To: lwagner@ tmc. com
From: lsun@ rainbowtex. com
Subject: Special Offer for Garment Fabric

Dear Ms. Wagner:

Thank you for your inquiry dated March 19, for 6,000 yards of Garment Fabric Art. No. 10 & 12.

As this is a repeat order from you, an old customer, you will enjoy a special offer which is 3% lower than our present market price, subject to your reply reaching us before March 30, our time.

Please find, in the attachment, our latest pricelist. The terms and conditions regarding payment and delivery remain the same as usual.

We appreciate your prompt reply.

Sincerely,

Lili Sun, Manager
Rainbow Textiles Co.
987 - 034 - 56768888
www. rainbowtex. com

5. Telephone conversation

Peter wants to increase the quantity of the order he has made. But it is already passed the office hour and all the staff are off work. So Peter left a voice mail to Jason's office.

Peter: Hello, Jason. This is Peter from Oriental Trade. I'm ringing to increase the purchase quantity by 150 pieces under order number 560, as we received another order from our client. Then, the total quantity is 550 pieces. I'll confirm by fax on Monday morning. Please change your sales confirmation accordingly, and let me know when you have done this. My phone number is 800 - 6656 - 5675. I repeat, 800 - 6656 - 5675. Thanks. Goodbye.

New Words and Phrases

offer [ˈɔfə] *n.* an act of proposing to sell certain goods or services at specific prices on certain terms and conditions 出价，报盘

firm offer 实盘

withdraw [wiðˈdrɔː] *v.* to remove or draw back 收回，撤销

revoke [riˈvəuk] *v.* to void or annul by withdrawing 撤回，废除，宣告无效

amend [əˈmend] *v.* to alter formally by adding, deleting, or rephrasing 修正，修改

The contract has been amended. 该合同已被修改。

expire [ikˈspaiə] *v.* to come to an end; terminate 期满，终止

The contract expires by the end of the year. 该合同年底到期。

non-firm offer 虚盘

quotation [kwəuˈteiʃn] *n.* the quoting of current prices for goods 报价单

counter-offer 还盘

destination [ˌdestiˈneiʃn] *n.* the place to which one is going or directed 目的地

valid [ˈvælid] *a.* legally acceptable 有效的

The quotation remains valid for tree days. 该报价有效期三天。

Odense [ˈəuðənsei] *n.* a port city in Denmark 欧登塞（丹麦）

captioned goods 标题中提到的产品

concerning [kənˈsəːniŋ] *prep.* in reference to 关于

I have no objection concerning the purchase of the goods.

关于购买这些货物我没有任何反对意见。

take advantage of 利用

We should take advantage of the good facilities. 我们应该利用这些良好的条件。

Notes

1. Unshelled Peanuts, 2006 crop 2006 年产花生仁

2. CIFC2% 成本费，保险费加运费，2%佣金

"C" refers to Commission

3. All Risks 全险

4. War Risk 战争险

5. Cooperation between us will not only benefit you in making export profits but also in expansion of your market. 我们之间的合作不仅可使你方出口获利,还可以扩大你方市场。

6. We, therefore, can not *accommodate* your request to reduce our price.

因此,我方无法满足你方要求降低我方的价格。

accommodate: to do a favor or service for 帮助,提供服务;施惠

7. Otherwise, we'll *have no alternative but* turn to other suppliers.

否则,我方将别无选择只好求助其他供应商。

have no alternative but + *v.*

e. g.: In this circumstance, we have no alternative but to give up. 在这种情况下,我们别无选择,只得放弃。

8. However, considering the long-term cooperation between our two firms we are willing to *make an exception* for you to allow you *3% discount* if your order for each specification reaches 1,000. 然而,考虑到我们两公司的长期合作,我们愿意破例给你方3%折扣,如果你方每一种规格的订货量达到1 000。

to make an exception 破例

3% discount 3%的折扣, 打97折

9. Our Commercial Counselor's Office in your country has *referred to* us your enquiry for cable as it falls within the scope of our business. 我方驻贵国的商会向我方介绍了贵方的电线询价,该商品正在我方的经营范围之内。

referred to: to direct to a source for help or information 引导……去求助

e. g.: You may refer to my employer for my integrity. 对于我的品行,你可向我的雇主咨询。

He referred her to a heart specialist. 他叫她找心脏病专家。

10. subject to our final conformation 以我方的最终确认为准

该短语为虚盘报价常用语,表示所报价格不确定,只供参考。

e. g.: The prices listed are subject to our final conformation. 所报价格以我方的最终确认为准。

11. Suwan 水原:韩国西北一城市

12. impose an ban 实施禁令

13. lift a ban 取消禁令

14. We are not *in a position* to purchase the products at present.

我们目前无法购买贵方产品。

to be in a position + infinitive (基于客观条件)能够

e. g.: Thanks to the advanced facilities, we are in a position to deliver the goods promptly. 因为有了先进的设备,我们能够迅速交货。

15. The terms and conditions regarding payment and delivery *remain the same* as usual.

有关付款和运输的方式与条件和往常一样。

remain the same 保持不变

e. g. : Everything remains the same except the price. 除了价格外,一切都没有变化。

Useful Expressions

1. Under separate cover, we are sending you our Catalogue No. 6 together with our price list.
2. We enclose our latest quotation, and trust that the prices quoted will lead to further business.
3. We should very much like to receive orders from you as our products can compete in both price and quality with those offered by other manufacturers.
4. We would like to make you, subject to your reply reaching us by April 5, the following offer for 200 dozens of woolen sweaters.
5. We regret to inform you that we are unable to provide a firm offer at the price you suggested owing to the fact that the prices for raw materials have increased considerably.
6. We regret being unable to accept your offer as we have in the meantime placed orders with other suppliers at a lower price.
7. We feel that your quotation is not proper because the price for such material is on the decline at present.
8. We would be pleased to purchase 300 cases if you could allow us 5% discount.
9. Unless you reduce your pieces by 10%, business prospect is rather remote. Please revise your offer.
10. The price for the shirts is US $ 15 each CIF London, totaling US $ 3,000.

Exercises

1. Answer questions.

(1) What is an "offer" and what is a "counter-offer" in business transaction?

(2) What is a "firm offer" and what is a "non-firm offer"?

(3) What is an order?

(4) What will be included in an offer in response to an inquiry?

2. Questions for discussion.

1) How shall we make a clear and accurate offer and counter-offer?

2) What are possible reasons for a counter-offer and a rejection?

3. Choose the best answer to complete the following statements.

1) At your ______, we are making you the following offer subject to your reply reaching here before July 15.

A. request B. requirement C. need D. offering

2) The above prices are on a CIF San Francisco ______.

A. offer B. basis C. counteroffer D. request

3) Please note that a 5% ______ applies to orders for each item exceeding 1000 instead of 5%

commission.

A. commission B. discount C. price D. cost

4) If you are interested in other models, please see the ______ illustrated catalogue.

A. inside B. closed C. enclosed D. including

5) Compared with your last quotations for North America, we find the current ______ rather high.

A. offer B. quotation C. order D. price

6) To be frank with you, the price we quoted you only allow us a very small ______ of profits.

A. quotation B. margin C. order D. price

7) ______ of your offer would make your bicycles uncompetitive with other stores in our region.

A. Receiving B. Acceptance C. Purchasing D. Ordering

8) In this case, we are willing to make a(n) ______ as an introduction of our bicycles on your market.

A. request B. offer C. exception D. wonder

9) It will not be possible for us to accommodate your ______ for a price reduction.

A. request B. requirement C. need D. offer

10) We are not in a ______ to accept your bid at the present state of the market.

A. way B. position C. state D. means

4. Decide whether the following statements are true or false. Write "T" for true, and "F" for false in the brackets provided.

1) Companies in international business often conclude a deal through a process of offer-counter-offer-acceptance. ( )

2) Once an offer is made, the buyer must accept it within the time limit given in the offer. ( )

3) An offer is the wish of the seller to sell particular goods under stated terms. ( )

4) In international business, offers can be divided into two kinds: firm offer and non-firm offer. ( )

5) An offer is called a "firm offer" if it is a definite promise to sell a certain kind of goods and the terms in the promise will not be changed within the validity period. ( )

6) Non-firm offers are not binding upon the sellers and the details of the offers may change at any time.

7) A counter offer is a partial or full rejection of original offer. ( ).

8) A counteroffer can be made by either a seller or a buyer in a business transaction. ( )

9) An expression of thanks should be given even if the offer is not acceptable. ( )

10) A seller can make either an offer or a bid in difference circumstances. ( )

5. Make sentences with the following phrases.

1) subject to 2) no longer 3) to be in a position 4) turn to (sb.)

5) base on (*or*: on the basis of)

6. Filling in the blanks with the words and phrases given below. Change the form when

necessary.

as follow	to reduce	in line with	be subject to	provided that
remain open	to one's regret	owing to	discount	acceptance

1) We intend to buy 300 "Flying Pigeon" Brand Bicycles at the prices ______.

2) We accept your offer ______ you cut your price by 2%.

3) The offer ______ until 12:00 a. m. November 21, Beijing time.

4) I'm sure our offer is ______ the prevailing market price level.

5) The L/C has not yet been opened ______ unforeseen circumstances.

6) Our offer is a non-firm offer. It ______ our final confirmation.

7) ______, we found the quality of the shipment is not satisfactory.

8) If you can ______ the price, we might place a large order.

9) We hope you can grant us a 3% ______ for any order of more than 100 bales.

10) Our offer is firm, subject to your ______ reaching us by March 1.

7. Translate the following sentences from Chinese to English.

1) 按你方要求,我方就以下产品做如下报盘,此报盘以我方最后确认为准。

2) 若你方对此报盘7日内不接受,该报盘将被撤销。

3) 此报盘以你方答复在本月底之前到达我方为准。

4) 我方发现你方报价比其他供应商略高,望你方降低价格以便能对付其他供应商的竞争。

5) 很遗憾,我方不能接受贵方报盘,因为贵方市场的其他供应商以比你方价格低3% 的条件向我方提供几乎同样的货物。

6) 虽然你方价格与市场水平一致,但交货日期太长。

7) 鉴于我们之间长久以来的贸易关系,特做此报盘。

8) 对于小量定购来说,你方还盘太低。

9) 我方货物优于市场上其他同类产品,其设计独特,款式新颖且价格合理,近年来一直畅销。

10) 若订货超过600件,可享受8折优惠。

8. Translate the following sentences from English to Chinese.

1) The discount prices you referred to when you make price comparisons were for volume purchases only.

2) The profit margin for these products is so thin that any price reduction would make business transactions pointless.

3) We are informed by retailers at our end that prices for air conditioners have dropped another 3% in large department stores here.

4) We would be willing to discuss a volume discount if the quantity of your order is doubled.

5) Enclosed please find our quotations which are open for two weeks only.

6) We are anxious to do what we can to help you to establish your new business and are prepared to allow you a special discount of 3% if payment is made within one month.

7) Thank you for your letter of December 23 asking us to offer you 10,000 metric tons of the

wheat in subject for shipment to Singapore in February.

8) We have received your inquiry of June 4 for our electronic toys and now make you the following offer for your consideration.

9) We regret to inform you that we cannot accept your offer, as we are obtaining goods of similar quality from other sources at a price 6% lower than yours.

10) Considering the quality of the suitcases offered we do not feel that the prices we quoted are excessive at all, but in view of the long-standing business relations between us, we have decided to offer you a special discount of 2% for an order exceeding US $ 20,000.

9. Write a letter based on the information given below.

Smith & Jones is an importer located in San Francisco, U. S. A. In a letter of inquiry, the company expressed its interest in Chinese cashmere sweaters and asked for an offer. Write a reply to the inquiry with the information given below:

Price: US $ 45 per piece, CIF San Francisco, 3% discount for orders over 500 pieces

Packing: In transparent plastic bags, 10 dozen bags in a carton

Payment: L/C at sight

Delivery: Within 45 days after receipt of covering L/C

Validity: 5 days

Attached: Catalogue and detailed specifications

10. Make a telephone conversation in pairs with two students sitting back to back, one calling the other to find out the detailed address to get to the company you want to visit. Please note that it is the first time for you to go to the company.

Lesson Eleven
Payment Terms

1. Introduction

In international trade, both the exporter and the importer face risks because of the possibility of default, the former risks not getting paid after delivering the goods, while the latter risks not receiving the goods after payment. So business people adopt various payment terms depending on how much risk is involved. The following are the basic methods of payment introduced in the order from the safest to the least safe.

(1) Letter of Credit (abbreviated as L/C)

A letter of credit is a letter written by the importer's bank to the exporter, verifying the bank's promise to pay the beneficiary (usually the exporter) upon presentation of documents relating to the dispatch of the goods, if the importer fails to effect payment. Thus it is protective of the exporter's interests. On the other hand, it protects the importer's interests too, because the importer receives the guarantee from the bank that the exporter will not be paid until the goods ordered have truly been dispatched and all the documents relating to the goods are in order. The documents mainly include the Contract between the exporter and importer, Bill of Lading, Insurance Policy, Inspection Certificate, etc.

The disadvantage of this method of payment is the cost, which is to be borne by the importer for opening an L/C, that is usually higher than other means of payment, and it takes a longer time.

(2) Bill of exchange (or draft)

A bill of exchange is also called a draft, which is an unconditional order in writing, usually drawn and signed by the exporter (also called a drawer), requiring the importer (or the drawee) to pay on demand, or at a fixed future time, a certain sum of money to the person specified.

A bill of exchange is either a sight or a term bill. The former is one that is payable on presentation to the drawee. The other type is payable at a fixed time in the future, or a number of months or days after the bill has been sighted.

In foreign trade the bill of exchange is mostly a documentary bill, that is, the bill of exchange is accompanied by the documents relating to the goods for which payment is to be settled. A documentary bill falls into two categories:

a. Documents against payment (D/P)

The exporter makes shipment and sends the shipping documents to the exporter's bank for collection. The bank then sends the shipping documents along with a bill of exchange to the importer's bank, which then sends the bill of exchange to the importer, who has to make payment immediately upon receiving the bill of exchange.

b. Document against acceptance (D/A)

Under the D/A term, the importer does not have to pay immediately when the documents are presented. Instead, the importer has to accept the bill of exchange to signify his formal commitment to pay on the due date. Thus, the accepted bill of exchange is paid by the importer on the day, which may be 30, 60, or 90 days later, as originally agreed upon with the seller.

Under the above terms, only after payment does the importer receive the original shipping documents and become the legitimate owner of the goods.

The major advantage of this method is the low cost, compared with a letter of credit. But, this is offset by the risk that the importer might for some reason or other reject the documents. Since the cargo would have already been loaded (to generate the documents), the exporter has little recourse against the importer in cases of non-payment. So, a D/A or D/P arrangement involves a high level of trust between the exporter and the importer.

(3) Remittance

The importer pays the sum for the transaction agreed upon with the exporter directly to the seller/exporter through a bank. This method is carried out in three ways.

a. Telegraphic transfer (T/T)

b. Mail transfer (M/T)

c. Demand draft (D/D)

This method is fast and of low cost, but is least safe since the payer does not have any guarantee whatsoever for receiving the goods after payment. It is mostly used when the amount of money involved is small.

(4) Electronic payment (e-pay)

Payment through electronic system is fast and the payer can pay at anytime, regardless of the business hour of the relevant bank or company of the importing country. Electronic systems support B-to-C and B-to-B transactions by means of credit card, magnetic strip card, electronic check and electronic money. But users of this payment system need to satisfy a number of requirements, including integrity, trust, anonymity, confidentiality, authentication, etc.

2. Writing strategy

(1) State the payment terms clearly and accurately

Always express your accepted terms explicitly and unmistakably in business correspondence in order to avoid misunderstanding and subsequent trouble. Take the letter of credit as an example, which takes different forms such as Irrevocable L/C, Confirmed L/C, Unconfirmed L/C, Transferable L/C, Sight L/C, Revolving L/C, Automatic revolving L/C, Back to back L/C, Reciprocal L/C, Anticipatory L/C, Standby L/C and each of them has different restrictions and requires different practices.

(2) Negotiate for changes

If the expected term of payment cannot be accepted, make a polite request and give the reason for a change. As far as the other party is concerned, if they have to give a negative reply, use the reader-centered "you" attitude and emphasize the positive.

3. Communication for results

On making request for a favor, use "you" attitude is more appropriate.

"we" attitude	"you" attitude
Since we are doing business on commission basis, we usually get 3% commission from our suppliers.	Would you please provide us 3% commission which is necessary to promote sales here.
We usually pay for our imports by D/P, and we hope you will accept the same payment term.	Would you please accept payment by D/P as we have been allowed by other suppliers.

4. Example letters

(1) Expressing terms of payment

September 18, 2010

Dear Sir:

Thank you for your order No. XP3210 for 500 dozen Cotton Shirts, Art. No. 036.

Please pay for the goods you ordered by Confirmed and Irrevocable L/C available by draft at sight, against a full set of shipping documents to be presented to the negotiating bank at the port of loading. The shipping documents consist of:

a. Clean "on Board" Bill of Lading

b. Commercial Invoice in triplicate

c. Inspection Certificate issued by ABC Inspection House

d. Insurance Policy in duplicate

Other terms remain unchanged.

Sincerely,

(Sigature)

(2) Buyer's counter-proposal for easier payment term

Dear Sir:

Thank you for your letter of Sept. 18, stating the terms of payment, for which we would like to give our proposal for your consideration.

Business transactions between us have been quite satisfactory during the past years. We have always honored the contracts and have made payment on time.

Therefore, we think we deserve easier terms of payment for this order of 500 dozen Cotton Shirts as well as for future orders.

Would you please accept payment by D/P as we have been allowed by other suppliers?

We believe this will further promote the mutually beneficial business co-operation between us.

We appreciate your favorable reply.

Sincerely,
(Signature)

(3) A reply to accept the proposal

September 22, 2010

Dear Sir:

We have carefully considered your proposal to pay with easier terms for your purchase of the 500 dozen cotton shirts.

In order to facilitate your efforts in sales, we've decided to make an exception and to accept D/P at sight for the total value of the goods shipped.

The decision is made in view of the friendly business relations between us over the years. We trust you will value this opportunity to promote our products on your market.

Sincerely,
(Signature)

(4) Aequest to the seller to accept payment by D/P

Dear Sir:

Order for 100 Motorbikes

We would like to place a trial order of 100 Motorbikes, model CJ125 at the price quoted in your offer which reached us on July 15, 2010.

As for the terms of payment, would you please give us some special treatment to pay by D/P instead of Confirmed Irrevocable L/C as required in your offer. Because issuing an L/C will tie-up our capital and increase the cost, leaving us a much narrower profit margin.

We would be most grateful if you could extend this favor to us. You can be rest assured that once we receive the shipping document for the captioned goods we will pay immediately the full amount of the purchase.

This is just an initial order. If the transaction goes on well, large orders will follow. We are looking forward to your favorably reply.

Yours faithfully,

(Signature)

(5) Refusing buyer's request of payment by D/P, but easing the term of payment

Dear Sir:

Payment for Order of 100 Motorbikes

We have received with thanks your order of July 20 for 100 Motorbikes, model CJ125.

Because we have kept it as a rule that payment exceeding USD $ 1,000 must be made by L/C, we cannot accept your proposal to pay by D/P.

However, with an eye to promoting friendly business cooperation between us. We shall give you a more favorable term — L/C at 60 day sight instead of L/C at sight, which is the best term we've ever offered.

Our products are very popular in many countries for the advantage of oil efficiency and reasonable price. Please confirm your order soon so that you and your customer will enjoy the fine quality and reliable after-sale service of our products at an early date.

Sincerely,

(Signature)

(6) Reply to a refusal

Dear Sir:

Payment under Order No. XT3810

We thank you for your order No. XT3810 for 100 tons of Peanuts.

Regarding the matter of payment for the captioned order, our general practice for business settlement is by confirmed and irrevocable L/C, so we are not in a position to accept your request to pay by D/A at 30 days sight.

Considering your problems with an urgent demand from your customer, we shall give you priority for the earliest possible delivery, which is within 20 days after receiving your relevant L/C.

Presently our stock is running low, please establish your relevant L/C soon so that the goods will be hipped by the first steamer.

Sincerely,

(Signature)

5. Telephone conversation

Peter wants to call Jason to make changes in the terms of payment. Karl is Jason's secretary.

Karl: Jason Lee's office. This is Karl.

Peter: Hello, Karl, this is Peter White.

Karl: Hello, Mr. White. How may I help you?

Peter: I need to talk with Jason.

Karl: Certainly. Hold on.

Peter: Thanks.

Jason: Hello, Peter. This is Jason.

Peter: Hi, Jason. I've just received your Sale's Confirmation which says that payment for our Order No. 560 is to be made by L/C. Would you consider payment by D/P for this repeat order?

Jason: Sorry, I can't. It is our rule that payment which exceeds $1,000 must be made by L/C.

Peter: You know our order this time is quite large, and to open an L/C for such a large amount is costly.

Jason: I understand your situation. But we can't take any risks. We have to insist on payment by L/C.

Peter: Can you be a bit more flexible for the repeat order from us? Shall we make a concession with 50% by D/P, and 50% by L/C?

Jason: Well, let me see. The best I can do is 70% by L/C, and 30% by D/P. This is really the biggest concession I've ever made.

Peter: All right, then. Thank you.

New Words and Phrases

default [di'fɔːlt] *n.* failure to do something demanded by duty or law; failing to pay 不履行(债务;义务),不支付

The firm is in default on a loan. 这家公司拖欠贷款。

verify ['verifai] *v.* prove 证明,证实

beneficiary [beni'fiʃəri] *n.* receiver of benefits 受益人

dispatch [dis'pætʃ] *n.* the act of sending off to a specific destination 派遣

draft [drɑːft] *n.* a written order directing payment of a specified amount of money 汇票

draw [drɔː] *v.* to make out; issue (a bill) 开出(票据)

to draw on sb. 向某人开出汇票

unconditional ['ʌnkən'diʃənəl] *a.* without condition 无条件的

drawer ['drɔːə] *n.* the person who make out a draft or bill 开票人

drawee [drɔː'iː] *n.* the person on whom a draft or bill is drawn 受票人,付款人

original [ə'ridʒənəl] *a.* initial, earliest 原始的,最初的

original document 原件

collection [kə'lekʃən] *v.* getting money on presentation of a draft or check for payment at the bank 托收

legitimate [li'dʒitimit] *a.* lawful 合法的,正当的

offset ['ɔːfset] *v.* 抵消

recourse [ri'kɔːs] *n.* possible source for help 求援,追索权

remittance [ri'mitəns] *n.* sending of money 汇款

credit card a card issued by a bank or business authorizing the holder to buy goods or service on credit 信用卡

magnetic strip card 磁卡

anonymity [ˌænə'nimiti] *n.* the state of being unknown or unacknowledged 匿名

authenticate [ɔː'θentikeit] *v.* to prove (sth.) to be authentic 证实……为真品

authentication [ɔːˌθenti'keiʃən] *n.* establishing the identity 证实……的真实性

facilitate [fə'siliteit] *v.* make easy, help 使容易

Your information has greatly facilitated our preparation for shipment.

你的消息极大地帮助了我们的装船工作。

To facilitate shipment, please see to it the stipulations in your L/C are in full conformity with those of our Sales Confirmation. 请注意你方信用证条款与我们的销售合同的条款完全相符以便于装运。

This agency agreement will surely facilitate your pushing the sale of our products.

此代理协议一定有助于你们推销我方产品。

(Note: No infinitive or "that clause" is used after the verb "facilitate".)

confirm [kən'fəːm] *v.* provide support for the truth or correctness 确认

motorbike ['məutəbaik] *n.* 摩托车

model ['mɔdl] *n.* a style or design of an item 型号

The car is last year's model. 这辆车是去年的车型。

Notes

1. ... the document relating to the goods are *in order* ……有关货物的单证已备好

in order 整齐,有条理,状况正常

e. g.: The ship is in (good) order for sail. 船已准备完毕,等待起航。

The machine is in (working) order now. 机器状况良好。

2. bill of lading (or blading) 提单

3. insurance policy 保险单

4. inspection certificate 检验证书

5. to open an L/C 开立信用证

Relevant expressions: establish an L/C 开立信用证; apply for an L/C 申请(开立)信用证; issue an L/C (银行)开出信用证

6. bill of exchange 汇票

"汇票"也常称为"draft",或简称为"bill"。

7. a sight bill 即期汇票

Other expressions: a draft at sight

8. a term bill 远期汇票

Other expressions: a draft after sight, a 30 (or 60, 90) day draft

9. documentary bill 跟单汇票

A bill that is attached to shipping documents

10. document against payment 付款交单

11. document against acceptance 承兑交单

12. The importer has to accept the bill of exchange to signify his formal commitment to pay *on the due date*. 进口商必须接受汇票,以表示正式承诺到期付款。

on the due date 到期日

e. g.: The goods must be delivered on the due date. 货物必须按时装运。

13. ... the exporter has little *recourse* against the importer in case of non-payment. 万一

进口人不付款,出口人几乎没有任何追索权。

Recourse: right to cover the loss

14. electronic transfer 电子汇款

15. telegraphic transfer 电(报)汇(款)

16. mail transfer 信汇

17. demand draft 票汇

18. letter of credit (L/C) 信用证

19. irrevocable L/C 不可撤销的信用证

20. confirmed L/C 保兑信用证

21. unconfirmed L/C 不保兑信用证

22. transferable L/C 可转让信用证

23. sight L/C 即期信用证

24. revolving L/C 循环信用证

25. automatic revolving L/C 自动循环信用证

26. back to back L/C 对背信用证

27. reciprocal L/C 对开信用证

28. anticipatory L/C 预支信用证

29. standby L/C 备用信用证

30. We require confirmed and irrevocable L/C available by draft at sight against full set of shipping documents presented to the negotiating bank at the port of loading.

我们要求的付款方式是凭附带全套装船单证的即期汇票开立的信用证,在装货港所在地银行议付。

31. clean on board bill of lading 清洁的、已装船提单

32. clean bill of lading 清洁提单

A bill of lading issued by a carrier for goods delivered in "apparent good order and condition", bearing no notations or added clauses which may limit the liability of the carrier.

Compare: foul bill of lading 不清洁提单

A bill of lading issued with notations, such as the goods were received damaged, or short, or improperly packaged, which limit the carrier's liability.

33. commercial invoice in triplicate 商业发票一式三份

34. inspection certificate issued by ABC Inspection House 由 ABC 商检公司开出的商检证书

35. We have carefully considered your proposal *to pay with easier terms* for your purchase of the 500 dozen cotton shirts. 我们认真考虑了你方建议用较宽松的付款方式支付你方订购的500打全棉衬衫。

to pay with easier terms 用较便利的付款方式付款

36. in view of 鉴于,考虑到

e. g.: in view of the facts 考虑到这些事实

in view of future business opportunities 考虑到将来的交易机会

37. We would be most grateful if you could *extend this favor to us*. 如果您能给我方提供这种优惠,我们将不胜感激。

extend the favor to us 给我方这种帮助

38. with an eye to 着眼于

e. g. : We did this with an eye to the exploration of the potential market. 我这样做是着眼于探查潜在市场。

39. Presently our stock is running low. 现在我们的存货在逐渐减少。

Useful Expressions

1. Please note that our terms of payment are by irrevocable L/C, payable by draft at 30 days sight accompanied by shipping documents, for negotiation at the Bank of China at the port of shipment.
2. To open an L/C is quite costly and will tie up the capital of our company. Can you allow us a more favorable term of payment such as document against acceptance?
3. Drafts drawn under this credit must be negotiated in China on or before October 31, 2006, after which this credit expires.
4. We write to inform you that we have now opened an irrevocable letter of credit in your favor for 20,000 Euro with ABC bank, London, valid until 31 December.
5. The letter of credit authorizes you to draw at 60 days on the bank in London for the amount of your invoice after shipment is made.
4. On accepting the draft, the bank requires you to produce the following documents: Bill of Lading in triplicate, Commercial Invoice, Packing List, Certificate of Insurance and Certificate of Origin.
5. Thank you for your remittance of US $600 in payment of the freight due under Invoice No. 37B.
6. We have to remind you that we have not yet received the amount of ¥1500 for the 20% of the freight still outstanding.
7. Please find enclosed our invoice for HK $5000 and note that we have drawn on you for this amount at 30 d/s attaching the shipping documents to our draft.
8. We note that you wish us to draw on your Tokyo agents for the amount of our invoice. This is acceptable to us and we shall forward them our draft for their attention as soon as the goods are ready for shipment.
9. Your proposal to pay by draft is acceptable to us and we shall accordingly draw on you at 2 months from the date of shipment of your order.
10. Our bank in Tokyo, Ohiro Bank, (东京大平银行) will accept your draft on them on our behalf.

Exercises

1. Answer the following questions.

1) What are the major credit risks in international trade? How to avoid the risks?

2) What are the advantages and disadvantages of the following terms of payment?

A. L/C. B. Draft. C. Remittance. D. Electronic payment.

2. Decide whether the following statements are true or false. Write "T" for true, and "F" for false in the brackets.

1) Bill of Exchange is a way used for payment in foreign trade. ( )

2) The writer of a draft is the drawer. ( )

3) The draft is to be accepted by the exporter in general practice. ( )

4) Payment by documentary bill is more risky for the exporter than the importers. ( )

5) A sight bill is to be paid immediately on presentation to the drawee. ( )

6) An L/C is a safer means of payment than a sight bill. ( )

7) A term bill is to be paid on a future date. ( )

8) Payment by draft is easier than mail transfer. ( )

3. Choose the best answer to complete the following statements.

1) An exporter will suffer great loss if the importer <u>defaults</u>.

The underlined part of the sentence means ______.

A. makes mistakes B. forgets C. fails to pay D. disappears

2) The risk for an importer in a business transaction is that ______.

A. he may not get the goods he wanted B. he may not be able to pay for the goods

C. he may not be believed by the exporter D. he may not find a suitable means of payment

3) A safe method of payment is ______.

A. L/C B. bill of exchange C. a draft at sight D. remittance

4) If payment is made by L/C the exporter is guaranteed for getting paid unless ______.

A. the goods are damaged B. the ship in damaged

C. the importer is bankrupt D. the opening bank is bankrupt

5) The beneficiary in an L/C is usually ______.

A. the importer B. the exporter C. the carrier D. the bank

6) A documentary bill is ______.

A. a document that is written and formal B. a bill that must be paid immediately

C. a bill that can be paid later D. a bill that is attached by documents

7) A D/P requires ______.

A. immediate payment after being presented to the importer

B. payment after 30 or 60 days

C. payment made by the bank

D. payment made by the shipper

8) The major advantage of remittance is ______.

A. it is cheap and fast

B. it is cheap and safe

C. it is cheap and profitable

D. not advantageous compared with other ways of payment

9) A clean bill of lading is a ______.

A. A bill of lading which confirms the goods delivered are in "apparent good order and condition"

B. A bill of lading which confirms the goods delivered are clean

C. A bill of lading which confirms the goods delivered are safe

D. none of the above

10) In writing a request for easier payment term it is always appropriate to ______.

A. adopt "you" attitude　　B. adopt a friendly attitude

C. give a deadline　　D. give a promise

4. Write out the full forms of the abbreviated payment methods and give the equivalent terms in Chinese.

Abbreviation	Full Form	Chinese
M/T		
T/T		
L/C		
D/A		
D/P		

5. Make sentences with the following words and phrases.

1) facilitate　　2) in view of　　3) extend the favor to　　4) honor (*v.*)

6. Translate the following sentences into English.

1) 我们认真考虑了你方要求放宽付款条件的建议,鉴于双方多年友好合作的关系,决定接受以即期付款交单的方式支付 AC500 号订单下货物。(in view of)

2) 由于存货不多,且行市趋涨,请速订购。(stock)

3) 如贵方能给予我们这项优惠,我们将非常感谢。(extend to)

4) 请把下列单据备好,以便我们向中国银行议付。(in order)

5) 你 1456K 号订单已于昨天装"金星"轮,现将有关发票付上。当你方银行向你们提示我们的汇票时,请予以支付。(honor)

6) 根据双方达成的协议,我们已开具了这批船货的即期汇票,通过此处中国银行转去,请见票即付。(draw on)

7) 你方皮鞋的价格可接受,若同意付款交单的付款条件,拟试订购 200 双。(trial order)

8) 你方 9 月 10 日所报男衬衫价格已接受,目前正在申请进口许可证。一旦获准,立即开立信用证。(apply for)

9)因这批货物涉及金额较大,付款交单的办法很难接受,请用信用证见票 60 天付款。(L/C at 60 days sight)

10)以保兑的、不可撤销的、金额为全部货款的即期信用证支付。(full amount)

7. Translate the following passage into Chinese.

Every exporter has problems of getting paid. There are even risks of buyer default in rich countries. The importers might go bankrupt or the government might not allow the importers to buy the payment currency. On the other hand there are credit problems. The sellers need to be paid in advance but buyers have no funds and need credit. The sellers must offer good terms, otherwise they will lose their customers who will look for other suppliers. There are also problems caused by exchange rates and changes of value of the payment currency. If it falls, the exporter loses money. Both sellers and buyers want to be sure that the other side will fulfill their side of the agreement. The exporters want to be paid in full at the right time and the importers want the right goods delivered on time. These problems can be solved by the banks acting as advisers.

8. Write a reply to the following letter.

Dear Sir:

Thank you for your letter of 8th of May.

We are grateful that you will ship our goods in good time but we are surprised that you still demand payment against documents. After long years of satisfactory trading we feel that we are entitled to easier terms. Most of our suppliers are drawing on us at 60 d/s, documents against acceptance, and we will appreciate it if you could grant us the same terms.

We are looking forward to your favorable reply.

Yours sincerely,

(Signature)

9. Make a telephone conversation in pairs with two students sitting back to back, one acts as a buyer and ask the other, who acts as a seller, to grant an easier term of payment.

Lesson Twelve
Payment by Letter of Credit

Part I Urging Establishment of L/C

1. Introduction

After the signing of a Sales Contract (or Sales Confirmation) which stipulates that payment is to be made by L/C, the importer should timely establish the L/C according to the contract. But sometimes they fail to do so due to various reasons ranging from negligence of the working staff to delay in receiving an import license from relevant authorities. On the part of the exporter, they cannot ship the goods without receiving the covering L/C. In this case the exporter has to urge the importer to open an L/C in time in order not to delay shipment.

2. Writing strategy

In writing the first letter urging the importer to open an L/C, you can write a gentle reminder considering that the importer may be too busy to remember the time, or the L/C may be on the way to the exporter.

Include in your letter the contract number and/or order number in the letter, and the time of shipment as well, so that the reader will have a clear idea which transaction you refer to, and of the urgency to speed up the procedures.

If the L/C is still not available after repeated reminders, write a strong request to the importer to open the L/C on time. Set a deadline and inform the buyer of any serious consequence.

3. Communication for results

You may feel frustrated not receiving the L/C at the expected time. But avoid using words that attack your reader's competence, intelligence or honesty.

Instead of saying	Say
You fail to observe the contract you have signed.	You must observe the contract you have signed.
At this point, the only sensible thing is to open the L/C immediately.	Please open the L/C immediately.
You claimed that your L/C will reach us on time, but you forgot it.	You have signed the contract which stipulates the time for opening the L/C.

4. Example letters

(1) A reminder to the importer to open an L/C

Dear Mr. Williams:

Re: Your Order No. FG2345

With reference to the above order under S/C No. 7788, we'd like to remind you that the date of delivery, September 15, is approaching, and the covering L/C should have reached us by August 15 according to the Sales Confirmation. But up to the present we have not received it yet. Please act promptly to have your L/C reach us within this month so that the above order will be shipped on time.

Your cooperation is appreciated.

Sincerely,
(Signature)
Chang Hong

(2) A strong request for the importer to open an L/C

Dear Mr. Williams:

Re: Your Order No. FG2345 under S/C No. 7788

Referring to the captioned order and our fax on August 25, requesting you to establish the relevant L/C, we have not received your L/C nor your explanation for the delay up to now.

Would you please give your attention to item 5 in the above Sales Confirmation which reads "The Buyer shall establish the coving Letter of Credit before 30th August, 2006, failing which the seller reserves the right to rescind the contract without further notice".

It is understood that both of us must observe and execute the contract once we have signed it.

We have already prepared for shipment according to the Sales Confirmation. The goods you ordered have been ready for some time, and demand has been great recently. It is hard for us to keep the goods for you any longer. However, in viewing of the friendly business relations between us, we shall wait for your L/C, which must reach us no later than September 6, 2006. If, by then, we fail to receive your L/C, we shall cancel our Sales Confirmation and ask you to refund to us the storage charges we have paid on your behalf.

Please attend to this matter with all speed.

Sincerely,
(Signature)
Chang Hong

New Words and Phrases

negligence [ˈneglidʒəns] *n.* carelessness 疏忽
authority [ɔːˈθɔriti] *n.* a person or body having administrative power 当局,官方
authoritarian [ɔːˌθɔriˈtɛəriən] expecting unquestioning obedience 专横的
urge [əːdʒ] *v.* impel, drive forcefully 催促,力劝
consequence [ˈkɔnsikwəns] *n.* the result or effect of an action 结果,后果
reserve [riˈzəːv] *v.* retain or secure 储备,保存,保留
rescind [riˈsind] *v.* cancel, abrogate 废除
observe [əbˈzəːv] *v.* keep, follow (esp. the law, stipulation) 遵守(法律,规定等)
  to observe the rule 遵守规则
refund [riˈfʌnd] *v.* pay back 退还,偿还
  We'll refund you the purchase price if you are dissatisfied. 若你方不满意我们将退还货款。
storage [ˈstɔridʒ] *n.* the storing of goods 贮藏,存储
on the way 在途中
  The shipment is on the way, and will reach you soon. 船正在途中,马上就到达你方。
with reference to 关于
on one's behalf (*or* on behalf of ...) 为……的利益,代表
  The party is given on your behalf. 这个晚会是专为你举行的。
  I'd like to express my sincere thanks to you on behalf of the members of my delegation. 我代表我的代表团成员向你们表示衷心的感谢。

Notes

1. **But sometimes they fail to do so due to various reasons *ranging from* negligence of *working staff to* delay of receiving import license from relevant authorities.** 有时由于各种原因,从员工疏忽到不能得到有关政府部门颁发的进口许可证等等,他们未能做到这一点。

   range from... to... (范围)涉及……

e. g. : The prices of the dolls range from $5 to $100. 那些布娃娃价格从5美元到100美元不等。

working staff 职员，工作人员

2. up to the present 至今

3. up to now 到目前为止

4. be aware of 明白，知道

e. g. : You must be aware of the fact. 你一定知道这个事实。

5. "The Buyer shall establish the coving Letter of Credit before 30th August, 2006, failing which the seller reserves the right to *rescind* the contract without further notice"

"买方必须在2006年8月30日以前开具信用证，否则，卖方保留撤销合同的权利，不另行通知"

6. rescind 运用权利废除或废止

e. g. : rescind a rule 废除一项制度

7. However, in viewing of the friendly business relations between us, we shall wait for your L/C, which must reach us *no later than* September 6, 2006. 然而，考虑到我们之间的关系，我们打算等您的信用证，您的信用证必须在2006年9月6日以前到达。

no later than (a certain date) 不迟于(特定日期)

e. g. : Payment must be made no later than October 15th. 必须在10月15日前付款。

8. *With reference to* the above order... 关于上述订单

The phrase "with reference to" is frequently used in business letters.

Similar expressions: as for, concerning, in (with) regard to, regarding, as regards

e. g. : *With reference to* the context we can understand what he means.

根据上下文，我们能够理解他的意思。

I don't have any further remark *as for* the schedule of the visit.

至于这次访问的时间安排我没有进一步说明。

Do you have any idea *concerning* their business conduct?

关于他们的商业做法，你是否有所了解？

I have something to say *in regard to* their business conduct.

对于他们的经营作风，我有话要说。

I don't have any objection *regarding* your proposal.

我对你的提议没有任何反对意见。

As regards the future prospects of our business, I'm full of confidence.

对于我们的生意前景，我充满信心。

9. We shall cancel our Sales Confirmation and ask you to *refund* to us the storage charges we have paid on your behalf. 我们将撤销销售合同，并要求您偿还我们为您支付的仓储费用。

refund *vt.* & *n.* 退款

e. g. : You'll be *refunded* if the delay is caused on our side.

如果延误是由我方造成的，我们会给你退款。

Or: You'll get a *refund* if the delay is cause on our side.

Useful Expressions

1. As a business person yourself, I know you appreciate those who meet their financial obligation in a timely manner.
2. Since we haven't received your L/C, we are wondering if there are any extenuating circumstances or if there is some misunderstandings in your statement.
3. You must be aware that failure to open the L/C on time will mean violation of contract.
4. From your letter of 5th July we learn that the L/C has been arranged, but up to now we have not received the banker's advice yet. Please push the confirming bank in New York for their soonest action.
5. You L/C is one month past due, and you've not responded to any of our requests. If we receive no reply by the end of the week, we'll have no alternative but to resort to arbitration.
6. Unless your relevant L/C reach es us within ten days from the date of this letter, we'll turn this matter over for arbitration.

Part II Amendment of Letter of Credit

1. Introduction

On receiving an L/C the exporter must examine thoroughly all the clauses against the terms and conditions stipulated in the sales contract to make sure they are in exact conformity with the contract, because any discrepancy, even a minor difference, if not amended timely may result in the exporter's difficulty or inability to get paid from the negotiating bank.

Besides, the exporter must also check to see if there are any necessary clauses that are not included in the contract, and if there are any unacceptable clauses so as to consult with the importer to amend them in order to avoid difficulties or problems in future.

Special attention must be given to the following clauses:

1) The type of the credit
2) The expiry date of the credit
3) The name and address of the importer (or applicant)
4) The name and address of the exporter (or beneficiary)
5) The amount of the credit both in numeral and in capital letters
6) The terms of price (FOB, CFR, CIF, etc.)
7) The specification and the quantity of the goods covered by the credit
8) The packing and shipping mark
9) Instruction of the documents against which payment is to be made (the terms in the documents must also be in conformity with those in the contract and the L/C)
10) Shipping instruction (whether partial shipment and transshipment is allowed)
11) Name of the place of shipment and delivery or discharge

12) The name of the party on whom the draft is to be drawn, and the type of the draft (a sight draft or a time draft).

13) Instruction to the negotiating bank

If any discrepancy between the terms in the L/C and those in the contract is found the exporter must notify the importer as soon as possible to ask for amendment.

During the implementation of the contract, the exporter or even the importer sometimes find it necessary to make some changes to the contract as well as the L/C due to something unexpected. In this circumstance, either side must get the approval from the other side before the changes are made. The change in the contract will cause corresponding change in the L/C in order for them to conform to each other. Therefore, the importer has to advise the opening bank for an L/C amendment.

2. Writing strategy

Since it is the importer who has to take the trouble, spend time and bear the cost to apply to the opening bank for any changes or amendments in the L/C, in requiring changes the exporter should write with courtesy and in a positive tone. For the sake of clarity, include the L/C number in the letter, and explicitly explain how the amendment is to be made.

If the importer requires amendment, adopt a persuasive tone to get the consent from the other side.

3. Communication for results

When you ask for an L/C amendment, refer to the L/C specifically to give your reader a clear idea which one you mention.

Instead of writing	Write
We have received your L/C now.	Your L/C No. AD678 covering 500 T-shirts has reached us now.

4. Example letters

(1) Exporter's requirement for L/C amendment

Dear Mr. Williams:

L/C No. BV4567

Thank you for your Letter of Credit No. BV4567 for the amount of 150,000,000 yen to cover your Order No. XY386 for 500 metric tons of walnut meat.

After checking, we have found that amendment is to be made in the following 3 points:

1) The packing clause in your Credit should read "corrugated paper cartons with 50 kilos to one carton" instead of "corrugated paper cartons with 30 kilos to one carton".
2) In the quantity of the commodity, please insert the words "5% more or less" after "500 tons", because it is impossible for us to ship the goods in the exact amount.
3) Your Credit stipulates "No transshipment and partial shipment allowed", but the term in the Sales Confirmation is "Transshipment and partial shipment allowed".

We'd like to inform you that a direct steamer is not available during the next two months. The earliest shipment to your port is via Hong Kong. Moreover, we have 300 tons ready for shipment now. It would benefit both of us if we ship it by the steamer sailing to your port next week and the rest of the goods by the end of the month.

In order to ship the goods on time please amend the above 3 points in the L/C immediately.

We thank you for your cooperation.

Sincerely,
(Signature)
Chang Hong

(2) Reply from importer

Dear Ms. Chang Hong:

L/C No. BV4567

Immediately after receiving your request on May 15 concerning the above L/C, we advised our bank, the Midland Bank, for the amendment. We now confirm the amended clauses read as follows:

1) Packing: Corrugated paper cartons with 50 kilos to one carton
2) Quantity: 500 tons with 5% more or less
3) Transshipment and partial shipment allowed

You will receive the amendment by cable from the advising bank soon. Please arrange for the first shipment in the first half of the month because we have promised our customers timely delivery of the goods.

We look forward to your early information about shipment.

Sincerely,
(Signature)
Karl Williams

New Words and Phrases

amendment [ə'mendmənt] *n.* miner alteration or addition to document, etc. 修改

expiry [iks'paiəri] *n.* the moment when sth. ends 期满，终结

capital ['kæpitəl] *a.* （字母）大写的

Type it in capital letters. 用大写字母打印。

conformity [kən'fɔːməti] *n.* being in compliance with 一致，符合

discrepancy [dis'krepənsi] *n.* inconsistency 差异，矛盾

Make sure there is no discrepancy between the two documents. 保证两份文件没有差异。

minor ['mainə] *a.* smaller, less important 较小的，次要的

pack [pæk] *v.* 1) to put things into a case, box, etc. 包装；收拾

Pack some paper around the dishes in the box so that they will not break.

用纸把箱子里的盘子四周充塞好，就不会打碎了。

They are packing for the holiday. 他们在为度假收拾行李。

n. 2) a small package 小包；小盒

a pack of cigarette 一包香烟；a pack of candy 一盒糖果

discharge [dis'tʃɑːdʒ] *n. & v.* unload(ing) 卸货

The goods will be discharged at your warehouse. 货物将卸在你方仓库。

implementation [ˌimplimen'teiʃən] *n.* fulfill, complete (esp. contract) 履行，执行

implementation of a policy 执行政策

approval [ə'pruːvəl] *n.* the act of approving 赞成，正式批准

The government has given their approval to our project. 政府已批准了我们的项目。

corresponding [ˌkɔris'pɔndiŋ] *a.* 对应的

There is no corresponding Chinese version for this English phrase.

这个英文短语没有对应的中文词语。

bear [bɛə] *v.* to carry; to support; to pay 承担，负担

bear the responsibility 承担责任；bear the cost 负担费用

courtesy ['kəːtisi, 'kɔː-] *n.* being polite 谦恭，礼貌

explicitly [ik'splisitli] *adv.* the state of being fully and clearly expressed 明白地，清楚地

State your requirement explicitly. 明确说明你的要求。

consent [kən'sent] *n. & v.* agree(ment) 同意，赞成，答应

give one's consent to 同意

Silence gives consent. 沉默表示认可。She consents to my proposal. 她同意我的提议。

corrugated paper carton 瓦楞纸箱

for the sake of 为了……缘故

for the sake of convenience (*or* for convenience sake) 为了方便

Notes

1. **150,000,000 yen** 150 000 000 日元

Short form of major world currencies:

USD: U. S. Dollar

GBP: British Pound

CAD: Canadian Dollar

EUR: Euro

CHF: Swiss Franc

AUD: Australian Dollar

HKD: Hong Kong Dollar

JPY: Japanese Yen

(For Chinese currency, we use RMB, the initials of Ren Min Bi.)

2. **The amount of the credit both *in numeral* and *in capital letters*** 用阿拉伯数字和大写字母表示的信用证金额

in numeral 用阿拉伯数字表示 in capital letters 用大写字母表示

为避免金额数量的差错、伪造或涂改,信用证以及发票、汇票等的金额须在阿拉伯数字之后,在括号内用大写英文字母重复该金额,并在大写文字前加上"SAY",意为"大写",在最后加上"ONLY"意思为"整"。

如:Party A shall pay Party B a monthly salary of US $1000 (SAY ONE THOUSAND UNITED STATES DOLLARS ONLY).

3. **FOB** Free on Board 船上交货价,离岸价
4. **CFR** Cost and Freight 成本加运费价
5. **CIF** Cost Insurance and Freight 到岸价
6. **shipping mark** marking on the outer packing of the goods showing special information about the goods, the destination, etc. 唛头
7. **shipping instruction** 运输说明
8. **negotiating bank** 议付银行
9. **opening bank** 开证银行 Also called: issuing bank, establishing bank
10. **please insert the words "5% more or less" after "500 tons"** 请在"500 吨"后面加上"增减 5%"
11. **direct steamer** 直达轮
12. **advising bank** 通知银行(它把开证事宜通知出口人) Also called: notifying bank
13. **partial shipment and transshipment** 分批装运和转运
14. **result in** 导致

e. g.: Their carelessness resulted in a great loss. 疏忽造成了巨大的损失。

The accident resulted in the sinking of the cargo ship. 事故造成货船沉没。

15. **the change in the contract will cause corresponding change in the L/C in order for them to *conform* to each other.** 合同的修改需要使信用证做出相应的修改,以便使二者相符。

conform 符合（ always followed by "to" or "with"）

e. g. :conform to the taste of the consumer 符合消费者的口味

conform with the interest of the people 符合人民的利益

16. For the sake of clarity, include the L/C number in the letter, and explicitly explain how the amendment is to be made. 为了清晰起见，信中要写明信用证号，并且明确地解释如何进行修改。

17. The earliest shipment to your port is *via* Hong Kong. 最早的一班到贵方港口的船是经过香港的。

via: by way of 途经

Useful Expressions

1. Please make sure that the L/C stipulations are in exact accordance with the terms set forth in our sales confirmation.
2. As we have placed a further order with our suppliers, will you please increase the credit to US $ 3900 in accordance with the attached instructions?
3. If, for any unpredictable reason, you are unable to dispatch during September, please inform us immediately as it may be necessary to use airfreight even at increased cost to insure the arrival of the shipment in time for our manufacturer's program. The relative credit will include "Airway bills Acceptable".
4. Please insert the word "about" before the quantity in your L/C No. 345.
5. As there is no direct sailing from Tianjin to your port during June and July, it is imperative for you to delete the clause "by direct steamer" and insert the wording "partial shipment and transshipment allowed".
6. The commission granted for this transaction is 3% as stipulated in our sales conformation, but we find your L/C demands a commission of 5%. Therefore you are requested to instruct your banker to amend the L/C.

Part III Extension of Letter of Credit

1. Introduction

An L/C has validity and all the business proceedings concerning the deal must be completed on time before the L/C expires. Otherwise, the L/C has to be extended. Very often, the postponement of the time of delivery, or time of negotiation, or time of presentation of shipping documents set in the L/C cause extension of the L/C, that is, the validity of the L/C has to be postponed accordingly.

2. Writing strategy

Messages requiring an L/C extension are unwelcome to the importer for the same reason as that of an amendment. In writing such request, explain the reason and write in a positive tone. If such amendment has to be made due to some problems caused by the person who requests extension, an apology in the letter is appropriate.

3. Communication for results

In writing a requirement for your reader to take action, focus on the following points.

1. Make it easy for your reader to understand.

Instead of writing	Write
You have to extend the L/C to August 31st and September 15th for shipment and negotiation respectively.	Please extend the time of shipment to August 31, and the time of negotiation to September 15 in your L/C No. BI330.

2. Write in a positive tone.

Instead of writing	Write
To our great regret, the goods cannot be shipped on time because of your delay in opening an L/C. Your L/C has to be extended.	In order to ship your goods early next month, please extend your L/C No. BI300 to October 31.

4. Example letters

Example 1. Exporter's requirement for L/C extension because of the buyer's delay

Dear Mr. Williams:

Re: L/C No. 3456

We have received the above L/C covering your Order No. 0506 on June 30, 2010.

We'd like to draw your attention to clause (6) in the S/C310 ~ 330: "Shipment between July 15—18 provided the L/C reaches the seller on/before June 15". However, we received your L/C only yesterday, 15 days later than the time stipulated.

Because July shipment is impossible, we advise you to extend the time of shipment and the validity of the L/C that reads as follows:

"Time of shipment: August 10 – 15, 2010"
"Validity of L/C No. 3456: September 30, 2010"

Please have your L/C amendment reach us no later than July 15.

We have arranged the goods for shipment, and we look forward to receiving the relevant L/C amendment in time.

Sincerely,
(Signature)
Chang Hong

Example 2. Requirement for L/C extension due to problem on the writer side

Dear Mr. Williams:

Re: L/C 7788 for 500 Metric Tons of Walnut Meat

We are sorry that owing to the delay on the part of our suppliers at the place of origin, the captioned goods will not be ready till the end of this month.

We have done our best to arrange the consignment to be shipped on S/S "Rickmas" sailing from Tianjin Port on/about April 10.

Would you please extend the date of shipment to April 15 – 18, 2006, and the validity of the L/C to April 30, 2010?

We apologize for the delay. Please send us the extended L/C before March 28 in order to ship the goods at the above time.

Your understanding and cooperation is appreciated.

Sincerely,
(Signature)
Chang Hong

5. Telephone conversation

Peter calls Jason again to talk about payment terms.

Jason: Jason Lee's office.

Peter: Hi, Jason, this is Peter.

Jason: Hello, Peter.

Peter: I've considered your request to pay by L/C. We think it would be better to pay by L/C after sight so as to avoid having our funds tied up for too long.

Jason: Well, you see, this time your order involves quite a sizable sum of money.

Peter: But we'll definitely make payment on time as we always do.

Jason: Sorry, I can't give you any definite answer right now. I'll have to consult the general manager.

Peter: Okay, could you give me a reply tomorrow?

Jason: Yes, I'll try.

Peter: Then I'll call back tomorrow. Have a good day.

Jason: You too. Bye.

(Peter calls back the following day.)

Peter: Hello, is it Jason?

Jason: This is he.

Peter: Good morning, Jason. This is Peter.

Jason: Good morning, Peter. I've talked over with the general manager. Now, I can give the decision about your payment.

Peter: Yes?

Jason: Since you are our old customer, we will make an exception to accept L/C after sight, but you'll have to pay the interest based on the current rate of the City Bank.

Peter: No problem. Then, it is settled.

Jason: Please have your L/C reach us on August 30th.

Peter: Sure.

New Words and Phrases

extension [iks'tenʃən] *n.* prolongation 延期

I made one week extension to my visit. 我把访问时间延长了一周。

extend [iks'tend] *v.* prolong 伸展,扩大,加长

My visit has been extended for another week. 我的访问又延续了一周。

proceeding [prə'siːdiŋ] *n.* action, conduct 进程, 事项

expire [iks'paiə] *v.* become void, reach its term 期满, 终止

My passport expires in a month. 我的护照一个月后到期。

postpone [pəust'pəun] *v.* put off 延期, 推迟

The journey is postponed because of the weather. 由于天气原因,旅行被推迟了。

metric ton 公吨

hand in 递交;上交

The document must be handed in no later than October 20th. 文件必须在10月20日前递交。

owning to 因为,由于

Owning to our joint efforts, the task was finished ahead of schedule.

由于我们的共同努力,任务提前完成了。

place of origin 原产地

Notes

1. ... **the postponement of the time of delivery, or time of negotiation, or time of presentation of shipping documents *set* in the L/C cause extension of the L/C, that is, the validity of the L/C has to be postponed accordingly.** 推迟信用证规定的交货期或议付期或提交货运单据的日期常常使信用证延期，即信用证的有效期须相应推迟。

   set in the L/C 作定语修饰 shipping documents。

   set: fixed　确定

   e. g.: The time has been set for the departure. 出发的时间已经确定了。

   Set a date for our meeting. 为我们的会议制定日期。

2. **letter of credit** 信用证

   Also called: credit, abbreviated as L/C, Ls/C for plural

3. **Messages requiring L/C extension are unwelcome to the exporter for the same reason as that of amendment.** 出口商不喜欢看到要求信用证延期信件，其原因和他们不喜欢修改信用证一样。

4. **on the part of somebody** (*or* on somebody's part)在(某人)一方；就(某人)而言

   e. g.: It was a mistake on your part to sign the agreement before reading it. 不看内容就签约，错误在你方。

5. **S/S** (*or* s/s, ss, s. s.): steamship 轮船（仅用于船名前）

   Similar expression: M/V(motor vessel)

Useful Expressions

1. As the sailing vessel s. s. "Norfolk" was cancelled because of serious damage, we are not in a position to ship the goods within the validity period of L/C No. QW889. We have to advise you to extend the L/C to the end of this month, and time of shipment to 18 August.
2. Because of the fire accident in our manufacturing company which resulted in some damage of the goods. We are forced to have part of goods remanufactured. We shall be grateful if you would persuade your customer to extend the covering L/C for 30 days.
3. We shall allow you a one-month extension of the L/C upon your suggestion and hope this will help you out of your present difficulty.

Exercises

1. Answer the following questions.

1) What should exporters do first of all on receiving Ls/C?

2) How to urge buyers to open the Ls/C in time if they fail to do so?

3) What is the consequence if the buyers delay the opening of L/C?

2. Choose the best words or phrases to complete the following sentences.

1) ______ our S/C No. 301, the goods will be shipped by October 10.

A. With reference to B. Refer to　　C. Referring　　D. With refer to

2) ______ we would like to supply you with the products, we are unable to fill your order owing to heavy commitments.

A. As much as B. Much as C. Very much D. As

3) We assure you of our full ______ in executing the contract.

A. cooperation B. attention C. intention D. appreciation

4) In writing the first letter ______ importer to open an L/C, the exporter can write a gentle reminder.

A. urge B. urging C. urged D. being urged

5) We wish to stress that shipment be made within the prescribed time limit, as a further ______ will not be considered by our end – users.

A. prolong B. protract C. extension D. expansion

6) With demand for the products growing ______ every year, business is trying to speed up production in order to meet the increasing market.

A. at millions B. with a million C. with one million D. by millions

7) If a letter of credit is "irrevocable", this means that ______.

A. an importer may cancel a bank's authority to make payment

B. an importer may not change his method of payment at any time

C. an importer may change credit terms by giving notice

D. an exporter will grant only the most favorable terms of credit

8) If the seller finds any discrepancies in the letter of credit, whom does he ask for an amendment?

A. The issuing bank. B. The advising bank. C. The buyer. D. The negotiating bank.

9) The description of merchandise on the letter of credit must be identical to that on the ______.

A. insurance policy B. sales contract C. invoice D. certificate of origin

10) ______ the late arrival of the L/C, we are unable to make shipment according to the date specified in the S/C.

A. Owing to B. As for C. Since D. Because

3. Decide whether the following statements are true or false. Write "T" for true, and "F" for false in the brackets.

1) After the signing of the sales contract, the importer should establish the L/C according to the contract without delay. ( )

2) As long as the working staff work carefully, the importer will not fail to establish the L/C in time. ( )

3) The phrase "observing the contract once you have signed it" is to remind the buyers to read the contract carefully when they are signing it. ( )

4) If gentle reminders fail, it is necessary for the exporter to set a deadline and inform the buyer of any serious consequence. ( )

5) The importer dislikes messages requiring L/C extension and amendment. ( )

6) The date of shipment and the validity of L/C should be extended to the same date. ( )

7) The exporter insists that "5% more or less" be added to the clause of quantity because it is impossible to ship the exact amount for bulk goods. ( )

8) Transshipment is needed if there is no direct steamer to the port of destination. ( )

4. Translate the following sentence into Chinese.

1) On receiving an L/C the exporter must examine thoroughly all the clauses against the terms and conditions stipulated in sales contract to make sure they are in exact conformity with the contract, because any discrepancy, even a minor difference, if not amended timely may result in the exporter's difficulty or inability to get paid from the negotiating bank.

2) The credit is a letter issued by a bank at the request of the importer in which the bank promises to pay upon presentation of relevant documents.

3) After confirming the letter of credit, the exporter delivers the goods to the shipper who then issues a bill of lading.

4) A letter of credit is called transferable if it can be transferred by its original beneficiary to one or more parties. The original beneficiary is called the first beneficiary, and the party (or parties) the credit is transferred to is called the second beneficiary.

5) The letter of credit may not be the most ideal method of payment for a particular transaction, and the contracting parties should make their best choice according to the specific conditions.

6) The seller may be unknown to the buyer, and his commercial integrity may be questionable.

7) As you are usually very prompt in settling your accounts, we wonder whether there is any special reason why we have not received payment for the above account, already a month overdue.

8) The flexibility of payment terms will definitely bring you more orders as well as suit the buyers' convenience.

9) We have completed our inquiries concerning the firm you mentioned in your letter of May 18 and must advise you to think twice in doing business with them.

10) When the exporter and the importer are trustworthy to each other, or when the sum in question is small, payment by T/T can be considered.

5. Translate the following sentences into English.

1)请在3月28日以前寄来延期信用证,以便能够按照上述时间准时给你发货。

2)很抱歉,由于原产地供应商方面的延迟,标题货物到本月末才能全部准备就绪。

3)在国际贸易中,时间因素至关重要,所以买方通常坚持货物必须在指定截止日期前或一段时间内装运是很自然的。

4)制造厂接的订货太多,我们只能答应3月份装船。

5)尽管买方已经在我处有过两三次订货,但是我们的规定不允许接受除信用证以外的其他付款方式。

6)出口人,即受益人,将对信用证的所有内容进行认真审核,如果发现任何与合同不符之处,可要求开证人进行修改,以确保交易安全和准时收到货款。

7）在执行合同的过程中，签约双方都应该遵守合同条款。任何一方如果不严格履行合同，就会给另一方带来麻烦，甚至使另一方遭受损失。

8）要么因为信用证金额过大，要么因为对开证行不完全信任，出口商有时可能需要保兑的信用证。

9）根据不同货物的性质及不同开证行的做法，信用证的形式、长短、语言和规定会有所不同。

10）如果信用证在6月15日之前到达销售方，发货时间可定于7月15日至18日。

6. Letter writing.

1) You receive a letter of credit from ABC bank, Tokyo. Upon inspection, you discover the following discrepancies:

a. The total amount of the credit is insufficient. The amount in the S/C No. 3678AS is US $38,500, but the amount in the L/C is US $38,000, the difference being US $500.

b. The port of destination in S/C is in Hong Kong, while in the L/C it is Kobe.

c. Payment term in S/C is "by irrevocable L/C 60d/s", but the L/C reads "by irrevocable L/C at about 60d/s", the word "about" should be deleted.

Now, write a letter to the buyer asking them to amend it.

2) When you receive the amended letter of credit, there are only 3 days left before the date of delivery. Loading the goods onto the ship needs 5 days. And the earliest ship available is 6 days later. So you write another letter asking for L/C extension.

7. Make a telephone conversation in pairs with two students sitting back to back, and discussing payment terms. The buyer asks for payment by L/C after sight instead of by L/C at sight.

Lesson Thirteen
Packing and Shipping Mark

1. Introduction

(1) Packing

Packing is very important in international trade. Appropriate packing avoids or reduces loss and disputes.

Export packing usually falls into two categories:

a. Outer packing: It is usually large. The main purpose is to ensure easy handling of the goods in loading, unloading and storage, and to protect the commodity from being damaged during transportation which can be very rough journeys sometimes.

b. Inner packing: It is the packaging for sales in shops and markets. Its function is to make the goods into nice and compact shapes, which attract consumers and enhance the competitiveness of products, besides the protective function of packing.

Different goods use different packing. The following packing is often used in overseas transportation.

Bag, sack, carton, case, box, crate are used for solid goods in general.

Drum and barrel are used for liquid goods in large quantity.

Can or tin are used for liquid goods and food in small quantity.

Bales are used for soft goods like cotton and wool.

Carboy is used for chemicals.

In addition, shipping companies provide containers and pallets to save time and facilitate handling of goods.

In recent years, environment-friendly materials are often required by importers. So packing materials must not only protect the goods in transportation, but also meet environment protection standards of importing countries.

(2) Shipping mark

Shipping marks are the information printed on the outer packing to distinguish certain goods from others and give warnings as to how to handle the goods. Shipping marks are mainly composed of the following parts:

a. The mark of the consignee or consigner.

b. The name of the port of destination. Some countries require marking the name of the country of origin.

c. Package number or case number, weight and dimensions.

In addition, for some special kinds of goods, warning marks are printed in capital letters for the carrier or the customer to handle the goods with special care. Examples of warning marks are:

HANDLE WITH CARE	THIS SIDE UP
INFLAMMABLE	EXPLOSIVE
ACID—WITH CARE	GLASS—WITH CARE
FRAGILE	FUSIBLE
KEEP DRY	KEEP COOL
NO HOOK	AWAY FROM HEAT
NO SMOKING	STOW AWAY FROM BOILER
OPEN HERE	PERISHABLE

(3) Neutral packing

Neutral packing means that the country of origin and the names of manufacturers are not marked on either the outer or inner packing. This method is sometimes adopted because the seller or the buyer wants to keep the origin of the goods unknown.

2. Communication for results

In writing routine business letters, provide your reader with accurate and specific information.

Too general	Specific
The packing is seaworthy and can stand rough handling.	The packing is water-proof, light in weight and equally strong as wooden cases.
Please use normal containers.	Please use wooden cases.

Talk more about the advantage of your method instead of the disadvantage of your reader's method.

Instead of writing	Write
We never use wooden cases to pack this kind of goods because it is heavy and very expensive.	This new kind of packing material can save you much expense on packages and freight.

3. Example letters

(1) Reply to customer's inquiry about packing

To: Miss Lucinda Lucas

From: Harry Jones

Date: November 15, 2010

Subject: Packing of the goods under Order No. 3366

Dear Miss Lucinda Lucas:

In reply to your inquiry about the packing of the desk fans under your Order No. 3366, we would like to give you a more detailed description below:

The fans will be packed with each in an air-proof polythene bag, and then each bag placed in a cardboard box stuffed with foam plastic, 4 boxes in a fiberboard case reinforced with metal bands.

You can be rest assured that this kind of packing is seaworthy enough for the safe arrival of the goods at your destination.

As it is stated in the contract that shipping mark is at buyer's option, please give us your instruction about it if you have any.

Sincerely,
(*Signature*)
Harry Jones

(2) Customer's further inquiry

To: Harry Jones
From: Lucinda Lucas
Date: November 16, 2010
Subject: Packing of the goods under Order No. 3366

Dear Mr. Jones:

Thank you for your reply about the packing. However, as we normally use wooden cases for the packing, some of our customers are doubtful of the safety of the goods for the following reasons:

1) When the goods are transshipped in Hong Kong, they are subject to pilferage as fiberboard is thin and easily cut open.
2) Rain water may get into the cases when the goods are stowed at the wharf in heavy rains.
3) The fiberboard cases are not strong enough to stand the heavy pressure when they are piled up during loading and unloading, this may cause breakage of the goods.

Due to the above reasons, please replace fiberboard cases with wooden cases.

As for the shipping mark, we prefer neutral mark, but stencil the warning "HANDLE WITH CARE" on the front side of the cases.

Yours sincerely,
(*Signature*)
Lucinda Lucas

(3) Further explanation to customer's inquiry

To: Miss Lucinda Lucas
From: Harry Jones
Date: November 16, 2010
Subject: Packing of the goods under Order No. 3366

Dear Miss Lucinda Lucas:

I understand your anxiety. But once you have received our goods and see the package you will be satisfied with it.

In recent years we have replaced wooden cases with fiberboard cases because they have more advantages.

1) They are of lower cost and light in weight, thus saving much freight.
2) They are water-proof and easy to handle.
3) The fiberboard cases are made with double lids and bottoms lined with shock-reducing materials which give further protection to the goods.

As a matter of fact, we have used these cases in our shipment to many continental ports to the complete satisfaction of our clients.

Sincerely,
(*Signature*)
Harry Jones

(4) Customer's requirement about packing

Wood, Harvey & Co.
182 Madison St.
Sydney, Australia

Mr. David Wang, Manager
Tianjin Food and Oil Imp. & Exp. Corp.
Tianjin, China

September 18, 2010

Dear Mr. Wang:

S/C No. CK2345

We acknowledge receipt of your letter on September 19th, enclosing the above sales contract in duplicate, but wish to state that the packing clause, which reads as follows in the contract, is not clear enough.

"Packing: Seaworthy export packing, suitable for long distance voyage."

In order to avoid future trouble, we'd like to make clear our requirement for packing as follows:

The fruit jam under the captioned contract should be packed in tinplate cans of 400 ml each in weight, with 46 cans in a wooden case. Mark the outer packing with our initials WHC in a diamond, under which print the port of destination and our order number. Indicate the warning mark "STOW AWAY FROM HEAT" on the front side.

We have made the above remark in the contract, and have sent one copy to you by EMS after duly countersigning it.

We look forward to your early reply.

Sincerely,
(*Signature*)
Eugene Halley

(5) Reply to the customer's inquiry

To: Mr. Euqene Halley
From: David Wang
Date: September 19, 2010
Subject: S/C No. CK2345
Attachment: Shipping mark design

Dear Mr. Eugene Halley:

Thank you so much for your countersigning of the contract. We accept your requirement about the packing of the goods.

We have attached a design of the shipping mark according to your instructions. Please check and confirm.

Sincerely,
(*Signature*)
David Wang

4. Telephone conversation

Mr. Smith, an importer of chinaware calls Mr. Black before shipment of the goods.

B: Hello, this is Alan Black from Oriental Industry.

S: Hello, Mr. Black, this is Barry Smith. I've got your shipping advice for our chinaware to be shipped on Monday. Could you tell me what kind of packing you plan to use for this consignment?

B: Cartons, as we usually do.

S: Cartons? I don't think cartons are strong enough for the fragile goods of chinaware.

B: We'll use metal straps to reinforce the cartons, and we'll stuff the cartons with hay for shock proof.

S: But the customs regulation in our country forbids using hay for packing. Could you use foam plastic instead?

B: Okay, no problem.

S: Good. For the outer packing, I don't want to take any chance. How about using wooden cases?

B: We'll use wooden cases if you insist. But wooden cases are more expensive and heavier than cartons. You'll have to pay the extra packing fee and freight.

S: How much will that be?

B: Well, let me calculate. The extra packing cost will be USD280, and the freight will be about USD320 higher.

S: That's an extra charge of USD $600 altogether. Well, I have to accept for the safe arrival of the goods.

B: Then, we'll pack the goods according to your instruction.

S: Thank you.

B: That's okay. Please fax me to confirm this instruction today.

S: I will. Oh, there is one more thing. Please don't forget to stencil the warning mark "fragile" and "handle with care" on the wooden cases.

B: No problem. If it will reassure you, we'll do that too.

S: Thank you very much. Bye-bye.

B: You are welcome. Bye.

New Words and Phrases

dimension [di'menʃən] *n.* a measure of spatial extent, especially width, height, or length 尺寸

inflammable [in'flæməbl] *a.* easily ignited and capable of burning rapidly 易燃的

Oil is an inflammable product. 油是易燃物。

fragile ['frædʒail] *a.* easily broken, damaged, or destroyed 易碎的

fusible ['fjuːzəbl] *a.* capable of being fused or melted by heating 可溶的

perishable ['periʃəbl] *a.* subject to decay 容易腐烂的

These goods are perishable and must be shipped in refrigerated containers.

这些物品易腐烂,必须用冷藏集装箱运输。

seaworthy ['siːˌwəːði] *a.* fit to put to sea 经得起风浪的,适合航海的

a seaworthy ship 适于航行的船

water-proof ['wɔːtəpruːf] *a.* something which not allow water to go through 防水的

Is this material water-proof? 这种材料防水吗?

Put on your water-proof coat when you go out in the rain. 下雨时出去要穿上雨衣。

fiberboard ['faibəbɔːd] *n.* board made of fiber 纤维板

pilferage ['pilfəridʒ] *n.* loss caused by stealing, esp. during transport or storage of goods 偷盗,行窃

wharf [(h)wɔːf] *n.* a landing place or pier where ships may tie up and load or unload 码头

stencil ['stensl, -sil] *v.* to copy by using a piece of paper, metal, etc. in which patterns or letters have been cut out 用模版印刷(标记)

Please stencil our initials on the outer packing. 请在外包装上印上我公司名称缩写。

Notes

1. **outer *packing*** 外包装

   packing:包装(尤指外包装,包装过程)

   Compare:package 包装(尤指包好的或用盒子装好的物件)

2. **rough journey** 颠簸的旅程,不平静的旅程
3. **inner packing** 内包装
4. **sack** 大袋子,大包
5. **crate** 板条箱
6. **barrel** 桶;一桶之量
7. **bale** 大包,大捆
8. **carboy** 一种大玻璃瓶或大塑料瓶,通常套装在一个保护性的篮子或板条箱内,用于盛装腐蚀性液体
9. **container** 集装箱
10. **pallet** 托盘

11. shipping mark 唛头(简称 mark)

12. consignee 收件人,收货人

13. consigner 发货人

14. port of destination 目的港

15. HANDLE WITH CARE 小心搬运

16. NO HOOK 请勿吊钩

17. AWAY FROM HEAT 远离热源

18. STOW AWAY FROM BOILER 远离锅炉

19. rough handling 野蛮装卸

20. pile up 堆积

21. The packing is seaworthy and can *stand* rough handling. 该包装适合海运并且能承受野蛮装卸。

stand *vt.* 耐受

e. g. : This material stands wear. 这种材料耐磨。

22. The fans will be packed with each *in* a polythene bag, and then placed *in* a fiberboard case stuffed with plastic foam, 4 fans *in* a fiberboard case reinforced with metal bands. 电扇用聚乙烯袋单独包装,每个纤维板箱装 4 台,内部填充泡沫塑料,纤维板箱用金属带加固。

in 用某种容器包装,装于……内

e. g. : Cement should be packed in double kraft paper bags. 水泥要用双层牛皮纸包装。

Men's shirts are packed in cardboard cartons of 10 dozen each.

男士衬衣用纸板箱包装,每箱 10 打。

Pens are packed in boxes of a dozen each, 100 boxes to a wooden case.

钢笔用盒装,每盒装一打,100 盒装一木箱。

Cotton socks are packed each pair in a plastic bag, 100 bags to a carton.

棉袜每双装一个塑料袋,100 袋装一纸箱。

23. As a matter of fact, we have used these cases in our shipment to many continental ports to the complete satisfaction of our clients. 事实上,我们用这种箱子装运,已经到过很多大陆港口了,客户完全满意。

24. The fruit jam under the captioned contract should be packed in *tinplate cans* of 400 ml each in weight, with 46 cans in a wooden case. 标题合同项下的水果应用马口铁罐头装,每罐 400 毫升,46 罐装一木箱。

tinplate cans 马口铁罐头

ml 毫升 (milliliter 的缩写)

Other abbreviations of weight and measurement:

L/T	long ton	长吨	kg	kilogram	公斤
M/T	metric ton	公吨	G. W.	gross weight	毛重
lb	pound	磅	N. W.	net weight	净重
DOZ	dozen	打 (a dozen has 12 pieces)			

ft. foot 英尺 yd yard 码

25. Mark the outer packing with our initials WHC in a diamond, under which stencil the port of destination and our order number. 在外包装上把我公司字首大写字母WHC标注在菱形框内,唛头下印上目的港和我们的订单号。

26. As for the shipping mark we have attached a design of it according to your instructions. Please check and *confirm*. 我方已根据贵方要求,附上唛头图样,请检查确认。

confirm: make certain, give proof 确认(已经说出或写下的内容)

e. g. : Please confirm your telephone message in writing. 请书面确认你在电话中所说的内容。

Useful Expressions

1. Please note that your packing must be able to withstand the long sea voyage.
2. Candles are packed 20 pieces to a paper box, 40 boxes to a carton.
3. Containers used for packing the glass should be lined with soft padding.
4. The packing should be strong enough to withstand rough handling in transit.
5. The packing and mark shall be at seller's option.
6. We use internationally standardized packing which is approved by our overseas clients.
7. We pack our shirts in plastic-lined, waterproof cartons, reinforced with metal straps.
8. I'm afraid we shall have to charge more for designated packing, as it calls for more labor and cost.
9. Unless otherwise instructed, please mark all the boxes as usual.
10. Our usual packing is in wooden cases of 112 lbs, each containing 16 packets.

Exercises

1. Answer questions.

1) What is the purpose of packing?

2) What is the purpose of shipping mark?

3) What information is usually given in a shipping mark?

2. Questions for discussion.

Suppose you are a consigner, what should you take into consideration for the goods to be shipped over a long voyage as far as the packing is concerned?

3. Choose the best answer to complete the following statements.

1) Please mark the initials on the ______.

A. inner packing B. outer packing C. product D. box

2) Our products are packed in cartons lined ______ poly sheet.

A. with B. in C. within D. among

3) The outer packing should be strong enough to ______ rough handling.

A. bear B. stand C. stop D. fight

4) The overall ______ of the case are 100 cm × 50 cm × 50 cm.

A. volumes　B. weights　C. capacities　D. dimensions

5) Our strong packing will certainly help ______ the sales of the product.

A. promotional　B. promotion　C. promote　D. promoting

6) Every buyer expects that his goods will reach him ______ perfect condition.

A. on　B. at　C. in　D. by

7) It's apparent that the goods have been damaged ______ your end.

A. at　B. off　C. in　D. to

8) It was found upon examination that nearly 20% of the ______ has been broken, obviously due to improper ______.

A. packing, packages　B. packages, packing

C. packing, packing　D. packages, packages

9) Which of the following is the most appropriate container for the transportation of crude oil?

A. Tank.　B. Water-proof bag.　C. Air-tight box.　D. Barrel.

10) The clause "Shipping Mark: at buyer's option" means ______.

A. the buyer makes decision on the shipping mark

B. the seller makes decision on the shipping mark

C. no shipping mark is needed

D. shipping mark is needed

4. Decide whether the following statements are true or false. Write "T" for true, and "F" for false in the brackets.

1) Inner packing plays the role of displaying rather than protecting the goods. (　)

2) People usually pay more attention to the quality of the goods. Therefore, the package is not a very important factor in pushing the sales. (　)

3) Cotton is usually packed in bales. (　)

4) Wooden cases are more seaworthy than cardboard boxes. (　)

5) Shipping mark plays the same role as warning mark. (　)

6) Warning mark is printed for the carrier or customer to handle the goods properly. (　)

7) Neutral Mark means not to mark anything at either the outer packing or the inner packing. (　)

8) Carboy is usually used for the packing of liquid goods. (　)

5. Translate the terms and expressions and make sentences with each of them.

1) rough handling　2) seaworthy

3) neutral packing　4) water-proof

5) stow away from boiler　6) be lined with

7) perishable　8) shipping mark

6. Fill in the blanks with the words and phrases given below and change the form when necessary.

rest assured	delay	catch the eye	rough handling
appreciate	be liable for	in perfect condition	to be lined with

1) We hope our goods will reach you ______ to the complete satisfaction of the end users.

2) You may ______ that we'll ship the goods by the first available steamer.

3) The seller must pack the goods in such a way that they will withstand ______.

4) The shipping company should ______ the damage of the goods.

5) As the goods are urgently needed, please dispatch them without ______.

6) We shall ______ it if you will inform us of the condition of packing as well as the arrival of the consignment at your end.

7) Each case ______ foam plastics in order to protect the goods against press.

8) A packing that ______ will help us push the sales.

7. Translate the following sentences into English.

1)纸箱作为一种容器已在国际贸易中广泛使用,因此对它的适航性,你们不必担心。

2)标题合同项下的毛巾包装为:同一种颜色,每半打装一塑料袋,每10袋装一纸板箱。

3)你们的包装必须具有适航性,并能经得起运输途中的野蛮搬运。

4)包装须符合我地市场的偏好。

5)我们已经把你方对包装的意见转告给厂方,他们同意下次交货时采纳你方意见。

6)我们已经特意加固包装,以便将货物可能受到的损失降到最低程度。

7)罐装货物装入纸箱,外面加两道箍。

8)请在外包装上标明"小心轻放"字样。

9)除非另有指示,请按常规标记所有盒子。

10)我们恐怕要对指定的包装多收费,因为需要更多人工和成本。

8. Translate the following sentences into Chinese.

1) If the cartons are not strong enough, we are afraid most of them will be liable to break on arrival.

2) All marks should be stenciled according to our requirement.

3) Please pack the goods as you did for the last shipment unless otherwise instructed.

4) We can meet your requirements to have the goods packed in wooden cases but you have to bear the extra packing charge.

5) Please mark the cases as per the stipulation given in the contract.

6) The machines must be well protected against dampness, moisture, rust and shock.

7) Your opinions on packing will be passed on to our manufacturers.

8) Our packing will be on a par with that of the Japanese.

9. Write a letter in English with the information given below.

1)感谢对方来信询问包装事宜,现告如下:

2)女士丝绸衬衣,塑料袋单独包装,每打一纸箱,纸箱内衬防水塑料布,每40纸箱装一集装箱。

3)按贵方要求,纸箱外的标记除印刷有重量、数量外,还包括贵公司名称及商标。

4)希望贵公司满意。

10. Make a telephone conversation in pairs with two students sitting back to back, one acts as an importer giving "shipping instruction" to the other, acting as an exporter.

Lesson Fourteen

Shipment

1. Introduction

The clause of shipment is an indispensable part in international business contract. It mainly includes: the time of shipment, the place of shipment, the place of delivery, the place of destination, and the shipping documents.

With the rapid development of international trade, shipment not only refers to ocean transportation, but also to land, rail and air transportation, though ocean shipping significantly outnumbers other modes of shipment, due to the low cost.

In general practice of shipment, the seller is obliged to notify the buyer in "shipping advice" the name of the ship and the time of departure when loading the goods on board the named vessel. After the goods are loaded, the seller will obtain the shipping documents (mainly the bill of lading) from the carrier and pass them to the buyer, so that the buyer will be able to effect the insurance (under FOB, CFR terms) and get ready to receive the goods. If the seller fails to do so in a timely manner, any damage and loss incurred to the goods because of his/her failure or delay in producing the shipping advice will be borne by the seller.

Many companies have printed shipping advice form for the seller to fill in the relevant information. This makes it easy to read and understand.

Before shipment, the importer may inform the exporter of his specific requirements for shipment, known as "shipping instructions", to specify the shipping mark, packing, mode of transportation, etc.

If the seller chooses to deliver a given lot of contracted goods in partial shipment and if direct sailing from the port of loading to the port of destination is unavailable and transshipment is necessary, the seller must get the buyer's consent and stipulate in the L/C such statement as "transshipment and partial shipment allowed".

2. Writing strategy

In writing a shipping advice the following information are usually included:

(1) Information of the consignment

The name of the goods to be shipped	The S/C number
The order number of the goods	The L/C number

(2) Information of the shipment

The name of shipping vessel — The place of shipment

The expected time of departure — The place of destination

The expected time of arrival

(3) The documents specified in the contract to be handed over to the buyer for receiving the goods and to go through the necessary procedures at the place of delivery.

Bill of lading — Commercial Invoice

Packing List — Insurance Policy

Customs Invoice — Inspection Certificate

(4) Sometimes information of the carrying ship is needed. This often includes the age of the ship and her nationality.

3. Communication for results

Business correspondence should be written in a matter-of-fact tone. Avoid using jokes and slang.

Inappropriate	Appropriate
Though we quote a higher rate, the quality of our service is *a notch above* the others.	Though we quote a higher rate, the quality of our service is better than the others.
If you want to tip the scales you've got to take drastic measures.	If you want to reverse the situation, you must adopt drastic measures.

Avoid giving promises on something over which you don't have much control or which is hard to predict.

Inappropriate	Appropriate
I'm sure the goods will arrive at your port in perfect condition.	We are doing our best to insure the goods arrive at your port in perfect condition.

Avoid the expressions which are considered insincere by native English speakers.

Insincere	Sincere
We sincerely hope that our delay in reply has caused you no inconvenience.	We will send our reply to you more promptly next time.

4. Example letters

(1) Urging the seller to effect shipment

October 18, 2010

Dear Mr. Simpson:

Re: 1,000 Sets of Dell Brand Computers Under S/C 8269

We have not received any information up to now about our ordered goods in question. We wish to draw your attention to the contract in caption which stipulates that the shipment is due on October 15, and we should have received your shipping advice by now.

You may recall that we explicitly stated in our order the importance of punctual delivery of the goods that are urgently needed by our end users.

We have to reiterate that your shipment must be within the stipulated time and we await your prompt reply.

Sincerely,
(*Signature*)
Susan Clark

(2) The seller's explanation for the delay

October 19, 2010

Dear Ms. Clark:

Re: 1,000 Sets of Dell Brand Computers Under S/C 8269

Our manufacturer will deliver the goods within this week. We have arranged to ship the goods by S. S. "Virgin Mary" which is scheduled to sail for your port on October 25.

We apologize for having not given you the shipping time for the present order sooner. The reason is that we have being urging our manufacturer to give us a definite delivery date for your order and would like to inform you about it when we receive some definite information from them.

We will give you further information about the shipment more promptly.

Sincerely,
(*Signature*)
Larry Simpson

(3) Shipping instruction from buyer

December 20, 2010

Dear Sir:

Re: Machines of Model AJ3650

We thank you for having booked our order for two Machines of Model AJ3650, which will be shipped by the end of this month.

As our purchase is made on FOB basis, we have arranged shipment with our forwarding agent, ABC Company, Denmark, who is going to take care of shipping the goods from Copenhagen to Tianjin. ABC Company will inform you tomorrow about the shipping space booked and the name of the ship.

We would like to specify that the machines must be packed in strong wooden cases that will withstand rough handling because some parts of the machines are susceptible to shock. Please see to it that the galvanized parts is covered by a coating of slush compound that will keep out dampness, but will not liquefy and run off when temperature goes up in hot weather conditions.

We are looking forward to the satisfactory arrival of the goods.

Yours sincerely,
(*Signature*)

(4) Shipping advice from seller

December 29, 2010

Re: Shipment per S. S. "Sunlight" covering your Order No. 3365 under S/C No. 860 for two Machines of Model AJ3650

Dear Mr. Simpson:

We have completed the loading of the above shipment in accordance with your instruction and the stipulations set forth in L/C No. GL5678.

The ship is going to set sail from Copenhagen on January 2, and the estimated time to arrive at Tianjin port is January 30.

We have mailed to you by air this morning (our local time) the following documents as required in the contract:
Our Invoice No. 3367 in duplicate
Packing List No. 789 in duplicate
Non-negotiable Bill of Lading No. BE1365
Insurance Policy No. BQ2346
Survey Report No. TA3300

We appreciate the friendly business cooperation between us and look forward to more opportunities to serve you.

Yours sincerely,
(*Signature*)
Susan Clark

(5) A shipping advice form

GWF Industrial Corp.

88 Queen's Road Suite 707
Copenhagen, Demark
tel: 1234 - 5678 Fax: 1234 - 5679
E-mail: export@ gwf. com

May 29, 2010

Dear Susan Clark,

We take pleasure to advice you that your Order No. *3365*
covering *two Machines of Model AJ3650* dated *November 28, 2010*
under L/C No. *L/C No. GL5678*
has been shipped via S. S. "Sunlight"
estimated time of departure from *Copenhagen* on *January 2*
estimated time of arrival at *Tianjin* on *January 30* enclosed please find the following copies of shipping documents:

√ Commercial Invoice

✓	Packing List
✓	Bill of Lading, Non-Negotiable Copy
✓	Insurance Policy/Certificate
✓	Inspection Certificate (Report)
	Certificate of Origin
✓	Customs Invoice
	Others

Thank you for your patronage. We look forward to the pleasure of receiving your valuable repeat orders.

Sincerely yours,

GWF INDUSTRIAL CORP.

5. Telephone conversation

Zhang Weihua calls Jason Lee to make sure of the location of Asuncion.

Zhang: Good morning. May I speak to Jason Lee please?

Lee: This is he.

Zhang: Oh, hi, Jason, this is Weihua, I didn't recognize your voice.

Lee: Hello, Weihua, nice to hear you. How can I help you?

Zhang: I've just got your order for mosquito repellent incense. The destination given in your order is Asuncion. Could you give me some idea where this Asuncion is exactly?

Lee: It is a landlocked city located on the bank of River Parana right next to the border line of Paraguay and Argentina.

Zhang: I see. But we can only ship the goods to a seaport. How about choosing a seaport that is close to Asuncion?

Lee: Well, how about Montevideo, Uruguay, then?

Zhang: Good. That can be arranged. I'll send you the quotation with the place of destination as Montevideo, Uruguay. Okay?

Lee: That's fine. Thank you very much.

New Words and Phrases

shipment [ˈʃipmənt] *n.* 1) the act or an instance of shipping goods 装运，装载货物

Please defer shipment until you receive our further instructions.

请延期装运，等待我方进一步通知。

Shipment can be effected within 30 days after receipt of your L/C.

收到信用证后可在 30 天内装运。

2) a quantity of goods or cargo that are shipped 装载量，装载的货物

shipping [′ʃipiŋ] *n.* the act or business of sending or transporting goods 运输

We are waiting your shipping instruction. 我们正等待你的装船通知。

The shipping space has fully booked up. 舱位已满。

ship [ʃip] *v.* transport on board a ship, or by airplane, truck or other vehicles 运输

The goods will be shipped in one lot. 这批货物将整批运输。

outnumber [aut′nʌmbə] *v.* exceed in number 比……多

vessel [′vesl] *n.* ship 船,船舶

punctual [′pʌŋktjuəl] *a.* observing appointed time, neither early or late 准时的

She is punctual to the minute. 她非常准时。

He is punctual in paying bills. 他准时付款。

susceptible [sə′septəbl] *a.* liable, vulnerable to 易遭受……的

The goods are susceptible to damage with rough handling. 野蛮装卸会使货物损坏。

galvanize [′gælvənaiz] *v.* coat with zinc 镀锌于

shush [ʃʌʃ] *n.* 润滑油

slush compound (机用)黄油

keep out 隔离,远离

liquefy [′likwifai] *v.* become liquid 液化

run off 使流出

set forth 提出,宣布

patronage [′pætrənidʒ] *n.* support 惠顾

landlocked [′lændlɔkt] *a.* 内陆的

Notes

1. shipping advice: a notice given by an exporter to an importer on information of the shipment 装船通知

2. shipping instruction: a notice given by an importer to an exporter on the way of handling the good to be loaded and shipped 装船须知,装船指示

3. a notch above (slang) 略胜一筹

4. tip the scales (slang) 扭转局势

5. on board 在船上

Goods *on board* the ship are to be exported to Canada. 船上装载的货物将运往加拿大。

6. *forwarding* agent 货运代理

Relevant expression: forwarding agency 运输行

forward *v.* 发货,寄送

e. g.: Your order No. 20 can be *forwarded* next week. 你方 20 日订单可在下周发货。

7. the galvanized part 镀锌的部位

8. *PackingList* No. 789 第 789 号包装清单

packing list 包装清单,它是注明每件货物的名称、净重、毛重、包装的尺码等内容的单据

9. our local time 我方本地时间

10. Commercial Invoice 商业发票

11. non-negotiable Bill of Lading: A non-negotiable bill of lading is issued to a named person, either the consignee or buyer. Under this bill, the carrier is responsible for delivering the goods at the destination of the consignee or buyer named in the bill of lading. 不可转让提单

12. Inspection Certificate (Report) 商检证书(报告)

13. "This is he." (电话用语)"我就是。"

14. mosquito repellent incense 驱蚊香

Useful Expressions

1. The goods are ready for delivery. Please give us your shipping instructions.
2. Please send us by return full instructions for the five cases of toys for San Francisco.
3. The goods are ready for immediate shipment and will reach your port within 10 days.
4. After receiving your instruction, we contacted your forwarding agent and regret to inform you that there is no container ship sailing to your port during the time you requested. For your information, the earliest vessel sailing to your port so far is S. S. "Rainbow", which is scheduled to leave on/about August.
5. Presently, we are doing everything we can to book places for your order to be delivered within the contracted time. As soon as shipping space is available we will notify you.
6. As we were told in your letter, your end user is urgently in need for these goods. We now propose a partial shipment of your order. We will deliver 1/3 of the order in the early part of May, and the remaining 2/3 by the time set in the L/C.
7. If we understand correctly you mean that you wish to have 80% of the goods shipped in December and the balance in January instead of two equal shipment in January and February.
8. We suggest the use of cartons with hinged lids to facilitate opening for inspection and examination.
9. The shipment of chemical fertilizer under Contract No. 3456 will be effected by S. S. "Taishan", which is scheduled to leave here on 16 March. Please arrange insurance for the cargo.
10. According to the terms of the contract No. 789, shipment is to be effected by the 20th January, and we must have the B/L by the 31st of January at the latest.

Exercises

1. Answer the following questions.

1) What is the difference between "shipping advice" and "shipping instruction"?

2) What clause must be written in the L/C if the goods cannot be shipped in one cot, and if the goods cannot be delivered directly from the port of loading to the port of destination?

3) Who is to bear the cost for any delay of shipment incurred by failure to produce in time the

shipping advice?

2. Choose the best answer to complete the following statements.

1) Which of the following is included in the clause of shipment?

A. The delivery of shipment. B. The time of shipment.

C. The destination of shipment. D. All of the above.

2) Which of following is the most often used mode of overseas transportation?

A. Express train. B. Container truck. C. Airline. D. Ship.

3) "Shipping advice" is a notice ______.

A. produced by the seller B. produced by the buyer

C. produced by the shipping company D. produced by the owner of the goods

4) Under FOB terms, if a shipping advice is not given in time, any negative consequences resulted from this will be borne by ______.

A. the buyer B. the seller C. the shipping company D. the importer

5) They emphasized <u>punctual</u> delivery of the goods.

The underline word means ______.

A. timely B. careful C. urgent D. fast

6) If direct steamer is not available for the transportation, ______.

A. the goods will not be shipped B. partial shipment should be allowed

C. the goods have to be transshipped D. the goods have to be separated

7) When goods are on board a shipping vessel, ______.

A. they are going to be loaded B. they are going to be unloaded

C. they have already been loaded D. they have already been unloaded

8) The goods <u>are susceptible to</u> shock.

The underlined part of the sentence means ______.

A. are dangerous to B. are damaged by

C. are suspicious of D. are vulnerable to

9) Which of the following way of transportation is most economical?

A. By air. B. By rail. C. By ship. D. By mail.

10) A shipping instruction can give information about ______.

A. way of packing B. shipping mark design

C. way of loading D. all of the above

3. Decide whether the following statements are true or false. Write "T" for true, and "F" for false in the brackets.

1) A business document should be written in a mater-of-fact yet friendly tone. (   )

2) Shipment only refers to transportation by ships. (   )

3) A shipping advice gives information about the name of the boarding vessel and its departure time. (   )

4) It is the seller's obligation to send a shipping advice to the buyer. (   )

5) The buyer is obliged to issue all the needed shipping documents. (   )

6) Transshipment is necessary if direct sailing from the port of loading to the port of destination is unavailable. (   )

7) The seller should inform the buyer of the time of shipment. (   )

8) A friendly business letter should be humorous and with some jokes. (   )

9) The buyer is to arrange shipping space under FOB terms. (   )

10) "Our local time" refers to the time used in the time zone where the speaker or the writer of the message is located. (   )

4. Translate the following letter into English.

辛普森先生：

500 台缝纫机

我们 2010 年 3 月 12 日签订的 HK8899 号合同规定，500 台缝纫机在 2010 年 5 月交货。但迄今未听到你方这方面任何消息。我用户急需此货，打算派"海花"轮去载货，该轮预计 5 月底左右抵达你方港口霍尔姆斯克(Kholmsk)。请立即传真告知我方你们是否同意此建议。若不同意，请告最早的、确切的、货可备妥的时间。

由于交货延误，我方遇到不少麻烦。如你们 5 月尚不能交货，我们只好向你们提出索赔，并保留取消合同的权利。

此致敬礼

5. Translate the following passage into Chinese.

The most important shipping document is the bill of lading, which is a document signed by or on behalf of the master of a carrying vessel, certifying that the goods have been received on board in good order for transportation and delivery as specified in the document.

When a consignment is loaded, an officer or agent of the shipping company signs the Bill of Lading that the goods have been "received in apparent good order and condition". In other words, the consignment must be exactly as written on the Bill of Lading and not different. The cases should be undamaged and sacks, if any, should not be torn or stained. Drums of liquid should not be dented or leaking. The number and kind or packages should be the same as on the Bill.

If there is any difference between what is said on the Bill and the actual condition of the consignment, the shipping company has to write a clause on the Bill giving the damage or loss. In this case, it is no longer a clean Bill of Lading and the bank representing the importer may not accept it. So the exporter's bank may not be able to get payment for the goods. For this reason, "foul" or "claused" Bill of Lading must be avoided at all costs and the exporter must make sure that their goods arrive at the docks in good order and condition.

6. Write a letter based on the following information.

Your order due to arrive on September 20, but now it is already September 30 and you haven't received it yet. You write a letter to urge shipment. Make sure to include all the necessary information.

7. Make a telephone conversation in pairs with two students sitting back to back, and making an arrangement for the place of destination.

Lesson Fifteen
Insurance

1. Introduction

In overseas transportation, consignments are subject to risks or perils of various kinds, such as heavy weather, accidents in loading, unloading and storage, breakdown of the ship. In order to cover losses or damages that might happen, buyers or sellers apply to insurance companies for insurance covering the goods in transit before transportation.

A contract of insurance, usually in the form of an insurance policy, is established between the insurer (insurance company or underwriter) and the insured (buyer or seller) after the insured pays the premium — a sum of money quoted as a percentage of the sum insured to cover certain risks.

Chinese firms and enterprises engaged in foreign trade usually adopt China Insurance Clause (CIC) which came into force on January 1, 1981, for marine insurance.

The risks covered by insurance falls into two categories.

(1) The principle risks:

1) W. A. (With Average) or W. P. A. (With Particular Average)

2) All Risks

3) F. P. A. (Free from Particular Average)

(2) Additional risks

After covering any one of the above principle risks, the insured can cover "Additional Risks", which include "General Additional Risks" and "Special Additional Risks".

1) General additional risks:

◇TPND (Risk of Theft Pilferage and Non-Delivery)

◇Fresh Water and /or Rain Damage Risk

◇Shortage Risk

◇Intermixture and Contamination Risk

◇Leakage Risk

◇Clash and Breakage Risk

◇Taint of Odor Risk

◇Sweat and Heating Risk

◇Hook Damage Risk

◇Breakage of packing Risk

2) Special additional risks:

◇War Risk

◇Strikes Risk

◇On Deck Risk

◇Rejection Risk

◇Aflatoxin Risk

◇Import Duty Risk

◇Failure to Deliver Risk

Since "General Additional Risks" are included in "All Risks", if the insured has already covered "All Risks", he/she doesn't need to cover "General Additional Risks".

In general practice, the insurance value is calculated as: The total value of the goods based on

CIF price + 10% of it, that is 110% of the total invoice value. If the insured requires more than 110% of the total value, he/she has to bear the additional cost.

An insurance policy is one of the important shipping documents that is to be presented to the bank at the time of negotiation if the goods are priced on CIF basis.

On arrival at the place of destination the goods shipped are to be inspected by the named inspection firm or organization agreed upon by the two parties within the time period specified in the sales contract. If any damage is found and is to be claimed, submit the insurance policy together with the relevant documents to the insurance company as promptly as possible.

2. Writing strategy

In writing a letters inquiring about insurance the following points are to be considered.

(1) The methods of insurance (whether it's a policy or an open policy)

(2) The risk or risks to be covered

(3) The consignment to be insured

(4) The voyage to be covered

(5) The premium rate

(6) The mode of payment

(7) The validity of the insurance

3. Communication for results

(1) Adopt "you" attitude in introducing your business.

Instead of writing	Write
We have expanded our insurance coverage to give you more selection of additional risks.	You have more selection of additional risks now thanks to our expanded insurance coverage.

(2) Don't talk about your feelings or your reader's feelings in routine business messages except to congratulate.

Instead of	Write
We are pleased to inform you that we have covered All Risks for 110% of the invoice value for your shipment.	We have covered All Risks for 110% of the invoice value for your shipment.
You will be happy to learn that we have arranged your goods to be shipped per S. S. "Fengqing" due to sail next Monday.	We have arranged your goods to be shipped per S. S. "Fengqing" due to sail next Monday.

4. Example letters

(1) Buyer seeking information about insurance

Dear Madam or Sir:

Thank you for your offer of Glazed Wall Tiles. We would like to place an order for 2,

000 cases (Art. No. 012) at the price you offered, which, we have noted, is on CIF terms.

Since we have an open policy with our local insurance firm at a favorable premium, would you please inform us about the premium charged by your insurance company and the scope of coverage handled at your end so that we can make a better decision on which firm we shall apply for the insurance of the shipment.

We look forward to hearing from you early.

Yours sincerely,
(*Signature*)
Harry Johns, Manager

(2) Reply from seller for insurance information

Dear Mr. Harry Johns:

We welcome your order of 2,000 cases of Glazed Wall Tiles (Art. No. 012). In reply to your request about our insurance we give you the following information:

We usually effect insurance with the People's Insurance Company of China, a prestigious enterprise enjoying a high reputation in settling claims promptly and equitably. The company has agents in almost all main ports and regions of the world, who are in a position to handle your claims at your end in case any damages occur to your goods.

We usually cover All Risks for Glazed Wall Tiles at a premium rate of ... % of the invoice value for voyage from Tianjin Port to Singapore. Should there be any claims, the insurance policy covers 110% of the total invoice value. However, if you require a higher percentage you can do so by paying extra premium.

Most of our clients are placing their orders with us on CIF basis as it saves time and simplifies procedures. You will enjoy the advantages if you follow the same practice.

We look forward to your reply.

Yours sincerely,
(*Signature*)
Lucinda Wilde

(3) The importer request the seller to arrange for insurance

TO: Ms. Lucinda Wilde
FROM: Harry Johns
DATE: March 12, 2010
RE: ORDER NO. 3511 FOR GLAZED WALL TILES

Dear Ms Lucinda Wilde:

Thank you for your information. We now wish to have the captioned goods insured at your end. Would you please arrange to insure the goods on our behalf against All Risks at invoice value plus 10%. The insurance will cover the consignment during shipment from Tianjin to our warehouse in Singapore.

We shall refund to you the premium upon receiving your debit note or you may draw on us at sight for the amount required.

We await your confirmation to cover the consignment and your insurance policy reaching us at the earliest possible time.

Sincerely yours,
(*Signature*)
Harry Johns, Manager

(4) An exporter request the insurer to arrange an open policy

Dear Madame or Sir:

We are going to start exporting electrical components to Singapore on regular basis from January 2010 to January 2011. Since the consignment will be shipped in one container per month, would you please arrange an open policy against All Risks for an amount of US $6,000 per shipment at the most favorable rate you can provide?

Your earliest reply is appreciated.

Sincerely yours,
(*Signature*)
Mike Johnson

(5) The seller accepts the request to arrange for an open policy

TO: Mr. Mike Johnson
FROM: Lucinda Wilde
DATE: January 10, 2010
RE: Arrangement for an open policy

Dear Mr. Mike Johnson:

We accept your request to arrange an open policy for the transportation of the electric fans. The open policy will be valid for voyages between Shanghai Port and Singapore. It will take effect from January 1 and remain valid till December 31, 2010.

As requested, we will cover the shipment against All Risks for full invoice value plus 10% at a premium rate of ... % of the total value of the consignment.

You will receive the open policy by the end of the week together with our debit note for the premium.

Yours sincerely,
(*Signature*)
Lucinda Wilde

5. Telephone conversation

Peter, a buyer of peanuts, wants to talk to Jason about covering additional risk for the goods. But Jason is not in.

Mary: Jason Lee's office.
Peter: Mr. Lee, please?
Mary: He is meeting a client. Would you leave a message?
Peter: No, I really need to talk to him personally.
Mary: Would you like to leave a message on his voice mail, then?
Peter: Yes, thank you.
Mary: Hold on please and I'll transfer you to his telephone.
Jason's answering machine: Sorry, I'm not available to take your call at the moment, please leave your name, number and a brief message.
Peter: Good afternoon, Jason. This is Peter. I'm calling to ask you to cover additional risk of aflatoxin for the 300 metric tons of peanuts, which is going to be shipped tomorrow,

because it's getting really hot these days. My phone number is 23456789. Again, 23456789. Please call back as soon as possible. Bye.

New Words and Phrases

insurance [inˈʃuərəns] *n.* the act, business, or system of insuring 保险行为,业务或系统

insure [inˈʃuə] *v.* 1) to cover with insurance 给……保险；保……险

insure sb.'s property against fire 给某人财产保火险

have one's life insured 给某人保人寿险

2) to make sure 保障；保证；确保

Carefulness insures you against errors. 谨慎细致可使你避免发生差错。

consignment [kənˈsainmənt] *n.* something consigned 托付物；货物

Synonyms: goods, cargo, shipment

be subject to liable, be exposed to 易遭受

The price is subject to change without notice. 价格很可能会出现变化,但我方不另行通知。

peril [ˈperil] *n.* serious or immediate danger 风险

storage [ˈstɔːridʒ] *n.* 1) the act of storing goods 存储；2) cost of warehousing 仓储(费)

breakdown [ˈbreikdaun] *n.* the state of being destroyed or damaged 损坏，破裂

insurer [inˈʃuə] *n.* person or organization that insures sb. or sth. against certain risks 保险人

insured [inˈʃuəd] *n.* person who asks for insurance 投保人,被保险人

underwriter [ˈʌndəraitə] *n.* insurer, insurance company 保险商，保险公司

premium [ˈpriːmiəm] *n.* money paid by the insured to the insurer in return for insurance cover 保险金

marine [məˈriːn] *a.* of or relating to the sea 海的，海事的

marine products 海产 marine transportation 海洋运输

marine animal 海洋动物 marine insurance 海运保险

inspect [inˈspekt] *v.* examine officially 检验

submit [səbˈmit] *v.* present 提交 (*usu. followed by* to)

glaze [gleiz] *v.* 上釉于，上光于

glazed wall titles 琉璃墙面砖

prestigious [ˌpreˈstidʒəs] *a.* having respect, reputation or influence derived from achievements, power, etc. 有声誉的

equitable [ˈekwitəbl] *a.* being fair; just 公平的，公正的

equitably [ˈekwitəbli] *adv.* 公平地,公正地,合理地

breakage [ˈbreikidʒ] *n.* damage caused by breaking 破碎

debit note 账单;借项清单

confirmation [ˌkɔnfəˈmeiʃən] *n.* the act of providing support for truth or correctness 确认

book [buk] *v.* engage in advance, make reservation 预订

Notes

1. **heavy weather** 恶劣天气
2. **cover** 承保（或投保）……险别
   e. g. :cover the risk of breakage 投保破碎险
   cover War Risk 投保战争险
3. **insurance policy** (*or* policy) 保险单，保险凭证
   Other expressions: cover note, insurance certificate
4. **open policy** 预约保单
   The difference between a "policy" and an "open policy" is that the former insures a single lot of shipment for one voyage, while the later covers all of the shipments automatically for more than one voyage during a specified period of time. 保险单承保指定航程内某一批货物发生的损失，而预约保单承保一定时期内发运的一切货物或几项货物。
5. **China Insurance Clause** 中国人民保险公司海洋运输货物保险条款
6. **principle risk** 主险
7. **W. A.** (With Average) or W. P. A. (With Particular Average) 水渍险
8. **All Risks** 综合险
9. **F. P. A.** (Free from Particular Average) 平安险
10. **Additional Risks** 附加险
11. **General Additional Risks** 一般附加险
12. **TPND** (Risk of Theft Pilferage and Non-Delivery) 偷盗及提货不着险
13. **Risk of Fresh Water and /or Rain Damage** 淡水雨淋险
14. **Shortage Risk** 短量险
15. **Intermixture and Contamination Risk** 混杂、玷污险
16. **Leakage Risk** 渗漏险
17. **Clash and Breakage Risk** 碰损、破碎险
18. **Taint of Odor Risk** 串味险
19. **Sweat and Heating Risk** 受潮、受热险
20. **Hook Damage Risk** 钩损险
21. **Breakage of Packing Risk** 包装破损险
22. **Special Additional Risks** 特别附加险
23. **War Risk** 战争险，兵险
24. **Strikes Risk** 罢工险
25. **On Deck Risk** 舱面险
26. **Rejection Risk** 拒收险
27. **Aflatoxin Risk** 黄曲霉素险
28. **Import Duty Risk** 进口关税险
29. **Failure to Deliver Risk** 交货不到险
30. **total invoice value** 发票总额

31. to bear the additional cost 承担附加费用

32. the scope of coverage 保险范围

33. for one's reference 以供某人参考

e. g. : These are my ideas for your reference. 这些是我的看法,供你参考。

34. We wish now to have the captioned goods insured *at your end*. 我们希望在贵方所在地为标题下货物投保

at one's end 在某人所在地

e. g. : The goods will be inspected at our end. 货物将在你方所在地检验。

35. Would you please arrange to insure the goods on our behalf against All Risks at invoice value plus 10%. 请代我方为这批货物投保一切险,保险金额为发票总额加10%。

36. We shall refund to you the premium upon receiving your debit note or you may *draw on us at sight* for the amount required. 我们收到你方借项清单后返还保险费,或者你方按所付的金额向我方开出即期汇票。

to draw on sb. 向某人开出汇票

at sight 即期 **e. g.** : a draft at sight 即期汇票

37. We accept your request to effect insurance on the captioned shipment *for your account*. 我们接受贵方要求为标题下货物办理保险,保费记入你方账户。

on someone's account 由(某人)付款

38. We have *booked the shipping space* for the goods on s/s Victor which is going to sail from Tianjin about the 28th of March. 我们已为这批货物订了"VICTOR"轮的舱位,该船大约3月28日离开天津。

book the shipping space 订舱位

Useful Expressions

1. Please cover All Risks for the goods listed below.
2. Please insure against leakage (breakage, fresh water damage, etc.).
3. Can you issue an open policy at a rate of about 1% for a total value of US $30,000 for shipment from Shanghai to Japanese main port?
4. Please see to it that shipment should be covered for 150% of invoice value against all risks. We know that according to your usual practice, you insure the goods only for 10% above invoice value, therefore the extra premium will be on our account.
5. Will you please arrange an insurance against all risks for us on the following consignment of transistor radios.
6. Owning to the fact that these bags of cement are frequently dropped into the water during the unloading in Kobe, the insurers have raised the premium to 2%.
7. Regarding insurance, the coverage is for 110% of invoice value up to the port of destination only.
8. Buyer's request for insurance to be covered up to the inland city can be accepted on condition

that such extra premium is for buyer's account.

9. Since the premium varies with the extent of insurance, extra premium is for buyer's account, should additional risks be covered.

10. We thank you for your instructions to arrange the shipment of bicycles. We take it that you wish us to insure this cargo against All Risks for the value of the goods plus freight.

Exercises

1. Answer the following questions.

1) Why is it necessary for business people to insure their goods before transportation?

2) What is the difference between "policy" and "open policy"?

3) What is premium?

4) What are principle risks?

5) How to cover additional risk?

6) In case any loss and damage occur to the goods and the damage is covered by the insurance policy, how to claim to the insurer to cover the loss?

2. Decide whether the following statements are true or false. Write "T" for true, and "F" for false.

1) It is always the seller who is responsible to arrange for insurance. (　　)

2) Loss and damage to the goods in transit is unavoidable due to the various risks of overseas transportation. (　　)

3) Breakdown of the ship is one of the perils in long-distance voyage. (　　)

4) An insurance policy may insures shipment for more than one voyage. (　　)

5) An open policy insures may lots of shipments for more voyages over a fixed period of time. (　　)

6) To cover additional risks you must cover principle risk first. (　　)

7) You don't need to cover General Additional Risks if you have covered All Risks. (　　)

8) You have to pay higher premium if you want to have higher insurance value. (　　)

9) Buyer can request the seller to effect insurance on their behalf. (　　)

10) A claim for insurance can be made at any time as the buyer wishes. (　　)

3. Choose the best answer to complete the following statements.

1) A contract of insurance is established in the form of ______.

A. policy　　B. confirmation　　C. order　　D. offer

2) In order to cover certain risks, the insured must pay the ______.

A. cost　　B. premium　　C. price　　D. shipping space

3) Which of the following is a Principle Risk?

A. TPND.　　B. Risk of Shortage.　　C. War Risk.　　D. All Risks.

4) Which of the following is Special Additional Risk?

A. Leakage Risk.　　B. Hook Damage Risk.

C. Strike Risk.　　D. Taint of Odor Risk.

5) Which of the following risks would you most likely to cover for shipment of grain?

A. Risk of Clash and Breakage.　　B. Leakage Risk.

C. Aflatoxin Risk.　　D. War Risk.

6) Under which of the following price terms the seller will arrange for insurance?

A. FOB.　　B. CFR.　　C. CIF.　　D. FAS.

7) All Risks include ______.

A. Special Additional Risks　　B. General Additional Risks

C. On Deck Risk　　D. Rejection Risk

8) The usual calculation of insurance value is ______.

A. total invoice value of the goods based on CIF price + 10% of the total invoice value

B. A certain part of the invoice value on CIF basis + 10% of the total invoice value

C. 10% of the total invoice value + total price of the goods

D. more than 10% of invoice value + a sum of money fixed by the buyer

4. Translate the following sentences into English.

1)如果保险公司接受,可以安排投保综合险及战争险以外的险别,但额外的保险费由买方付。

2)关于保险,按发票金额110%投保到目的港为止。

3)当客户无明确要求时,我们一般投保水渍险和战争险。若你方愿保综合险,我们可办理,但保险费稍高些。

4)根据我公司海洋运输货物保险条款的规定,承保上述货物综合险包括战争险的现行费率是0.50%,现附上上述条款请参阅。

5)关于我公司3306号订单下按CIF条款订购的200台电脑,我们希望你方投保一切险。

6)我方认为这类保险对价值较高、易破碎的货物来说是必要的。

7)兹确认收到你方3月6日来函,要求我方将标题货物以发票金额的130%投保。

8)如果你方愿意,我们也可以受理更广的保险范围,条件是额外的保险费由买方负担。

9)我公司定期由国际航运公司的班轮运送瓶装啤酒到新加坡,请你公司为这些货物签发综合险预约保单。

10)请告知如果我们答应每月按期运货,你公司能否给我们特惠费率。

5. Translate the passage into Chinese.

The history of insurance goes back as far as the twelfth centaury, when marine insurance was known to exist in North Italy. In the fourteenth century, Italian merchants came to Britain and brought their system of insurance to safeguard ships and cargo with them. In those days, of course, there were no insurance companies; merchants would group together and write their names under a promise to pay for ships or cargoes lost in storms or taken by pirates, and this is how the term "underwriters" came into existence. If the ship was lost, the financial loss was spread and no single merchant risked all his money.

6. Write a letter in English based on the information given below.

我方将开始定期出口摄像机(camera)到加拿大。因我们每月发运一批货,请保险公司办理预约保险,险别为一切险,保值为每批8万美元,从2月1日开始生效,有效期一年,并请给予最优惠费率。

7. Leave a voice mail for insurance coverage of 2,000 TV sets.

Lesson Sixteen
Complaints and Claims

1. Introduction

After the establishment of a contract, both the buyer and seller are obliged to observe all the terms and clauses in the contract. If one party violates or fails to carry out the contract, the other party is entitled to claim indemnity for any loss or damage. Sometimes the party may just make a complaint, i. e. to express dissatisfaction, instead of lodging a claim if the loss or damage is not serious in order to keep the friendly relations. The purpose is to require the defaulting party to take measures to prevent such loss from happening again.

It is usually the hope of both sellers and buyers that any problems or disputes between them be solved through friendly discussion.

However, if a satisfactory solution can not be reached between them through friendly discussion, a claim may be filed to the court specified in the contract for arbitration.

Complaints and claims are usually caused by

◇ The wrong goods have been sent.

◇ The quality is inferior than that stated in the contract.

◇ The goods arrived late, short or damaged.

Before lodging a claim, it is always necessary to make clear which party is responsible and should compensate for the loss or damage. Make sure that the claim is made against the party responsible for the loss and within the time of validity in the contract.

Claims can be made against

◇ The seller if the damage is caused by the seller's mistake or improper packing

◇ The shipping company if the damage is caused by the carrier's negligence or improper handling during transportation

◇ The insurance company if the damage or loss is covered by the insurance policy

2. Writing strategy

The purpose of a claim letter is to convince the reader that you have a legitimate complaint that deserves a desired response. The more professional a claim letter is the better chance you have of receiving positive feedback in your favor. For an effective solution, adopt the following strategy when writing a claim letter:

◇ **Identify the product or service** Giving accurate information as to the order number, the date of delivery, and description (specification) of the goods in subject

◇ **Explain the problem** Giving detailed description as to the damage, loss, or inconvenience incurred

◇ **Propose a solution** Asking for an explanation and adjustment

◇ **End the letter respectfully** Never use negative words to vent your anger though you may be frustrated.

You may attach a "Survey Report" made by an inspection organization and relevant business documents to support your letter.

If the worst happens, that is, if the responsible party refuses to compensate and gives no justifiable reasons, you may state that you are resorting to arbitration.

3. Communication for results

In writing letters of complaints and claims avoid accusing your readers. It is more effective to focus on the problem which needs to be addressed.

Instead of writing	Write
You shouldn't pack the goods in cartons.	The packing is not seaworthy enough.
You failed to deliver the goods satisfactorily.	The goods delivered were damaged by rain water.

4. Example letters

(1) Buyer's claim for damaged goods

Dear Mr. Hugh:

We have received the 500 MT peanuts under our Order No. B566 you shipped per S. S. Victor. But much to our regret we found one third of the peanuts damaged by mold.

Presently, the peanuts are urgently needed by our customers and we are unable to provide quality and satisfactory goods as we have promised. We have received claims from our customers, and as a result, we have to request that you compensate us for the loss.

To support our claims, we enclose two copies of Survey Report No. 6789 and No. 6790 together with our Statement of Claim which amounts to US $ 120,000.

As a long-term customer of yours we believe you will give our claims your most favorable consideration and early settlement.

Sincerely,
(*Signature*)

Michael Bigelow, Manager

Incl. :2 copies of Survey Report

2 copies of Receipt of Indemnity from our customers

A Statement of Claim

(2) Buyer's complaint about unreliable goods and ask for exchange

Dear Sir:

We bought 10 Olympic Brand, Model PRS – 2, CD-RW drives from your company at the price of US $ 800 with 5% discount. The goods were delivered on November 15th. These drives are urgently needed for our project to be completed by the end of this year. But when we first used the drives with our program 3 of them didn't work. You can imagine our frustration.

We took the 3 drives immediately to the authorized service center in our area. The service representative fixed the drives, but a week later we had to have them fixed again — other problems with the motor and some loose connection. Though they are working now, they are not working well. The response is still very slow.

What is your policy on exchanging unsatisfactory merchandise? Although all the repairs have been covered by the one-year warranty, we are not satisfied with the drives. We would like to exchange them for a similar model of another brand. If the new drives cost more than the old ones, we will pay the difference, even though we generally look for equipment with substantial discounts.

We are counting on you to live up to your reputation for good after-sale service. Please let us hear from you soon.

Sincerely,

Philip Brown, Administrative Assistant

(3) Buyer's complaint about inferior quality and ask for replacement

Dear Mr. Hugh:

We are greatly disappointed at the last delivery of our Order No. AF3300 for 200 dozen Men's Shirts, which are not up to your usual standard. The material is loosely woven and is inclined to pull out of shape. We have sent you by EMS a shirt from this consignment and another one from the previous consignment, so that you can see the difference in texture.

Because of the inferior quality, the shirts of this consignment have been rejected by our customer, leaving us no alternative but to return them to you and request you to send us the kind we ordered.

We look forward to your early reply.

Sincerely,
(*Signature*)
Michael Bigelow
Manager

(4) A buyer's strong claim for delay in delivery

Dear Mr. Hugh:

Re: Final notice for S/C No. 3618

This is the third time I have written to you concerning our order of 2,000 Table Lamps under the captioned contract. The goods are due to be delivered on 25 July according to the contract.

However, up to now we have not received your shipping advice, nor have we got any explanation from you for the delay.

We have to point out that your delay has seriously interrupted our business. As our present stock is exhausted, we are unable to meet our customer's demand, some of whom have consequently placed their orders elsewhere. This has caused us great loss in profits and damage in reputation.

Unless you ship our goods within this week we will have to cancel the contract, and take legal action against you.

Sincerely,
(*Signature*)
Michael Bigelow
Manager

5. Telephone conversation

Peter is calling to complain about the damage to the glassware he purchased.

Mary: Jason Lee's office.

Peter: Jason Lee please.

Mary: Just a second.

Peter: Thanks.

Jason: Hello. This is Jason.

Peter: Hello, Jason. This is Peter. I've got to tell you about the glassware I received yesterday. Two boxes are badly damaged.

Jason: Sorry to hear that. Have you got a survey report?

Peter: Yes. The report shows that improper packing caused the damage. There were not enough shockproof pads inside the boxes.

Jason: Please fax the survey report to me first, and we'll do whatever we can to prevent it from happening again.

Peter: As these goods are badly needed by our clients, please send another two boxes to replace the damaged ones.

Jason: Okay, I'll arrange for that.

Peter: When shall we expect the replacement to arrive?

Jason: If we ship them by air, they'll arrive in a couple of days.

Peter: Fine. Please let me know the flight number as soon as possible.

Jason: Sure. Now, I'll check the Survey report. And I'll inform you immediately.

New Words and Phrases

claim [kleim] *n.* & *v.* (a) demand for compensation

They lodged a claim against the shipping company. 他们向船公司提出索赔。

Their claim for money is absolutely unreasonable. 他们的赔偿金要求是毫无道理的。

complaint [kəm'pleint] *n.* a statement of dissatisfaction 怨言;控告

Our customer's complaint is not unreasonable. 我们的客户的抱怨不是没有道理的。

complain [kəm'plein] *v.* 抱怨,不满,诉苦

They complained about late delivery. 他们抱怨延误交货。

indemnity [in'demniti] *n.* compensation for loss; sum paid by way of compensation 赔偿,赔偿金

arbitration [ˌɑːbi'treiʃən] *n.* the settlement of a dispute by an arbitrator 仲裁,公断

compensate ['kɔmpənseit] *v.* to serve as or provide a substitute or counterbalance 偿还,补偿

justifiable ['dʒʌstifaiəbl] *a.* having sufficient grounds for justification 有理由的

vent [vent] *v.* 1) to give often forceful expression 发泄

2) to release or discharge (steam, for example) through an opening 排放(蒸汽等)

frustrated [frʌ'streitid] *a.* feeling discouraged or baffled 感到受挫,泄气

resort (**to**) [riˈzɔːt] *v.* to have recourse 求助；诉诸

If friendly discussion fails to solve the problem, we'll have to resort to arbitration. 如果友好协商不能解决问题,我们只好求助仲裁。

overdue [ˈəuvəˈdjuː] *a.* coming or arriving after the scheduled or expected time 过期的，迟到的

Your payment is two months overdue. 你的付款延误了两个月。

an overdue airliner 晚点的班机

mold (or mould) [məuld] *n.* fungus on food that has been kept too long or on objects that have been left for a long time in warm wet air 发霉

drive [draiv] *n.* (计算机)驱动器

texture [ˈtekstʃə] *n.* a structure of interwoven fibers or other elements (纺织品的)质地

inferior [inˈfiəriə] *a.* low or lower in quality or value 差的；次的；劣等的

The price is lower for goods of inferior quality. 品质差一些的商品价格较低。

Notes

1. **If one party violates or fails to carry out the contract, the other party *is entitled to* claim indemnity for any loss or damage.** 如果一方违反或没有旅行合同,另一方有权对所受的损失提出赔偿。

   to be entitled to: have the right to 被授予……的权利

   e. g. : I'm entitled to a compensation as I've covered the risk. 因我已投保这项险别,我有权要求得到赔偿。

2. **to lodge** (***or* file**) **a claim** 提出索赔

3. **The goods arrived late, *short* or damaged.** 过去分词短语"arrived late, short or damaged"作"the goods"的定语。

   "short" here means scanty, below the degree of 短重,短量

   e. g. : short weight 重量不够 be short of food 缺乏食物

   We are five miles short of our destination. 我们离目的地还差5英里。

4. **The more professional a claim letter is the better chance you have of receiving positive feedback *in your favor.*** 你的索赔信写得越符合商业规范,你得到对你有利的回复的可能性就越大。

   in one's favor 对某人有利，以某人为受益人

   We hope the decision will be made in our favor. 我们希望这个决定对我们有利。

   Payment will be made in your favor. 付款将以你方为受益人。

5. **Never use negative words to *vent your anger* though you may be frustrated.** 尽管你很生气千万不要用负面的词语发泄你的怒气。

   to vent one's anger 发泄愤怒

   e. g. : He slammed the door to vent his anger. 他摔门以发泄他的愤怒。

6. **survey report**: a report issued by an inspection organization to certify the degree of damage to certain goods or products (商检部门出具的,确定货物损坏程度的)鉴定报告

Compare: "inspection certificate" a certificate issued by inspection organization to certify certain goods or products are up to certain standard （商品质量）检验证书

7. . . . our present stock is *exhausted* ……我们现在的存货已经售完

exhausted: used up, sold out 用尽,售完

8. take legal action against: file a claim against 起诉

e. g. : We have no alternative but to take legal action against you. 我们别无选择,只能对你方进行投诉。

9. authorized service center 授权服务(维修)中心

10. loose connection 接触不良

11. one-year warranty 一年保修

12. If the new drives cost more than the old ones, we will pay the *difference*. . . 如果新的驱动器比旧的贵,我们愿意付差价……

difference: the amount by which one quantity is greater or less than another 差额

e. g. : The difference between this recorder and that one is RMB 120. 这台录音机和那台录音机的差价为120元。

13. counting on: 1) to be confident of; anticipate 对……有信心,预期

e. g. : She counted on getting a refund. 她期待获得退款。

2) to rely on; depend on 依靠,依赖

e. g. : You can count on my help. 你可以依赖我的帮助。

14. live up to one's reputation 名副其实

15. We are greatly disappointed at the last delivery of our Order No. AF3300 for 200 dozen Men's Shirts, which *are not up to* your usual standard. 我们收到的AF3300订单下的最后一批货——200打男衬衫没有达到你们以往的质量标准,对此我们感到很失望。

to be up to: to reach (certain standard, degree, etc.) 达到(标准或程度)

e. g. : The quality is not up to standard. 质量没有达到标准。

16. The material seems to be loosely woven and is inclined to pull out of shape. 衣料看起来织得很松,且容易变形。

Useful Expressions

1. As the contracted time of delivery is rapidly falling due, it is imperative that we hear from you without any further delay.
2. We must stress that unless the consignment we have ordered arrives before 31 August, we will have to cancel it.
3. The goods we ordered from you on May 15 are now considerably overdue, and we lost a wonderful opportunity of sales.
4. On opening the case we found it contained completely different articles. As we need the goods we must ask you to arrange for the dispatch of replacements at once.
5. The 500 computers we ordered arrived today. On opening the containers we found that the

goods were short by 30 sets.

6. We have noticed a shortage in weight totaling 50 tons.

7. Our clients have lodged complaints against us about breakage of the chinaware delivered last May 19th.

8. 3 cartons of the consignment are damaged because they are soaked by sea water. Would you arrange replacement to arrive by the end of this week?

9. We have to ask for a compensation to cover the loss incurred as a result of inferior quality of the goods in question.

10. We are compelled to express our strong disapproval of the way you handle our order. If the order is not fully refunded, we would be forced to stop our business relations.

Exercises

1. Answer questions.

1) What is the difference between a claim and a complaint?

2) What are the main reasons for complaints and claims?

3) What do you think are the best ways to solve a business dispute?

2. Topic for discussion.

Which do you prefer, "complaint" or "claim" in the following situation? Give your reasons for your answer.

1) On receiving the goods from an exporter with whom you have kept a friendly business relations for 5 years, you found 20% of the goods are damaged.

2) You have purchased a pair of shoes for 500 yuan, but later discovered they are not as good as what is said in the ads.

3. Choose the best answer to complete the following statements.

1) Which of the following parties are usually involved in a business transaction?

A. Buyer. B. Seller. C. Carrier. D. All of them.

2) If one party violates or fails to carry out the contract, the other party is entitled to claim <u>indemnity</u> for any loss or damage.

The underline part of the sentence means ______.

A. a sum of compensation B. a sum of premium

C. a sum of security D. legal exemption from penalty

3) What is usually the first solution to a business dispute?

A. To lodge a complaint. B. To lodge a claim.

C. To discuss in a friendly way. D. To buy another lot of goods.

4) Which of the following is not a direct reason for a claim?

A. The wrong goods have been sent.

B. The quality is inferior than that stated in the contract.

C. The late arrival of the goods.

D. The fluctuation of the prices.

5) The goods arrived short.

The underlined part of the sentence means ______.

A. faster than stipulated B. less than stipulated

C. partly damaged D. partly wrong

6) If the goods are damaged because of rough handling during transportation, claims can be made against ______.

A. insurance company B. seller C. buyer D. carrier

7) What information should be given in a letter of claim?

A. Description of the goods. B. Order number.

C. Degree of damage. D. All of the above.

8) A "survey report" is issued by ______.

A. shipper B. insurance company C. inspection company D. seller

9) Our stock is exhausted.

The underlined part of the sentence means ______.

A. sold out B. damaged C. lost D. disappeared

10) The goods are not up to standard.

The underlined part of sentence means ______.

A. disagrees with B. move upward C. are inferior to D. are superior to

4. Decide whether the following statements are true or false. Write "T" for true, and "F" for false.

1) Claims are always made by the buyer against the seller. ( )

2) Any party of a contract is entitled to claim indemnity if they suffer a loss. ( )

3) To make a complaint is always more effective than lodge a claim. ( )

4) Friendly discussion should be the first choice for the solution of trade disputes. ( )

5) To file a claim is the last resort to solve business problems. ( )

6) Claims should be made against the party that is responsible for the loss. ( )

7) Sometimes the shipping company should shoulder the responsibility for loss. ( )

8) Buyers never have any responsibility for loss. ( )

9) A survey report plays the same role as an inspection certificate. ( )

10) One can always claim for compensation if he/she had insured the goods before transportation. ( )

5. Fill in the blanks with the following words in their appropriate form.

find	break	lose	short	inspect	store	liable	examine	handle

1) On opening the case, it was found there was serious ______.

2) The insurer should be responsible for the ______ of the tape recorders.

3) We will make due compensation according to ______ in the survey report.

4) We will send a public ______ to investigate this matter.

5) When we unloaded the chemical fertilizer yesterday, a ______ in weight of 200 kg. was reported.

6) A thorough ______ showed that the short weight was due to improper packing.

7) According to the report, the damage was caused by rough ______ in transit.

8) The delay in delivery has caused us difficulties in ______ and marketing.

9) We therefore hold no ______ for the claim on account of lack of evidence.

6. Make sentences with the following words and phrases.

1) justify 2) overdue 3) complain 4) claim 5) warranty 6) count on 7) live up to

7. Translate the following letter into Chinese and write a letter of reply to settle the problem.

Dear Mr. Brown:

As someone who has worked with your company for over 3 years, we were very disappointed to see the documents you produced for our publicity campaign.

As our written agreement stipulated, we expected full color leaflets with fancy explanatory texts, but instead, we found that black and white photos had been included in the prepared leaflets.

We would like you to send out a photographer to provide us with the promised color coverage, or provide us with a refund.

Yours truly,

Thomas R. Smith, Director

8. Translate the following letter into English.

敬启者:

我方订单第 AV68 号

标题下订单的100套咖啡器皿已于昨天收到。但是很遗憾,15 套已被严重损坏。货物包装的外观表面完好,所以我们就签字接受了。我们小心翼翼打开包装后发现里面防震衬垫不够厚,估计这是造成损坏的原因。

希望你们尽快更换这15套。另外我们保存了被损坏的咖啡杯,以便你们向供应厂家索赔时提供证据。

此致商安

9. Write a letter of claim based on the information given below.

1) The 300 transistor radios under our Order No. AS321 have been delivered on Feb. 20th.

2) One-third of them are not up to the quality of the sample you sent us.

3) Please replace the radios of inferior quality.

4) Otherwise, we'll cancel the order, and claim compensation.

5) We attach a survey report.

6) The survey report is issued by China Commodity inspection Bureau.

10. Make a telephone conversation in pairs with two students representing the buyer and the seller respectively. The buyer complains about the damage of the goods delivered. The seller is trying to find an acceptable solution.

Lesson Seventeen

Adjustment to Claims

1. Introduction

On receiving a letter of claim you must analyze and investigate in detail whether the claim is justified and within your range of responsibility for compensation, then timely inform the reader that attention has been paid to the matter and further reply will follow.

There are usually three alternatives to settle a claim:

1) Do as the claimer required, such as effecting compensation.

2) Refer the claimer to a third party, the insurance company for instance, if the loss or damage is covered by the insurance.

3) Reject the claim if it is unfounded or unjustifiable. For example, sometimes the buyer may just try to find faults with the goods because they no longer want the goods, or they can get them cheaper elsewhere. They complain or make a claim for the purpose of escaping their obligation to fulfill the contract.

2. Writing strategy

The best result for settling a claim is to solve the problem without damaging the friendly relations between the two parties. Therefore a reply should be made timely and politely with clear explanations of the damage or loss. Take the following steps for the above three alternatives in writing the letter:

(1) Effect compensation

◇ Acknowledge receipt of the claim

◇ Express regret or apologize for the damage or inconvenience caused to the reader

◇ Provide compensation and offer preventive methods for future business

◇ Close with good will for keeping business relations

(2) Refer the buyer to a third party

◇ Acknowledge receipt of the claim

◇ Explain the cause for the damage or inconvenience

◇ Advise the buyer to cover the loss from the third party (insurance company, carrier, etc.)

◇ Provide the buyer with detailed contact information to the third party if necessary

(3) Reject the claim

◇ Acknowledge receipt of the claim

◇ Explain that the damage or loss or inconvenience was not caused by your company

◇ Provide proofs or evidence such as relevant business document, contract clauses

◇ Persuade the buyer to follow the business procedure with an eye to long term business relations

3. Communication for results

In settling a claim and giving apology don't use passive voice and evading sentences, which sound as if you are hiding yourself behind your words. Your readers may suspect your sincerity and willingness to take up responsibility. So use "we", "I" or "our" in active voice. Compare the following sentences:

Passive voice	Active voice
This matter will receive our immediate attention.	We will give our immediate attention to the matter.
You will be assured of our full commitment.	We assure you of our full commitment.
You'll get a replacement for the damaged goods, which will be sent to you on July 15th.	We will send you on July 15th a replacement for the damaged goods.

Adopt a tone that is decisive and final in settling a claim. Avoid closing your letter with the following sentences, as they may create an undesirable idea in your reader that more problems will arise.

Instead of writing	Write
If you have any more problems please feel free to contact us.	we'll solve the problem to your satisfaction.
Don't hesitate to call me if you need further information.	we'll give our full attention to this matter.

4. Example letters

(1) Seller's suggestion to the buyer to cover the loss from the shipping company (Refer to example letter 1 in lesson 16)

Dear Mr. Bigelow:

Having received your letter as well as the Survey Report and the receipts, we regret to learn that one third of your order of 500 MT of peanuts shipped per S. S. Victor have gone moldy on arrival at your port.

We have been exporting peanuts for many years. All our goods are subject to strict inspection before export and enjoy good reputation on international markets. But for any possible deterioration for which we are found liable, we shall always be ready to compensate.

As for the goods in subject, they were inspected by the prestigious ABC Inspection Company just three days before loading, and the goods were loaded onto the carrying vessel in perfect condition, which is clearly stated by the Inspection Certificate and the clean B/L. We, therefore, suggest that you file a claim against the shipping company for compensation.

Should you wish to place an order to make up for the damaged goods please let us know, and we'll be willing to do so.

Sincerely,
(*Signature*)
Dennison Hugh
Manager

(2) Supplier refers the buyer to a third party (Refer to example letter 2 in lesson 16)

Dear Mr. Brown:

Thank you for letting us know about your experience with the Olympic CD-RW drives delivered to you on November 15. It is important that we learn of unusual problems with the equipment we stock.

As you know, regularly priced equipment returned to our company's authorized service center within 30 days starting from the date of delivery can be exchanged unconditionally. This has been our tradition for 20 years. Your drives have passed 30 days and they were bought at discount during our holiday sales. However, they are still covered by the warranty of the manufacturer, who has a branch office at your area. Your needs will receive immediate attention if you write to

Mr. George Kean
Olympic Systems
P. O. Box 100087
Beijing, China

From my experience, I know that the people at Olympic truly care about having satisfied customers.

We, too, value your business. Please find the enclosed catalogue for our new products.

Sincerely,
(*Signature*)
Jack Smith

(3) Seller's agreement to change the goods (Refer to example letter 3 in lesson 16)

Dear Mr. Bigelow:

Re: 200 Dozen Men's Shirts of Order No. AF3300

We have given our full attention to your complaint about the shirts under your Order No. AF3300 as this is a rare case. We examined the two samples you sent us, and found that the wrong goods were packed for your consignment by mistake. We apologize for the inconvenience caused to you.

We will send you immediately the right kind of goods, Art. No. 365, to replace the present goods of Art. No. 375. They will reach San Francisco within this month.

As for the goods of Art. No. 375, they are made of thinner material, which are especially suitable for the up-coming summer season. If you care to sell them we'll offer you a special price. As soon as we receive your positive reply, we'll send you the specification and a credit note for it.

We apologize sincerely for the trouble caused to you, and will take measures to prevent such mistake from happening again.

Sincerely,
(*Signature*)
Dennison Hugh
Manager

(4) Seller's reply to buyer's complaint of late delivery (Refer to example letter 4 in lesson 16)

Dear Mr. Bigelow:

Re: Delivery of the goods under S/C No. 3618

In response to your fax message of 10 August concerning the late delivery of S/C No. 3618 please accept my apology for not being able to deliver your order and also for the inconvenience caused to you.

We were involved in an industrial dispute in the factory. Production had come to a complete standstill and the office building was closed, so I couldn't reply to your message immediately.

The dispute has been settled and we are back to normal production now. We are doing our best to fill your order as soon as possible. However, the earliest shipment available is Wednesday next week. Our workers are working overtime in order to make the shipment.

Clause 7 in the contract states clearly that in the event of unforeseen circumstances, we cannot be held liable for any delay in delivery. The industrial dispute is indeed something unexpected and we have little control over it. Therefore we should not be held legally liable on this matter.

However, I can assure you we will lose no time in prompt delivery.

Sincerely,
(*Signature*)
Dennison Hugh
Manager

5. Telephone conversation

Jason is settling the complaint for the damaged goods. He calls Peter for giving compensation.

Peter: Peter White, ABC Ltd.

Jason: Hi, Peter. This is Jason. I'm calling for our compensation of the damaged glassware under your order number AB338. We have sent you two boxes of well-packed glassware by express train CK56. They are expected to arrive at the Central Station, Amsterdam at 14:00 p.m. your local time on July 20th.

Peter: Please let me repeat. It will arrive at the Central Station, Amsterdam at 14:00 p.m. our local time on July 20th.

Jason: That's right. And I've sent you the Bill of Lading No. 801 by EMS this morning.

Peter: Thank you.

Jason: My pleasure.

New Words and Phrases

justify ['dʒʌstifai] *v.* to demonstrate sufficient legal reason for (an action taken) 证明……是正当的

implement [ˈimplimənt] *v.* to put into practical effect; carry out 执行

to implement the new procedures 执行新的程序

claimer [ˈkleimə] *n.* one who claims 索赔者,申请者

carrier [ˈkæriə] *n.* a person or an organization that deals in the transport of passengers or goods 承运人

reject [riˈdʒekt] *v.* to refuse to consider or grant; deny 拒绝

evade [iˈveid] *v.* avoid, escape 规避,躲避

to evade tax 逃税;to evade responsibility 回避责任

unfounded [ˌʌnˈfaund] *a.* not based on fact or sound evidence; groundless 没有事实根据的,没有理由的

unjustifiable [ʌnˈdʒʌstifaiəbl] *a.* impossible to excuse, pardon, or justify 不符合道理的

find faults with to seek, find, and complain about faults 挑错

preventive [priˈventiv] *a.* intended or used to prevent 预防性的

refer(to) [riˈfəː] *v.* to submit to an authority for arbitration, decision, or examination 提交

standstill [ˈstændstil] *n.* complete cessation of activity or progress 停止,停顿

Work came to a standstill for lack of fund. 由于缺乏资金,工作陷于停顿。

unforeseen [ˈʌnfɔːˈsiːn] *a.* not felt or realized beforehand; unexpected 无法预料的

We are faced with unforeseen difficulties. 我们面临着前所未有的困难。

to be held liable be responsible 负有责任的

moldy [ˈməuldi] *a.* covered with or containing mold 发霉的,腐臭的

The bread has gone moldy. 面包发霉了。

Notes

1. Advise the buyer to *cover the loss* from the third party. 劝告买方向第三方索赔。

to cover loss 得到赔偿

e. g. :to cover a loss from insurance company 从保险公司得到赔偿

2. Provide *proofs* or *evidence* such as relevant business document or contract clauses. 提供证明或证据,如有关商业文件或合同条款。

proof *n.* an evidence or argument that compels the mind to accept an assertion as true 证实,证明

e. g. :He was asked for proof of his identity. 他被要求证实他的身份。

She had an employment history that was proof of her dependability. 她有可证实她的可靠性的工作经历。

evidence *n.* things helpful in forming a conclusion or judgment 证据,证物

e. g. :The broken parts inside the package were the evidence that the goods had experienced heavy shock during transportation. 包装箱内被打碎的部件就是货物在运输途中曾经历严重振荡的证据。

He submitted the photograph in evidence. 他呈送照片作为证物。

3. Our workers are working *overtime*. 我们的工作人员在加班。

overtime *adv.* (working hours) in addition to those of a regular schedule 加班

The newspaper staff worked overtime. 新闻工作人员超时工作。

4. **credit note**: a formal printed note given to a purchaser requiring the payment for goods received 付款通知

Useful Expressions

1. Thank you for your letter of February 6 calling our attention to the damaged goods. I am investigating the case now and will give an answer to you within the next two weeks.
2. I'm sorry to learn that the shipment of your order of May 15 did not correspond with your order.
3. I suggest you ask for compensation from the insurance company, who has a branch at your area, so as to cover the loss.
4. In our examination, we did not find any evidence of inferior quality or workmanship, and the material used was of superior quality.
5. In the meantime, would you please send me a copy of the invoice? The additional information will be helpful to process this claim quickly.
6. Our further investigation shows the damage is caused by poor ventilation and high temperature in the ship hold.
7. As your letter of December 12 pointed out, Invoice No. 678 was indeed in error. The discount of 5% does apply to your latest purchase, and a revised invoice will be sent to you shortly.
8. We apologize for this unpleasant experience. We are taking additional precautions to make certain that this does not happen again.
9. We will give our immediate attention to the matter, and we assure you of our full commitment.
10. In order to settle the matter, we would like to send a representative to conduct an inspection. You may rely on our fair handling of the case to your satisfaction.

Exercises

1. Questions for discussion

1) What are you going to do when you receive complaints and claims from your customer?

2) How will you write a reply to a claimer?

2. Group discussion

Are you going to accept the suggestion given by the writer of example letter 4 if you were the customer? Give reasons for your answer.

3. Decide whether the following statements are true or false. Write "T" for true, and "F" for false in the brackets.

1) A compensation is the best way to settle a claim. (　　)

2) Reply to a letter of claim should be made after an investigation is carried out into the case.

(   )

3) It is not necessary to answer a claim that is not justified. (   )

4) Reply to a claim should start by acknowledging receipt of the claim. (   )

5) You don't need to reply to a letter of claim sent to you if you are not responsible to the loss or damage incurred. (   )

6) The writer of example letter 4 apologizes to the claimer and offers to compensate the loss. (   )

7) It can be inferred from example letter 1 that the seller ask the buyer to cover the loss from the shipping company. (   )

8) The writer of letter 3 suggests the buyer to return the wrong goods and get a refund from the seller. (   )

9) It can be inferred from example letter 4 that the dispute is caused by the seller's inability to deliver the goods on time. (   )

10) A credit note is a formal printed note given to a purchaser requiring the payment for goods received. (   )

4. Choose the best answer to complete the following statements.

1) We have to ______ a claim ______ ABC Company for the delay in delivery.

A. file, against　　B. reach, for　　C. carry, against　　D. issue, for

2) The goods under Contract No. 3561 ______ shipped already if your L/C had reached us on time.

A. have been　　B. would have been　　C. has been　　D. will have been

3) The quality of the goods was found inferior ______ that of the sample.

A. than　　B. at　　C. to　　D. over

4) We will investigate ______ the matter before giving you any definite answer.

A. with　　B. through　　C. about　　D. into

5) The case has been suspended for lack of ______.

A. proofs　　B. facts　　C. truth　　D. evidence

6) Our business motto is "______ or your money back".

A. satisfaction　　B. satisfied　　C. satisfactory　　D. satisfying

7) We have substituted the ______ goods for the ______ ones.

A. faulty, right　　B. right, faulty　　C. fault, right　　D. right, fault

8) The goods ______ your L/C No. 3366 will be delivered by the end of the month.

A. in　　B. under　　C. of　　C. within

9) All claims will receive our best attention and, whenever possible, will be ______ within 60 days.

A. answered　　B. solved　　C. replied　　D. settled

10) Please inform us ______ the market trend in your area.

A. for　　B. in　　C. of　　D. with

5. Make sentences with the following words and phrases.

1) to be liable 2) unfounded 3) to find faults with 4) unconditional 5) apologize

6. Improve the following sentences for better communicating effect.

1) You will get a refund of USD $ 300 in compensation for the damaged goods.

2) You can have our promise of a fair settlement of the claim.

3) Three packages of men's shirts of standard size will be sent to you early next week to replace the wrong goods.

4) It is found that the damage is caused by high temperature in the ship's hold.

5) High quality and quick delivery of the goods is promised by our company.

7. Translate the following sentences into English.

1) 我方发现货物的受损是由于运输途中遇大雨引起的。

2) 要不是这些困难,交货条件毫无疑问是可以遵守的。

3) 我方得知贵方收到的货物中有 85 袋与原样品不符,感到很遗憾。

4) 关于短重的问题本公司不能承担任何责任,请贵公司就此事向运输代理索赔。

5) 请将此货损坏的样品寄给我方,我们将仔细检查,然后寻求解决办法。

6) 我方将采取有效措施,防止此类事情再次发生。

7) 由于缺乏证据,无法证明货物的被损坏的原因。

8) 只有当双方都同意所有的条款时,才能签署这份合同。

9) 我方向你们保证将公正地解决这项索赔。

10) 对于你方目前的订货,我方没有早些给你方消息,为此我方应向你方道歉。

8. Translate the following sentences Chinese.

1) On receiving a letter of claim one must analyze and investigate in detail whether the claim is justified and within his or her range of responsibility for compensation.

2) Sometimes the buyer may just try to find faults with the goods because they no longer want the goods, or they can get them cheaper elsewhere.

3) As for the goods of Art. No. 375, they are made of thinner material, which are especially suitable for the summer season. If you care to sell them we'll offer you a special price of US $ 10 each.

4) However, the goods were inspected by the prestigious ABC Inspection Company here two days before loading, and the goods were loaded onto the carrying vessel in perfect condition, which is shown by the Inspection Certificate and the clean B/L attached.

5) The industrial dispute is indeed something unexpected and we have little control over it. Therefore we should not be held legally liable on this matter.

6) We will send you immediately the right kind of goods, Art. No. 365, to replace Art. No. 375. They will reach San Francisco within this month.

7) We very much regret that we cannot accept your claim on the coffee sets since evidence of improper handling during transportation as you complained is inadequate.

8) All disputes arising in connection with the execution of this contract shall be settled through friendly discussion.

9) We are sorry that we have to submit the case to arbitration.

10) It seems that the critical point of the dispute is whether the cause of late delivery should be taken as unpredictable circumstances.

9. Write a reply to the following letter.

Dear Sir:

I am writing with reference to the food processing machine under Order No. CK139. It was delivered to us last week. We noticed some damage to the outer packing, and when we turned it on it did not work. As we need the machine badly. Please replace it immediately.

Enclosed please find the copy of invoice. I look forward to hearing from you soon.

Yours Sincerely,

10. Make a telephone conversation in pairs with two students representing the buyer and the seller respectively. One makes a complaint for damaged goods, and the other tries to find an effective way to solve the problem.

Lesson Eighteen

Sales Promotion

1. Introduction

Business companies often need to write sales letters to potential customers and existing ones in order to penetrate into a new market, to enlarge sales, or solicit repeat orders.

In addition to the general purpose of increasing sales, a sales letter has two specific purposes:

1) To inform potential customers and buyers of new products or services and the benefits they can receive to persuade them to buy the products or services.

2) To remind existing customers of new benefits and improvements in the products, or solicit business from former customers.

Letters for the first purpose are usually unsolicited. They include advertisements. Letters for the second purpose are called "follow-up letters".

2. Writing strategy

(1) Writing unsolicited letters

The most difficult sales letters to write about are those that are unsolicited and not expected by readers. If not appealing to the reader at first sight, the letters are often neglected or treated as junk mails. In order for your letter to get noticed, get read, and be remembered adopt the AIDA plan.

◇ **Attention**: Get your reader's attention by starting your letter with an attractive opening line. If you use an envelope, include a compelling remark on it.

◇ **Interest**: Build interest by describing some of the products' unique features.

◇ **Desire**: Increase desire by emphasizing the benefits that are most appealing.

◇ **Action**: Motivate action by closing your letter with a suggestion of the action you want your reader to take, after you have built up enough interest.

To catch reader's attention, you must know what they need. This can be done by:

◇ **Analyzing your target readers and learn their demographics.** Know their sex, age, occupation, geographic location, and financial situation.

◇ **Seeing your products or service from the eyes of your reader.** Appeal to your reader's emotions and understand what they need — comfort, prestige, enjoyment, convenience, health, or loyalty.

◇ **Determining the key selling point.** Know your products' selling points, which can be better appearance, convenience, durability, price, comfort, education, etc., and how they benefit your particular readers who may be in poor health, living on a small income, using out-dated hardware and software, or paying inflated prices. For an effective sales letter, your products' distinguishing benefits must correspond to your readers' primary needs and emotional concern.

(2) Writing follow-up letters

Make contact if you haven't got business from a former customer for a while. Include the following points in a follow-up letter:

◇ Refer to the business opportunity you had with the customer at an earlier time.

◇ Inquire about the customer's degree of satisfaction.

◇ Highlight any new features, improvements, or more benefits readers will receive for a repeat order.

(3) Writing subject line for E-mail message

If you send your sales letters by e-mail, write a subject line that catches your reader's attention. Remember, there are people who get hundreds of e-mail messages a day, and they can't possibly read them all. So, if your subject line doesn't interest your readers, the readers may never open your message.

Instead of writing	Write
Meeting	Enjoy meeting new people
Our new product	Taste the difference
"Good memory"	Success starts with "Good Memory"

(4) Postscript

A postscript is a very effective way to call attention. You can withhold one last convincing argument for emphatic inclusion in a postscript.

(5) Envelope with a compelling remark

If the message is sent by post mail, an envelope with a compelling remark can be effective to catch your reader's attention and inform your reader. See the following example with a remark at the bottom-left corner.

Company Name
Street Address
City, Country

Valuable documents enclosed

3. Communication for results

In writing sales messages substitute euphemisms for words that have unpleasant connotations.

Instead of writing	Write
We provide *cheap merchandise* at Wonderland Store.	We provide *barging prices* at Wonderland Store.
Shannon Brand *toilet paper* is extremely suitable for baby care with extra softness and water absorption.	Shannon Brand *bathroom tissue* is extremely suitable for baby care with extra softness and water absorption.
We supply *high-calorie food* to winter sports lovers.	We supply *high-energy food* to winter sports lovers.
We welcome all people, esp. *the elderly*, to participate in our health improvement program.	We welcome all people, esp. *senior citizens*, to participate in our health improvement program.

4. Example letters

(1) A letter of sales promotion written to a potential customer

Skyline Company

56 Quan Street, Tianjin, China

0086 - 22 - 2336 5566

July 27, 2010

CERTIFIED MAIL

Ms. Dawn Roberts
General Manager
Free Travel Hotel
100 King's Road
Hanoi, Vietnam

Dear Ms Roberts:

Re: Excellent Opportunity to Buy Classy Bathroom Appliances

We have learned from Susan Hills from B & J Corporation that you are setting up a new hotel in the east part of your city. We believe you will benefit from Skyline, a major producer of high-and-medium-end bath fixture.

We develop products with seasoned engineers and marketing professionals to ensure that what we offer is not only aesthetically appealing, but also functionally superior.

I would like to invite you to tour our facilities and see first hand the design, craftsmanship and technology of our company and learn why we stand above the competition in delivering our line of products and supporting services.

I'm enclosing a copy of our latest catalogue for your reference. You will also see how we can assist you in meeting your specific requirements and the significant savings you can realize by purchasing from Skyline.

We are looking forward to fulfill our mission of improving the hardware of your hotel with our products and services.

Sincerely,
(*Signature*)
Anna Katherine, Sales Manager

AK/ml

Enclosure

You will get the most favorable price for our new model of Bubble Massage Bathtub by ordering between October 6th and 16th.

(2) An unsolicited sales letter written to visitors after a convention

LETTERHEAD

Dear customers and friends:

Thank you for visiting our booth at the recent Light Industrial Products Convention in Tianjin, China. We hope you enjoyed it as much as we did. Many who visited our booth commented on extraordinary benefits of White Lamb Brand Cashmere Sweater for:

◆Extra-softness and warmth with 100% super quality cashmere
◆A variety of colors and sizes for men & women
◆5% discount before Christmas and New Year

Please see the enclosed brochure that describes White Lamb Brand Cashmere Sweater in greater detail. If you're interested in learning more about our products and service, please call us toll-free at 86 – 800 – 23568906. You may also check our website at www. our company. com.

Sincerely,
ABC Textile & Apparel Co.
Encl.

(3) An unsolicited sales letter

Star Printers, Inc.

May 15, 2010
Dear Friends:

Are you trying to upgrade your color printing capabilities but have hesitated to make that big investment in a new color laser printer?

Are you tired of waiting on that old printer to finish that flyer or presentation?

Are you looking for a new way to promote your business that won't cost you a fortune?

You will be excited about Star Printers. The company provides the color printers and programs you are looking for with unique features focused on:

- High speed
- Wide format
- Multifunction

Star Printers utilize the latest technology in color laser and solid ink. The X7170 type all-in-one printer has multifunction performance with scanner, printer, copier, and image processing capabilities.

The C2626 type improves the image with incredible and vivid color printing that gets people to take notice, and makes a true difference in your business. Studies by experts proves that using professional looking color brochures, flyers, and bulletins can attract 66% more readers and hold their attention longer than a plain black and white document.

Star Printers incorporated in 1980. Today it continues to provide thousands of customers with new color printers each year. We focus on providing the best solutions for you with the best possible service. Contact us now to have a new high performance color printer for your business today!

Tel: 00 - 000 - 23457788
Website: www. starprinters. com

P. S. : *For purchase within this week, the printers are available with 10% discount.*

(4) A follow-up letter for after-sales service

Skyline Company

56 Quan Street, Tianjin, China
0086 - 22 - 2336 5566

Dear Mr. Brian Jones:

We appreciate the opportunity of being able to supply your store with our kitchen and bath fixture in December, 2010.

Skyline is fully committed in providing you not only fine quality products but also high quality after-sales service.

Since we are in business we have been striving to improve the lives of everyone who is touched by our products. However, we are aware that there is always room for improvement. We welcome your valuable comments and suggestions.

If you have any questions or problems with our products please contact Mike Johnson, our representative of customer assistance, by calling our toll-free number at 0086 - 800 - 7655678.

Sincerely yours,
(*Signature*)
Mark Miller
Director

MM: sw

(5) A follow-up letter to solicit new orders

To: Brian Jones < bjones@ tradefirm. com >
From: Mary Sill < msill@ skyline. com
Date: December 20, 2010
Subject: Bathtub fit for a queen
Attachments: 1. A customer questionnaire
2. A catalogue

Dear Brian Jones:

It has been quite some time since we had the pleasure of providing you with our bathroom appliances. We appreciate the pleasant business cooperation with your firm.

For your information, we attach a catalogue of our new products, among which the Bubble Massage Bathtub designed with the latest craftsmanship and technology is very popular among our consumers and many big hotels for VIP rooms. It is especially beneficial in saving energy, improving health and removing fatigue.

We are looking forward to receiving your new order.

Mary Sill
Manager of Customer Service

P. S. : For orders of any products in the catalogue within this month we offer 5% discount.

(6) A follow-up letter seeking customer's feedback

LETTERHEAD

June 12, 2010

Ms. Pat Long
535 Castle Hill
White Castle, PA14567
USA

Dear Ms. Long:

Subject: You are our valued customer

We regret to see that you didn't renew your contract for the purchase of our products this year. If you had a problem, please let us know. We will do our best to remedy it.

Your commons and feedbacks are valuable to us in improving our products and services. Please tick the questions and send your reply with the postage-paid and addressed envelope enclosed.

( ) Have you been dissatisfied with our service?
( ) Did you have a problem with our working staff?
( ) Were you dissatisfied with payment terms?
( ) Others ______________________________

As the summer season is drawing near, we enclose a brochure of our latest products for summer sports and look forward to new business opportunities.

Sincerely,
(*Signature*)
Morgan Lee
Manager of Customer Service

Encl.

P. S. Please note that we have extended our service hours and are now on call 24 hours a day at 800 – 123456.

5. Telephone conversation

Alice Wang calls for information about the arrival of the books she ordered.

Wang: (Dials the number of the book company.)

Recorded voice: Universal Book Ltd. Please dial 1 for Sales Department; dial 2 for Manager's Office; dial 3 for Claims; dial 4 for after-sales service; dial 5 for an operator.

Wang: (dials 1)

Recorded voice: This is the Sales Department. Please leave a message.

Wang: This is Alice Wang from Tianjin University of Science and Technology. I ordered 10 sets of "The Complete Collection of Business Letters" on October 15th, but I haven't received them yet. Please call back between 9 a. m. and 5 p. m. our time to tell me the definite time of arrival. My phone number is

0086 - 22 - 3355 6688, again, 0086 - 22 - 3355 6688. Thanks. Bye-bye.

New Words and Phrases

penetrate [ˈpenitreit] *v.* to enter and gain a share of (a market) 穿透，渗透

penetrated the home-computer market with an affordable new model 以大众可以买得起的新机型打入家用电脑市场

demographics [ˌdeməˈgræfiks] *n.* the characteristics of human populations and population segments, especially when used to identify consumer markets 人口统计学

follow-up letters （售后）跟踪信

durability [ˌdjuərəˈbiləti] *n.* the quality of being durable 经久，耐久力

compelling [kəmˈpeliŋ] *a.* urgently requiring attention 强制的，强迫的，引人注目的

withhold [wiðˈhəuld] *v.* to refrain 抑制，忍住

emphatic [imˈfætik] *a.* expressed or performed with emphasis 强调的，语势强的

He responded with an emphatic "no". 他斩钉截铁地回答"不"。

euphemism [ˈjuːfəmizəm] *n.* substituting a mild, indirect, or vague term for one considered harsh, blunt, or offensive 委婉，委婉的说法

connotations [ˌkɔnəuˈteiʃn] *n.* the set of associative implications constituting the general sense of a word in addition to its literal sense 含蓄，内涵

craftsmanship [ˈkrɑːftsmənʃip] *n.* 技能，技术

seasoned [ˈsiːznd] *a.* with a great deal of experience in the stated activity 经验丰富的，阅历很深的

a seasoned news reporter 经验丰富的新闻记者

aesthetical [iːsˈθetikl] *a.* concerning, or showing a sense of beauty 美学的，审美的，有审美感的

aesthetically [iːsˈθetikli] *adv.* 审美地，美学观点上地

questionnaire [ˌkwestʃəˈneə] *n.* a printed form containing a set of questions as a way of gathering information for a survey 调查表，问卷

convention [kənˈvenʃən] *n.* general agreement on certain practices or customs 例，习俗

scanner [ˈskænə] *n.* 扫描仪

copier [ˈkɔpiə] *n.* 复印机

incorporate [inˈkɔːpəreit] *v.* to cause to form into a legal corporation 使组成合法的公司

to incorporate a business 组建公司

VIP very important person 重要人物

Notes

1. **selling point**: the most attractive features of a product 卖点
2. **For an effective sales letter, your products' distinguishing benefits must *correspond to* your readers' primary needs and emotional concern.** 对于一封有效的销售信来说，你方产品独特的优点必须符合你的读者的主要需求和情感关注点。

correspond to: to be in agreement 符合;相对应

e. g. :His reply does not correspond to the request. 他的回答与要求不符。

3. **Highlight any new features, improvements, or more benefits readers will receive for *repeat order*.** 突出读者将会得到的任何新的特征、改进或是更多的优点,以便吸引回头客。

   repeat order 再次订货

4. **You can withhold one last convincing argument for emphatic inclusion in a postscript, or type the postscript in a different font or color.** 你可以保留最后一点有说服力的论证,把它写在附言中,使它起到强化的效果,或是用不同的字体或颜色来写附言。

5. **I would like to invite you to *tour* our facilities and see first hand the design, craftsmanship and technology of our company to learn why we stand above the competition in delivering our line of products and supporting services.** 我想邀请您参观我们的设备,并亲眼看一看我公司的设计、工艺和技术,以便了解我们为什么能够在提供系列产品和售后服务的竞争中立于不败之地。

   tour :*v.* to make a tour of 巡视,到……进行旅游

   e. g. :They toured Europe last summer. 他们去年夏天在欧洲观光。

   The government officials toured the scene of the disaster. 政府官员巡视受灾现场。

6. **high-and-medium-end bath fixture** 高中档浴室设备
7. **bubble massage bathtub** 气泡按摩浴缸
8. **kitchen and bath fixture** 厨卫设备
9. **toll-free number** 免费电话号码
10. **bathroom appliances** 浴室设备
11. **You are our *valued* customer** 您是我们尊贵的顾客

    value: *v.* regard highly 珍重

    e. g. :He valued health above money. 他把健康看得比钱更重要。

12. **to cost a fortune:** to cost a lot of money 花许多钱

    e. g. :I guess it will cost a fortune to travel around the world. 我认为周游世界需要许多金钱。

13. **an all-in-one printer:** a printer with many functions 多功能打印机
14. **to renew a contract:** to extend a contract 为合同延期

    e. g. :I'd like to renew my contract for another year. 我想将合同延期一年。

15. **P. S. Please note that we have extended our hours of service and are now *on call* 24 hours a day.** 附言:请注意,我们已延长了服务时间,现在全天24小时服务。

    to be on call ... 随叫随到的,待命的

    e. g. :physicians who were on call for 48 hours 48小时随叫随到的医生们

Useful Expressions

1. We always appreciate comments from you and your customers.
2. As you are a loyal customer, we offer 5% discount for your new orders.

3. Our latest catalogue is enclosed, in which you will find new colors and patterns.

4. We are able to offer you 3% discount on the retail price of our leather shoes. If your order is over 1000 pairs in a month, we'll consider offering you a higher discount.

5. We can assure you that, for any trial order you may place with us, the goods will be carefully selected as if you personally made the choice.

6. Our company has been operating in Asia since 1980, and has more than 100 staff working from offices in major cities of all Asian countries.

7. With 40 years experience in the field of international trade, we provide superior products and reliable service.

8. With a history dating back to 1884, the company has grown to become one of the 100 largest industrial companies in the US, with annual sales in excess of $2 billion.

9. In the spirit of friendship, equality and mutual benefit, we look to a continued business relations between our two firms.

10. We strive for your satisfaction with superior quality products and reliable after-sales service.

Exercises

1. Answer the following questions.

1) Why do business companies need to write sales letters?

2) What's a "follow-up" letter?

3) What's the writing strategy for a sales letter?

4) How to write an opening of a sales letter that catches your reader's attention?

2. Read the following advertisements and then discuss.

1) What products or services does each of them sell?

2) What is the selling point in each of them?

3) Are they effective enough for readers to take the expected actions? Why?

Ⅰ.

Fly non-stop to Sydney for just ¥5180

Take advantage of Qantas' special fares from now until 30 April, and you'll receive a free domestic transfer to either Melbourne or Brisbane.

Melbourne 墨尔本(澳大利亚港市) Brisbane 布里斯班(澳大利亚港市)

Ⅱ.

Can't Take Your Eyes off It?

Just one look and it sets your heart racing.

Graceful. Alluring.

The Mercedes-Benz E-Class captivates like no others.

When eyes meet soul, everything seems clear —

The agility within the charisma, the ingenuity within the calm.

Finally, there is something in life you want to be at once with.

Why wait?

agility [əˌdʒiləti] *n.* 敏捷　　Mercedes-Benz 奔驰(汽车商标)
charisma [kəˈrizmə] *n.* 领袖气质，超凡魅力　　Captivate [ˈkæptiveit] *v.* 迷人；诱惑
ingenuity [ˌindʒiˈnjuːəti] *n.* 精巧；灵活性

Ⅲ.

Racing against time just for you

Time is our greatest competitor, which is why our global team of more than 400,000 employees, 90,000 delivery vehicles and 500 planes work tirelessly round the clock to ensure all your delivery and logistics needs are met. After all, as the Official Logistics and Express Delivery Sponsor of the Beijing 2008 Olympic Games, we are constantly racing ahead to deliver more.

3. Translate the terms and expressions from Chinese into English.

1) 促销信
2) 招揽生意
3) 潜在客户
4) 目标客户
5) 产品促销

4. Use the following phrases in making sentences.

1) find a good / ready market
2) view sth. from the eyes of your reader
3) determine the key selling point
4) customer's degree of satisfaction

5. Choose the best answer for each of the statement.

1) A demographical analysis of your readers can be made by knowing their ______.
A. age　B. geographic location　C. occupation　D. all of the above

2) Which of the following is **not** a selling point of a product?
A. Convenience.　B. Durability.　C. Comfort.　D. Higher price.

3) They sell well in more than fifty countries and have won favorable ______ from home and abroad.
A. reception　B. respect　C. reputation　D. popularity

4) You may be sure that your order of our carpets will prove ______ to you.
A. advantages　B. good　C. profitable　D. benefit

5) The carpet is not yet in our ______, so we enclose a color picture for your reference.
A. content　B. context　C. contract　D. catalogue

6) We will send you our best ______ as soon as we hear from you.
A. quotation　B. quota　C. quote　D. quality

7) You can motivate your readers action only after ______.
A. you have given enough introduction of the benefit of your product
B. you have aroused enough interest to your product
C. you have created enough desire for your product

D. all of the above

8) The first step in writing a sales letter is to ________.

A. arouse the interest of your reader　　C. build up the desire of your reader

B. catch the attention of your reader　　D. ask the reader to take action

6. Decide whether the following statements are true or false. Write "T" for true, and "F" for false in the brackets.

1) A follow-up letter is a form of sales letter. (　　)

2) The aim of sales letters is to sell particular kinds of goods or services to target customers and thus expand your business. (　　)

3) By writing a sales letter, you seek to get the attention and arouse the interest of readers (the prospective buyers), convince them that the goods or service you are to supply are beneficial to them, and confidently ask for the action you want. (　　)

4) Sales letters are only given to those who know very little about your products or services. (　　)

5) In writing to unsolicited customers, your preliminary job is to get attention and then arouse interest so that your reader will be eager to see what you have to say and then make his/ her decision to buy. (　　)

6) To promote sales you must adjust the key selling points to correspond to different needs of different buyers. (　　)

7) In writing sales letter, you should emphasize the benefits the buyer will get from the product or service. (　　)

8) You may also use promotion materials such as a brochure to illustrate the details of the products or service. (　　)

7. Translate the following sentences into English.

1) 我们热情邀请您参观本届时装展,我们最新的羊绒衫系列在38号展台展出。

2) 有了这"世界各国百科全书",你所有的问题都解决了,所有问题的答案都在这部书里!

3) 我们将在半导体的零售价格基础上给您10%的折扣,如果您的购买量超过1000台,我们将考虑提供更高的折扣。

4) 感谢贵公司的友好合作,请填写附件中的调查问卷,并发回我方,以便我们了解贵公司客户的满意度。

5) 自从你方7月订购500台照相机后我们再也没有得到你方任何订单,对此我们十分遗憾。

6) 本公司的新厂已开始生产电子计算器,欢迎询价和订购。

7) 我们确信您会把握此次机会,向贵公司客户提供一流的产品。

8) 为了便于您了解,随函附上我们的图示目录、价格表及订单。

8. Translate the following sentences into Chinese.

1) Although we sent you our catalogue on March 9th we have not received any orders from you, and we should like to know if there is any additional information you need about our products.

2) May I draw your attention in particular to our Vertical Filling System, which permits quick and easy reference while holding correspondence securely in dustproof, fireproof drawers.

3) We are an exclusive exporter of parts and components of various types of motorcycles in this district and would take the liberty to send a quotation sheet covering our current range of products for your reference. We hope you will find it interesting.

4) In order to popularize these products, all the prices in the catalogue are subject to a special discount of 10% during the month of May.

5) You will note that we are making you a special reduction in prices owing to your support in the past. These reduced prices remain good within a week.

6) With a view to supporting your sales, we have specially prepared some samples of our new makes and are sending them to you, under separate cover, for your consideration.

7) For an old customer like you, we are willing to allow a 5% commission on each machine, plus a discount of 8% on all orders received before the end of this month.

8) We enclose the latest designs of our products, which are superior in quality and moderate in price. They will surely find a good market at your end.

9. Rewrite the following sales letter with AIDA plan.

Dear friends:

THE WORLDWIDE ENCYCLOPAEDIA

I am writing to introduce a new book just published by Universal Books Ltd.

The above book is very competitively priced and we offer attractive discounts. If you buy 60 copies you'll get free transportation and prompt delivery.

After years of research, we have now produced THE WORLDWIDE ENCYCLOPAEDIA, an important new work for the home, containing information on thousands of subjects. It is available as a set of three volumes or as a one volume shortened edition.

The book is very suitable for both adults and children with more than 100 full-color pictures. Children can read it quickly and easily. They can also see the tables covering all the countries of the world, their populations, capitals and sizes.

Please buy now!

Yours sincerely,

UNIVERSAL BOOKS LTD.

Betty Wood

Sales Representative

10. Make a telephone conversation in pairs with two students sitting back to back, one inquiring to the other about the arrival time of an order he/she has placed but has not received yet. The other student explains the reason and gives a satisfactory answer.

Lesson Nineteen
Business Report

1. Introduction

Business report writing is an essential part in business communication. The function of the report is to convey information, assist decision-making and solving problems. People in various departments and organizations need timely and accurate information to keep business running smoothly and maintain satisfied customers, and much of the information comes in the form of reports. The ability to be proficient in report writing is critical to pursue commercial success.

Reports can be long documents of over hundreds of pages, or short ones in just a few pages. They can be formal, or informal depending on your subject, your purpose, the culture of your organization, and your relationship with your audience. They mainly fall into the following types.

1) **Informational report.** It is mainly used for providing data and facts. Such reports include sales reports, quarterly reports and annual reports.

2) **Analytical report.** It mainly analyzes and interprets data and facts. Audit reports are examples of this type.

3) **Recommendation report.** It identifies business opportunity or problem and recommends action or solution. Feasibility reports and problem-solving reports fall into this type.

Some business report contain all of the above three types. For instance, it first informs the reader of a business opportunity, followed by an analysis of its possibilities, and then, recommends an action.

2. Writing strategy

A formal report may include the components given bellow, while an informal one is simpler with fewer components.

1) **Title page.** It contains the title, the author's and the recipient's name and the date in which the report is released.

2) **Table of contents.** It shows the headings of all the sections in the report and the pages in which they appear.

3) **Summary.** It gives a brief account of what the report is about.

4) **Background.** It gives the background of situation or the history of the problem.

5) **Introduction.** It gives the purpose and scope of the report.

6) **Body.** It presents all the findings.

7) **Conclusion.** It summarizes the main points.

8) **Recommendations.** It suggests the actions to be taken and solutions to the problems.

9) **Appendix.** It includes a glossary of all the technical terms.

10) **Acknowledgement.** It expresses thanks to people who have helped in writing or preparing the report.

11) **References.** It lists the materials (books, papers, documents, website, etc.) the author referred to for preparing and writing the report.

3. Communication for results

To present information effectively in writing formal reports, follow the tips given bellow:

(1) Use a fairly formal style. Avoid using contractions and slang.

Instead of writing	write
The problem might've been caused by inappropriate use of the equipment.	The problem might have been caused by inappropriate use of the equipment.
The concert held last week was off the hinges.	The concert held last week was excellent.

(2) Avoid using "you", as your multiple audience may include people not related to the project.

Instead of writing	write
It would benefit you to adopt the solution.	It would benefit ABC Company to adopt the solution.

(3) Include all the definitions and documents needed to understand the report. As the multiple audiences may include readers who refer to the report month or years later and they don't share your special knowledge.

Instead of writing	write
They accept CPL for settling payment of the project.	They accept CPL (the Chilean Peso—the currency of Chile) for settling payment of the project.

4. Example reports

(1) Informational report

Annual Report

Spring Valley Home for Senior Citizens

31 December 2010

Introduction

The purpose of this report is to inform the local authority, the senior citizen and all those who care for the development of the Spring Valley Home for Senior Citizens (the Home) the objective, the major activities, the financial state in 2010, and our commitment in future.

Objective

The objective of the Home is to provide care and a shelter for the needy, aged, and the sick and aged irrespective of race and religion.

Finance & funding

The Home is funded by the government and from public donations. The Home also collects nominal fees from the family members of the resident. Such fees are based on the family's financial background and their ability to pay.

Residence Accommodation

In 2010, we received 25 applications for admission to the Home. However, due to space constraint, we were only able to admit 20 residents —— 7 on Public Assistance. Thirteen of the residents are charged at a fee between RMB 700 and 900 per month.

Major Activities

January, Residents visited the Bird Park.

February, Chinese New Year celebration.

August, National Day celebration.

September, Mid-Autumn Festival celebration. .

November, Senior Citizens' Week entertainment

December, Christmas celebrations.

Weekly physiotherapy sessions are conducted by physiotherapists from General Hospital for the residents.

Financial State

The Home recorded a surplus of RMB 228,000 in the year 2010. We have spent RMB 50,000 to purchase health equipments for the physiotherapy room.

Construction of the new wing which can house another 50 beds has begun in June 2010. The new wing is expected to be completed by June 2012. The Government will be funding 90% of the construction costs and the Home will bear the remaining 10%.

Conclusion

The fund from the local government and donation from warm-hearted people from all works of life in the form of capital and voluntary work has helped the development and progress of the Home. We'd like to thank the local government, our donors, friends and supporters who have made significant contributions to the Home and the Home's Building Fund. We will make more efforts to accommodate more residents and provide better service.

(2) Analytical and recommendation report

Title page

Feasibility report

Web Based Chinese tutoring for Iceland

29 October, 2010

Prepared for

Ms. Sarah Long, Director

Language Teaching Department

Prepared by

Jennifer Yang, Professor

Joanna Zhao, Professor

Contents

Introduction

This report seeks to evaluate the overall importance and possibility of a website that coherently presents the Chinese language to Icelanders. The website's target audience would be Icelanders planning trips to China or Icelanders simply interested in learning the language. The rapid development in modern technology and communication dramatically reduced the distance between the two countries. As a result we would like to make learning Chinese as accessible for Icelanders as possible.

Background

It is important to recall that China has one of the oldest civilizations and there are approximately 1,052,000,000 people that speak Chinese. (Source: *http://www.nationsonline.org/oneworld/most _ spoken _ languages.htm, 1999*) Moreover, China and Iceland established diplomatic relations on 8th December 1971. In May 1972, China assigned the first resident ambassador to Iceland. For decades since then, we see drastic increase in trade between the two countries.

Problem

It is not trouble-free to have an access to material that teaches Icelanders Chinese. One of few ways to learn Chinese in Iceland is to sign up for expensive course. This is available at the local language learning schools. The course offered there has 18 hours of lessons and is taught in a period of nine weeks. A course of that type most certainly does not apply to everyone. Let us assume that a family is going for a vacation for two weeks in China, it is definitely not suitable for a family member to go on a nine-week course to pickup the basics in Chinese.

Objectives

The main aim of this project is to develop a web based system which introduces and teaches the Icelandic population Chinese and to encourage Icelanders to learn the essential day to day dialogues. This website will ensure that Icelanders should be capable of interacting in Chinese with basic understanding of the language.

Methods

The design of the website will have the following features:

a) Instructions that the user can quickly refer to if he needs assistance with a given problem.

b) Audio &video aids that help users watch the dialogues in action and observe to pronunciations.

c) The website will be broken down into a few categories such as pronunciation, vocabulary, grammar, and topics such as getting around, shopping and other activities.

d) Exercises will be used for the user to see how adequate he has become after a few lessons.

Feasibility analysis

Java scripts/applets are programs that can be executed by web browser. The statements in the programs can be made part of an HTML source file to enable some interactive features such as mouse clicks and input to forms. Flash is a graphics animation program, it can be viewed in a web browser, or user may "play" them. Flash files occur most commonly in animated web pages and rich-media websites.

Conclusion

The benefits of this website are undeniably profound. First there exists a definite lack of self teaching language websites directed at Icelanders. Secondly there is a growing interaction between Iceland and China in both business and tourism. Lastly the overall costs of the website will be minimal as the development and maintenance requires only a few staff members.

Recommendation

We as a group apply for implementing the project. Our group of four consists of a programmer, a website designer and two native Chinese speakers. We believe we are perfectly adequate to satisfy a project of this kind.

Summary

This website will open new doors for those who want to get to know Chinese and explore the endless treasure that the Chinese can offer. Therefore this website's feasibility resides in both the growing demand and relatively low cost structure. This project is practical and applicable from all points of view.

References

Dix, Finlay, Abowd, Beale. (2004). *Human-Computer Interaction* (3rd ed.). Pearson.

Mark, Allen, Weiss. (2002). *Data structures & Problem Solving using Java* (2nd edition). Addison Wesley.

New Words and Phrases

manuscript [ˈmænjuskript] *n.* A typewritten or handwritten version of a an article, a document, or other work 手稿，原稿

analytical [ˌænəˈlitikəl] *adj.* 分析的，解析的

analysis [əˈnæləsis] *n.* 分析

analyze [ˈænəlaiz] *vt.* 分析

appendix [əˈpendiks] *n.* A collection of supplementary material, usually at the end of a book 附录，附属品

acknowledgement [əkˈnɔlidʒmənt] *n.* 承认，确认，感谢

admission [ədˈmiʃən] *n.* The act of admitting or allowing to enter 允许进入，承认

constraint [kənˈstreint] *n.* The state of being restricted or confined within prescribed bounds 约束

entertainment [entəˈteinmənt] *n.* Something that amuses, pleases 款待，娱乐，娱乐表演

physiotherapy [ˌfiziəuˈθerəpi] *n.* 物理疗法

physiotherapist *n.* 理疗师

donor [ˈdəunə] *n.* One that contributes something, such as money, to a cause or fund 捐赠人

accommodate [əˈkɔmədeit] *vt.* To hold comfortably without crowding 供给，容纳

feasibility [ˌfiːzəˈbiləti] *n.* 可行性，可能性

iceland [ˈaislənd] *n.* 冰岛(欧洲岛名,在大西洋北部,近北极圈)

icelander [ˈaɪsləndə(r)] *n.* 冰岛人

browser [braʊzə] *n.* 浏览器

Notes

1. off the hinges: [American slang] great, wonderful, excellent

2. Senior Citizens: euphemism for old people

3. ... due to space constraint, we were only able to admit 20 residents. ……由于地方

有限,我们仅能收容 20 人。

residents here refer to the people staying in the old people home.

4. sign up 签约参加 e. g. :He signed up for the trip to the West.

5. Audio & video aids 视听设备

6. flash 原指 Macromedia 公司开发的动画编辑工具，现在常常用来表示动画或幻灯短片。

7. Java script, applet （计算机）应用程序

Useful Expressions

1. This report will cover several topics about real estate market development in China.
2. Our recommendation is based on the assumption that the profit margin will increase by 10% in the coming year.
3. The information from this report comes from research of the local market and online resources.
4. This research was limited to materials available via the Internet and from our university's library.
5. The aim of this report is to evaluate the success and expansion feasibility into the market in the West.
6. As far as our research shows, expanding into the new market is likely to be a profitable decision for a few reasons.
7. To ensure a successful development, ABC firm recommends the following.
8. Research has been made on the economic feasibility of the change of ownership.
9. Time constrains have limited the possibility of an exhaustive search for information regarding the market expansion.
10. I recommend the following process to ensure the success of the project.

Exercises

1. Answer the following questions

1) What are the major types of reports, and what are their functions?

2) Why are reports needed in business communication?

2. Translate the following passage into Chinese.

(1)

Formal reports usually have a section that gives the background of the situation or the history of the problem. Even though the current audience for the report probably knows the situation, reports are filed and consulted years later. These later audiences will probably not know the background, although it may be crucial for understanding the options that are possible.

(2)

Setting up a shop on the Internet is a big decision for our company. We do not have the computer staff that our larger competitors have, and our business development team is stretched rather thin already. But more and more people are shopping online, and we do not want to be left out of this mode of retailing. After studying the issue for several weeks, I concluded that we should go ahead with a site but that we should be careful about how we implement it.

3. Translate the following sentences into English.

1)商业报告是管理人员工作中常见的、不可或缺的书面沟通手段。

2)商业报告分为很多种类,如说明性报告、分析报告、建议书等。

3)写报告要有明确的目的,没有目的的报告是毫无意义的。

4)报告可以是正式的,也可以是非正式的,这要看你的主题、目的、企业文化以及你与读者的关系。

5)一篇正式的报告必须依照一定的格式,而且尽量少用人称代词。

6)如果你的报告是写给广大消费者的,最好用正式的格式;如果写给助理或同事,最好用非正式格式。

7)报告可以帮助你向上级分析项目的可能性,说明项目进展,推销你的构想。

8)写报告时,可以以目录标题为基础,把每个重点词扩展为一个句子,并用来作为每个段落的第一句或最后一句话。

4. Write a report on the following topic.

Carry out a research to find out the problems in English study among your classmates, and analyze the causes of the problems. Then, propose a solution.

Hints: Refer to the "Writing Strategy" in this lesson and include but may not be limited to the following points.

Introduction (the purpose for writing the report)

Recommendations (some suggestions to improve student's way of study)

Background (the background of the students, their level of English)

Problem (the difficulties and problems in English study)

Objectives (the main goal for learning English)

Methods (the methods adopted for the research, such as interview or questionnaire, etc.)

Feasibility analysis (possibility and effectiveness of your recommendation)

Conclusion (a brief account of the main parts of your report)

Summary (the central idea of your report)

References (books, magazines, newspapers, website, etc. consulted)

Lesson Twenty
Business Contracts and Agreements

1. Introduction

International sales and purchases are normally conducted through contracts, which are agreements reached between the seller and the buyer concerning the establishing, modifying and terminating the rights and obligations between the two parties during a business transaction. A contract is a legal document enforceable by law and binding on the parties involved, therefore, it must be observed and implemented once the terms and conditions of the contract are reached and the document is signed between the parties. The importance of a contract can never be overstated due to this binding nature. And all the clauses of a contract must be created and reviewed carefully.

There are different types of contracts that serve different kinds of business transactions. And the clauses vary depending on the types of contracts. But most of them include the following parts:

1) Title of the contract

2) Preamble of the contract

◇Date of signing

◇Signing parties

◇Place of signing

3) Body of the contract

◇Terms and conditions

◇Duration

◇Termination

4) Conclusion of the contract

◇Concluding sentence

◇Signature

Additional parts of a contract mainly include:

◇Number of the contract

◇Force Majeure

◇Arbitration

◇Governing law

◇Jurisdiction

As parties in an international trade are usually from different countries, good knowledge about international business law and practices, and the cultures, policies, regulations, political and economical conditions of relevant countries are necessary for writing international business contracts. In addition, knowledge on the language style is also needed for such documents are often full of technical terms, special expressions, and complex sentences.

Nowadays some experts and scholars in the US are advocating using simple and everyday language in legal documents. Some big American companies even rewrite their contracts in non-technical language. As learner of English, you should be aware of this trend, but at the same time understand the traditional type of contracts, because they are widely used and accepted.

2. Writing strategy

To conform with the legal and solemn nature, a business contract is usually written with the following language characteristics:

(1) Use formal words

For example:

1) If renewal of this Agreement is desired, notice in writing should be given by either party within one month *prior to* its expiry. ("prior to" is used instead of "before")

2) All disputes arising from *the execution of* this Agreement shall be settled through negotiation between both parties. ("the execution of" is used instead of "carrying out")

3) Party B shall *endeavor* to push sales of not less than 30,000 of "Younger" brand Men's Shirts. ("endeavor" is used instead of "make efforts")

4) The employer may object to and require the contractor to replace *forthwith* any of its authorized representatives who is incompetent. ("forthwith" is used instead of "immediately")

5) The Company may *terminate* this agreement at any time upon 30 days' written notice to the employee. ("terminate" is used instead of "end")

(2) Use special words and phrases

For example:

1) *Witness whereof* the parties *hereto* have *hereunder* set their respective hands and seals.

2) Now, it is *hereby* agreed and understood as follows.

3) *In the event* that all of the events described in paragraph 12 *hereof* have not taken place within 30 days after the parties' signing of the Agreement, then any expressed or implied *undertakings set forth herein* shall terminate.

(3) Use special terms and business jargons.

For example:

1) Payment is to be made by *Confirmed*, *Irrevocable*, *Transferable*, *and Divisible Letter of Credit* to be available by *sight draft*, to reach the sellers before November 30, 2010 and to remain valid for *negotiation* in China until the 20th day after the aforesaid Time of Shipment.

2) Full set of clean on board, "*freight prepaid*" for *CFR/CIF* Terms, or "*freight to collect*" for *FOB/FAS* Terms, *Ocean Bills of Lading*, made out to order, notifying the buyer at the port of destination.

(4) Use modal verb "shall" instead of "will" or "should", meaning "should", "must"

For example:

1) Neither party *shall* cancel the contract without reasonable causes.

2) The second party *shall* be provided by the first party with the air tickets from Guangzhou to Bamako, and from Bamako the Guangzhou upon terminating the service.

3) All payments *shall* be made in accordance with this contract and the agreements relating to this clause.

(5) Capitalize the name of relevant parties, organizations and the goods in question

For example:

1) The *Seller* shall keep close contact with the agent or the *Buyer*.

2) Name of Commodity: Snow White Brand Cashmere Sweater

(6) Often use long sentences

For example:

With the exception of late delivery or non-delivery due to "Force Majeure" causes, if the Seller fails to deliver the goods in accordance with the terms and conditions of this Contract, the Seller shall indemnify the Buyer for all losses, damages, including but not limited to purchase price and/or purchase price differentials, dead freight, demurrage, and all consequent, direct or indirect losses.

3. Communication for results

In writing a business contract you must give the exact and precise meaning, leaving no loopholes and possibility of misunderstanding. For example:

Instead of writing	Write
Shipment must be made before August 31, 2010.	Shipment must be made on or before August 31, 2010.

(In the custom of native English speakers "before August 31" does not include the day of 31st.)

Instead of writing	Write
Payment shall be made in 10 days.	Payment shall be made within 10 days after receiving the draft.

("in 10 days" may mean "within 10 days" or "after 10 days".)

Instead of writing	Write
The Seller shall undertake to load the goods on board the vessel on time.	The Seller shall undertake to load the *contracted* goods on board the vessel *nominated by the Buyer* on any date *notified by the Buyer*, *within the time of shipment as stipulated in Clause 8 of this Contract*.

(The sentence under "Write" uses 5 modifiers, as is shown by the italicized parts, to restrict the meaning of the nouns to make it as clear as possible.)

4. Example contracts

(1) A sales confirmation

ORIGINAL

ORIENTAL TRADING COMPANY

www.oriental.com

Tel: 00-00-00000000 Fax: 00-00-00000000 E-mail: orient@otc.com

Address: 56 Hainan Road, Tianjin, China

SALES CONFIRMATION

Seller: ORIENTAL TRADING COMPANY:

Seller's address: 56 Hainan Road, Tianjin, China

Tel:00 - 00 - 00000000

Fax:00 - 00 - 00000000

E-mail : orient@ otc. com

Buyer: K & D CO. LTD.

Signed at: Tianjin, China

Validity: 12 months

The Sales Contract is made between the undersigned Seller and Buyer whereby the Seller agrees to sell and the Buyer agrees to buy the under-mentioned goods according to the terms and conditions stipulated below:

1) Name of commodity and specification: Dawei Brand Men's shirts

2) Quantity: 2,000 pieces

3) Unit price: US $ 28. 00/piece CIF Los Angeles

4) Total value: US $ 56,000. 00 CIF Los Angeles

5) Packing and shipping mark: Each piece in a polythene bag, 40 pieces in a carton. No mark

6) Time of shipment: July 8 - 10, 2010

7) Port of loading: Tianjin, China

8) Port of destination: Los Angeles, U. S. A.

9) Insurance: To be effected by the Sellers covering All Risk for 110% of invoice value.

10) Terms of payment: L/C at sight

The covering Letter of Credit must reach the Sellers before June 10, 2010 and is to remain valid in the above indicated Loading Port 15 days after the date of shipment, failing which the Sellers reserve the right to cancel this Sales Contract and to claim from the Buyers compensation for losses resulting from it.

TERMS:

1) QUALITY/QUANTITY DISCREPENCY: In case of quality discrepancy, claim should be filed by the Buyers within 30 days after the arrival of the goods at port of destination, while for quantity discrepancy claim should be filed by the Buyers within 15 days after the arrival of the goods at the port of destination. In all cases, claims must be accompanied by Survey Reports of Recognized Public Surveyors agreed to by the Sellers. Should

the responsibility of the subject under claim be found to rest on the part of the Sellers, the Sellers shall, within 20 days after receipt of the claim, send his reply to the Buyers together with suggestion for settlement.

2) The Seller reserves the option of shipping the indicated percentage more of less than the quantity hereby given in (2) of this contract, and the covering Letter of Credit shall be negotiated for the amount covering the value of quantity actually shipped. (The Buyer is requested to establish the L/C in accordance with the indicated percentage over the total value of the order as per this Sales Contract.)

3) The contents of the covering Letter of Credit shall be in strict accordance with stipulations of the Sales Contract; in case of any variation thereof necessitating amendment of the L/C, the Buyer shall bear the expenses for effecting the amendment. The Sellers shall not be held responsible for possible delay of shipment resulting from awaiting the amendment of the L/C, and reserve the right to claim from the Buyers compensation for the losses resulting from this.

4) Except in cases where the insurance is covered by the Buyers as arranged, insurance is to be covered by the Sellers with a Chinese insurance company. If insurance for additional amount and/or for other insurance terms is required by the Buyers, prior notice to this effect must reach the Sellers before shipment and is subject to the Seller's agreement, and the extra insurance premium shall be on the Buyer's account.

5) INSPECTION: The Certificate of Origin and/or the Inspection Certificate of Quality/Quantity/Weight issued by China Commodity Inspection Bureau shall be taken as the basis for the shipping quality/quantity/weight.

6) The Sellers shall not be held responsible if they, owning to Force Majeure, fail to make delivery within the time stipulated in this Sales Contract or cannot deliver the goods. However, the Seller shall inform the Buyer immediately by fax. The Seller shall deliver to the Buyer by registered letter, if it is requested by the Buyer, a certificate issued by the China Council for the Promotion of International Trade or by any competent authority, certifying to the existence of the said cause or causes. Buyer's failure to obtain the relative Import License is not to be treated as Force Majeure.

7) ARBITRATION: All disputes arising in connection with the execution of the Sales Contract shall be settled amicably by negotiation. In case no settlement can be reached, the case under dispute shall then be submitted for arbitration to the Foreign Trade Arbitration Commission of the China Council for the Promotion of International Trade in accordance with the Provisional Rules of Procedure of the Foreign Trade Arbitration Commission of the China Council for the Promotion of International Trade. The decision of the Commission shall be accepted as final and binding upon both parties.

8) Remark:

The Buyer: The Seller:

(signature) (signature)

K & D CO. LTD. ORIENTAL TRADING COMPANY

(2) A purchase contract

PURCHASE CONTRACT

No. GH899

Date of Signing: Oct. 13th, 2010

Place of Signing: Shenyang, China

The Buyers: Shenyang Brilliance Co. , 567 xxx road, Shenyang, China,

Telephone: .... E-mail: .... Fax: ....

The Seller: JingZhou HengLong Automotive Parts Co. , Ltd. , Kan Hing Bldg, 20 Hilwood rd. Hong Kong, China,

Telephone: .... E-mail: .... Fax: ....

This contract is made by and between the Buyers and The Sellers, whereby the Buyers agree to buy and the Sellers agree to sell the under-mentioned commodity according to her terms and conditions stipulated below:

1) COMMODITY & SPECIFICATIONS: 16′ DISPLAYERS

QUANTITY: 120 SETS

UNIT PRICE: US $ 80. 90 CFR SHENYANG

TOTAL PRICE: 9,708. 00 (PACKING CHARGES INCLUDED)

2) COUNTRY OF ORIGIN AND MANUFACTURES: JAPAN

3) PACKING: To be packed in strong wooden cases suitable for long distance ocean transportation and the change of climate, well protected against moisture and shock. One full set of operating instructions for each instrument or machine shall be enclosed in the packages. The Sellers shall be liable for any damage of the commodity and expenses, incidents thereto on account of improper packing and for any rust attributable to inadequately or improperly protective measures taken by the Sellers in regard to the packing.

4) SHIPPING MARK: The Sellers shall mark on each package with fadeless paint the package number, gross weight, net weight, measurement and the wordings: "KEEP AWAY FROM MOISTURE", "HANDLE WITH CARE", "THIS SIDE UP", and the shipping mark: "89FL-6500ICK, SHENYANG, CHINA".

5) TIME OF SHIPMENT: During October, 2010

6) PORT OF SHIPMENT: Hong Kong

7) PORT OF DESTINATION: Shenyang

8) INSURANCE: To be covered by the Buyers

9) PAYMENT: The Buyers shall, about 20 days prior to the date of delivery, open an irrevocable Letter of Credit with the Bank of China, Shenyang, in favor of the Sellers. The Credit shall be payable against the presentation of draft drawn on the opening bank and the shipping documents specified in Article 10 of this Contract. The Letter of Credit shall be valid until the 15th day after the shipment is effected.

10) DOCUMENTS: The Sellers shall present to the paying bank the following documents for negotiation:

a. One negotiable copy of clean on board ocean Bill of Lading marked "FREIGHT PREPAID" indicating shipping mark, made out to order, blank endorsed, and notifying the Buyer.

b. 3 copies of Invoice with the insertion of Contract number and the Shipping Mark.

c. 3 copies of Packing List showing gross and net weight for each package.

d. 1 copy of Certificate of Quantity and Quality issued by the Manufacturers.

e. Certified copy of telex to the Buyers, advising shipment immediately after shipment is made.

The seller shall, after the shipment is effected, send by airmail one set of the same copies of each of the above-mentioned documents to the Buyer.

11) SHIPMENT: The Sellers shall ship the goods within the shipping time from the port of shipment to the port of destination. Transshipment is not allowed unless specially specified. The carrying vessel shall not fly the flag of a certain nationality unacceptable to the Buyers.

12) SHIPPING ADVICE: The Sellers shall, immediately upon the completion of the loading of the goods, advise by telex the Buyers of the Contract Number, commodity, quantity, invoice value, gross weight, name of the vessel, port of shipment, port of destination and date of sailing. In case the Buyers fail to arrange insurance in time due to the Sellers not having advised in time, all losses shall be borne by the Seller.

13) GUARANTEE OF QUALITY: The Sellers guarantee that the commodity hereof is made of the best materials with first class workmanship, brand new and unused, and that complies this Contract. The guarantee period shall be 12 months counting from the date on which the commodity arrives at the port of destination.

14) CLAIMS: Within 90 days after the arrival of the goods at destination, should the quality, specifications or quantity be found not in conformity with the stipulations of the Contract except those claims for which the insurance company or the owners of the vessel are liable, the Buyers shall, on the strength of the Inspection Certificate issued by the China Import and Export Commodity Inspection Bureau, have the right to claim for replacement with new goods, or for compensation, and all the expenses (such as inspection charges, freight for returning the goods and for sending the replacement, insurance premium, storage and loading and unloading charges) shall be borne by the Sellers. As regards

quality, if, within 12 months from the date of arrival of the goods at destination, damages occur in the course of operation by reason of inferior quality, bad workmanship and the use of inferior materials, the Buyers shall immediately notify the Sellers and put forward a claim supported by Inspection Certificate issued by the China Import and Export Commodity Inspection Bureau. The Certificate so issued shall be accepted as the basis of the claim. The Sellers, in accordance with the Buyers' claim shall be responsible for immediate elimination of the defect(s), or replacement of the defective portion of the shipment, or shall reduce the price according to the state of the defect(s). Where necessary, the Buyer shall be at liberty to eliminate the defect(s) themselves at the Sellers' expense. If the Sellers fail to answer the Buyers within one month after receipt of the claim, the claim shall be reckoned as having been accepted by the Sellers.

15) FORCE MAJEURE: The Seller shall not be held responsible for delay in shipment or non-delivery or the goods due to Force Majeure that has occurred during the process of manufacture or in the course of loading or transit. The Sellers shall advise the Buyers immediately of the occurrence and within fourteen days thereafter, shall send by airmail to the Buyers for their acceptance a certificate of the accident issued by the competent Government Authorities or the Chamber of Commerce of the place where the accident occurs as evidence thereof. Under such circumstances the Sellers, however, are still under the obligation to take all necessary measures to hasten the delivery of the goods. In case the accident lasts for more than 10 weeks, the Buyers shall have the right to cancel the contract.

16) LATE DELIVERY AND PENELTY: Should the Sellers fail to make delivery on time as stipulated in the Contract, with exception of Force Majeure cases as specified in Article 15 of this Contract, the Buyers may agree to postponement of delivery on condition that the Seller agree to pay a penalty which shall be deducted by the paying bank upon negotiation of the L/C. The penalty, however, shall not exceed 20% of the total value of the goods involved in the late delivery. The penalty is charged at the rate of 1% for every seven days, odd days less than seven should be counted as seven days. In case the Sellers fail to make delivery within ten weeks after the time of shipment stipulated in the Contract, the Buyers shall have the right to cancel the Contract and the Sellers, in spite of the cancellation, shall still pay the aforesaid penalty to the Buyers without delay.

17) ARBITRATION: All disputes in connection with the execution of this Contract shall be settled friendly through negotiation. In case no settlement can be reached, the case may then be submitted for arbitration to the Foreign Economic and Trade Arbitration Commission of the China Council for the Promotion of International Trade in accordance with the Provisional Rules of Procedures promulgated by the said Arbitration Commission. The Arbitration shall take place in Beijing and the decision of the Arbitration Commission shall be final and binding upon both parties, neither party shall seek recourse to a law court or other authorities to appeal for revision, of the decision. Arbitration fee shall be

borne by the losing party.

18) SUPPLEMENTARY CONDITION(S): Should any of the articles stipulated in this Contract be in conflict with the following supplementary condition(s), the supplementary condition(s) should be taken as valid and binding.

IN WITNESS THEREOF, this Contract is signed by both parties in two original copies; each party holds one copy.

THE BUYER	THE SELLER
(signature)	(signature)

(3) An employment agreement

EMPIOYMENT AGREEMENT

The Foreign Language Department of the AAA University, Guangdong, China (the engaging party) has engaged Professor Lisa Wang (the engaged party) as a teacher of English and American Literature. The two parties, in the spirit of friendship and cooperation, hereby sign this contract subject to the following terms and conditions:

1) The term of service is one year beginning on September 1, 2009 and ending on August 31, 2010

2) The work of the engaged party is decided through mutual consultation as follows:
   a. Training teachers of English, research students and students having advanced studies;
   b. Conducting senior English and American Literature classes and advising students on extracurricular activities of English;
   c. Compiling English textbooks and supplementary teaching materials;
   d. Having 8 to 10 teaching periods a week.

3) The engaged party works five days a week and seven hours a day. The engaged party will have legal holidays as prescribed by both Chinese and American Governments. The winter vacation is fixed by the school calendar.

4) The engaging party pays the engaged party a monthly salary of RMB 6,000 and provides various benefits as prescribed by the Chinese Government for foreign teachers working in China.

5) The engaged party shall abide by the laws and regulations of the Chinese Government concerning residence, wages and benefits, and travel for foreigners when entering, leaving and passing through the territory of the country, and shall follow the working system of the engaging party.

6) Neither party shall cancel the Contract without reasonable causes.

   If the engaging party finds it imperative to terminate the Contract, then, in addition to bearing the above-mentioned wages and benefits, it shall pay the engaged party three months' extra salary as compensation allowance, and arrange at his own cost for her and her family to go back to their country within one month.

If the engaged party submits her resignation in the course of her service, the engaging party will stop paying her salary from the date when her resignation is approved by the engaging party, and the engaged party will no longer enjoy the benefits. When leaving China, the engaged party and her family will have to pay for everything themselves.

7) This Contract comes into effect on the first day of the engaged party's arrival at the AAA University and ceases to be effective at its expiration.

If either party wishes to renew the Contract, the other party shall be notified in writing one month before it expires. Upon agreement by both parties through consultation, a new contract may be signed between the two parties.

8. This Contract is made in English and Chinese, both versions being equally valid.

The engaging party　　　　The engaged party

(signature)　　　　(signature)

Signed at Guangdong, China on August 10, 2009

New Words and Phrases

preamble [priː'æmbl] *n.* a preliminary statement, especially the introduction to a formal document that serves to explain its purpose 序言

Force Majeure [fɔːsmɑː'ʒɑː(r)] *n.* an unexpected or uncontrollable event 不可抗力，人力不可抗拒

arbitration [ˌɑːbi'treiʃən] *n.* the process by which the parties to a dispute submit their differences to the judgment of an impartial person or group appointed by mutual consent 仲裁

jurisdiction [ˌdʒuəris'dikʃən] *n.* the extent of authority or control 管辖权，控制权

indemnify [in'demnifai] *v.* make compensation for damage, loss, or injury suffered 赔偿，补偿

penalty ['penəlti] *n.* a sum of money, required as a forfeit for an offense 罚金

submit [səb'mit] *v.* to commit (something) to the consideration or judgment of another 将(某事)交于某人来考虑或判断

defect [di'fekt] *n.* the lack of something necessary or desirable for perfection; deficiency 瑕疵，毛病

revision [ri'viʒən] *n.* the act or process of revising 修订，校订，修改

Notes

1. freight prepaid 预付运费

2. freight to collect 到付运费

3. FAS: Free Alongside the Ship 船边交货价

4. where, here, there + preposition

whereas = considering that　鉴于

whereby = by what, by which　凭那个

wherein = in what, in which　在那里,在那点上

whereof = of what, of which　关于那事,关于它

whereon = on what; on which　在那上面

hereafter = after this　在下文

hereby = by means of this; by reason of this　特此

herein = in this　于此;在此中

hereinafter = later in this contract　在下文

hereinbefore = in a preceding part of this contract　在上文

hereof = of this　于此;关于此点

hereto = to this　对此,至此

hereunder = under this　在下面

hereupon = at this point; in consequence of this　关于这个,于是

herewith = with this　以此,同此

thereafter = later in the same contract　以下,在下文

thereon = on that　在其上

thereof = of that　因此

thereto = to that　此外,又

thereupon = then; as the result of that　随后,因此,关于那

5. China Council for the Promotion of International Trade　中国国际贸易促进委员会

6. operating instructions　使用说明书

7. . . . rust attributable to *inadequately or improperly* protective measures taken by the Sellers in regard to the packing.　……由于卖方在包装方面所采用的防护措施不当而产生的锈迹。

In writing contracts, two synonyms are often used together for emphasis.

For example:

1) This Agreement *made* and *entered into* by and between ABC Co. and UVW Co.
ABC 公司和 UVW 公司双方签订本协议。

2) Each party to this Agreement shall *fulfill* or *perform* any of the obligations under this Agreement.　本协议的双方应履行本协议规定的义务。

3) The *amendments to* or *alterations of* this Contract become effective only after they are signed by both parties and approved by the relevant authorities.　本合同的修改,只有在双方签字并经有关主管机关批准后才能生效。

8. Where necessary, the Buyer shall *be at liberty* to eliminate the defect(s) themselves at the Sellers' expense.　必要时,买方有权自行消除缺陷,但费用由卖方承担。

be at liberty: having the right (to do something)　有做……的权利

9. . . . odd days less than seven should be counted as seven days.　……不足 7 天的,将按 7 天

算。

10. the Foreign Economic and Trade Arbitration Commission 对外经济贸易仲裁委员会

11. Provisional Rules of Procedures 仲裁程序暂行规定

12. One negotiable copy of clean on board ocean Bill of Lading marked "FREIGHT PREPAID" indicating shipping mark, made out to order, blank endorsed, and notifying the Buyer. 可转让的清洁已装运海洋提单一套,注明运费已付,说明装运唛头,做成指示提单,空白背书,通知买方。

13. on the strength of 凭借,依赖

14. in witness thereof 以此为证,作为……的证据

Useful Expressions

1. The Contract, made out in Chinese and English, both version being equally authentic, by and between the Seller and the Buyer whereby the Seller agrees to sell and the Buyer agrees to buy the undermentioned goods subject to terms and conditions set forth hereinafter as follows.
2. The shipping space for the contracted goods shall be booked by the Buyer or the Buyer's shipping agent.
3. The age of the carrying vessel chartered by the Seller shall not exceed 15 years. In case her age exceeds 15 years, the extra average insurance premium thus incurred shall be borne by the Seller.
4. The Seller shall maintain close contact with the carrying vessel and shall notify the Buyer by fastest means of communication about any and all accidents that may occur while the carrying vessel is on route.
5. Within 48 hours immediately after completion of loading of goods on board the vessel the Seller shall advise the Buyer by cable or telex of the contract number, the name of goods, weight (net/gross) or quantity loaded, invoice value, name of vessel, port of loading, sailing date and expected time of arrival (ETA) at the port of destination.
6. Should the Buyer be unable to arrange insurance in time owing to the Seller's failure to give the above mentioned advice of shipment by cable or telex, the Seller shall be held responsible for any and all damages and/or losses attributable to such failure.
7. The signed purchase order becomes a part of the contract and have the same legal power as the contract.
8. Any supplementary terms and conditions that may be attached to this Contract shall automatically prevail over the terms and conditions of this Contract.
9. One month prior to the time of shipment the Buyer shall open with the Bank of ______ an irrevocable Letter of Credit in favor of the Seller payable at the issuing bank against presentation of documents as stipulated under Clause 18.
10. 10 – 15 days prior to the date of shipment, the Buyer shall inform the Seller by cable or telex of the contract number, name of vessel, ETA of vessel, quantity to be loaded and the

name of shipping agent, so as to enable the Seller to contact the shipping agent directly and arrange the shipment of the goods.

Exercises

1. Answer the following questions.

1) What should a business person consider when negotiating for a business agreement?

2) What are the major differences between legal documents and routine business letters?

2. Discuss on the following topic.

Some experts of commercial law in the US and Europe call for a reform in the writing of legal documents and advocate the use of simple words and everyday language. As a learner of English as a second language, what is your idea in drafting a business contract?

3. Translate the following clauses from a sales contract into English.

1)本售货确认书项下的货物装船前在装货港由中国商品检验局检验,该商检局出具的质量和数量/重量证明书将是最后的,对双方都有约束力的。

2)货物到达目的港卸货后,买方有权向中华人民共和国进出口商品检验局(中国商检局)或中国进出口商品检验公司(中国商检公司)申请检验。

3)如果发现质量和数量/重量与合同或发票或质量证书不符,买方有权根据中国商检局出具的检验证书在目的港卸货后90天内向卖方提出索赔。赔偿责任在船公司和/或保险公司方面除外。

4)若出现争议,双方应友好协商解决,协商不成时,提交中国海事仲裁委员会仲裁。

5)如果由于卖方没有及时通知而造成买方未能及时办理保险,卖方将承担责任。

6)被雇用方每天正常工作时间为8小时,工作超过8小时,作为加班,加班费按标准工资150%支付。

7)如果聘方中途提出终止合同,除按上述条款承担工资福利待遇外,须给受聘方增发3个月的工资作为补偿。

8)本合同自受聘方到校之日起生效,到聘期届满时失效。

4. Translate the following part of an agreement into Chinese.

AGREEMENT ON EMPLOYMENT

This Agreement is made and entered into this first day of March 2005 between the AA plant, Bamako (hereinafter called Party A) and Mr. Zhang Ming (hereinafter called Party B).

Whereas Party A is willing to employ Party B and Party B agrees to work as Party A's engineer in Bamako, it is hereby mutually agreed as follows:

1) The employment is for a period of two years from July 1, 2005 to June 30, 2007, exactly functioning from the date Party B arrives at the AA Plant and he will return to his country when he has completed his two years service.

2) Party B's monthly salary is USD 2,000.00 which shall be paid monthly in Bamako and can be remitted to China at the discretion of Party B. Party B's housing shall be provided by Party A during the service period.

3) Party B shall be provided by Party A with the air tickets from Guangzhou to Bamako, and from Bamako to Guangzhou upon terminating the service.

4) Party B shall obey the laws and regulations of Mali.

5) This Agreement is made both in English language and Chinese language in duplicate, each of which shall be signed kept by either party.

5. Rewrite the following sentences for exactness and free of ambiguity.

1) The Sellers shall deliver the goods before July 31.

2) Payment shall be made by Party B in 10 days.

3) Party A shall send technicians to train Party B's personnel.

4) The goods are to be shipped by a steamer at a port or ports on the West Coast as per bill or bills of lading dated or to be dated not later than April 30, 2010.

5) Shipment is to be effected bimonthly at 600 metric tons each.

6) All activities of ABC Co. shall be governed by laws and pertinent rules and regulations.

6. Work in groups with two parties of sellers and buyers in each group to negotiate on the terms and conditions given below for a named product and draft a sales or purchase contract.

Name of Commodity
Specification
Quantity
Unit price
Total Price
Packing
Port of shipment
Port of destination
Insurance
Terms of payment
Inspection
Force Majeure
Arbitration

Key to the Exercises

Key to Lesson One

2. Choose the best answer to complete the following statements.

1)D 2)D 3)A 4)A 5)C 6)A 7)D 8)B

3. Decide whether the following statements are true or false. Write "T" for true, and "F" for false.

1)F 2)T 3)F 4)F 5)T 6)T 7)T 8)F

4. Translate the following phrases into Chinese.

1)商务沟通 2)信息交流 3)电话留言 4)达成交易 5)以读者为中心的方式

6)面对面地谈话

6. Fill in the blanks with words and phrases given below. Change the form when necessary.

1)Correspondence 2)punctual 3)eliminated 4)persuasive 5)responded 6)counts

7) enhance 8)refer to 9)irrelevant 10)convenient

7. Translate the following sentences into Chinese.

1)商务函电从广义上讲指的是为商业目的而传递的信息。

2)有效地撰写商业信函能帮助你达成交易,增进客户的满意度,促销产品,维持公司的良好形象和促进工作效率。

3)写商务信函时,避免使用容易混淆、造成误解的含糊词语,冗长的句子,商业套话和陈词滥调。

4)简洁并不是完全使用短句或删除必要的细节,而是要使每个字都有意义。

5)撰写商业信函时,最吸引读者的语气是既友好又有效,让读者感到对方对他们所关心的事情既重视又感兴趣。

6)信文使用好的句子结构、正确的英语语法和单词拼写能够使你以及你的公司给读者留下良好的印象,另外还能使信文通顺流畅,避免误解。

8. Translate the following letter into Chinese.

尊敬的王先生:

感谢您在我们最近到北京访问时对我们的热情款待,这使我们此次访问更加愉快。

我和我的同事对 CBS 出版公司给予中国赠书基金会的帮助深表谢意。显然,我们工作的成功在于能使我们的书到达需要阅读这些书的人们的手中,因此,你们的帮助对于我们的工作是非常必要的。

我们基金会在这次访问中,除了这项有意义的工作外,最大的收获就是结识了远方和附近的朋友,我们很高兴地把你们作为我们最尊敬的朋友。我们不仅期待着将来与你们一起工作,而且希望能够经常享受你们的陪伴。希望早日在加州见到你们。

此致敬礼

马克·约翰逊

9. Revise the following sentences for better effect.

1) Please hand in your application in time so that you will be considered as a candidate.

2) In order to handle your case properly, please give us all the relevant information.

3) Please fill in the form provided in our questionnaire.

4) Please bring your résumé when you come for an interview.

5) You will get 10% discount if you make payment within a week.

6) We have direct cargo services from Shanghai to San Francisco twice a month.

7) You will find that I'm the right person for the job with my excellent school record and one-year work experience in this field.

8) You will get a discount for the purchase though our goods are well received in the market.

9) We have put off the meeting till next week.

10) Both parties must observe the rules and regulations.

11) This kind of goods shouldn't be loaded on deck.

12) The windows must be shut properly before you leave the office.

13) Your order can be filled next month.

14) Wool sweaters cannot be washed in hot water.

15) Your machine can be repaired tomorrow.

Key to Lesson Two

3. Decide whether the following statements are true or false. Write "T" for true and "F" for false.

1) F 2) F 3) F 4) T 5) F 6) T 7) F 8) F

4. Choose the best answer to complete the following statements.

1) D 2) D 3) C 4) A 5) D 6) B 7) B 8) C

5. Translate the following sentences into English.

1) Much business communication now occurs electronically, and this trend is certain to increase.

2) Electronic commerce is altering not only traditional styles of communication, but also the nature of the workplace itself.

3) With electronic communication, a manager can, at any place other than his/her office, compose a message that will be on the boss's or subordinate's electronic desks the next morning.

4) Faxes can overcome the barrier of different time zones, and, moreover, it can transmit the original document.

5) Internet electronic commerce can enhance customer service by electronically providing infor-

mation about product specification, quantity and price.

6) One of the advantages of e-mail is that when someone is saying something you are not interested and you prefer not to respond, it is easier not to respond their e-mail than not to answer their telephone.

7) The business manager decided to install a message filter to deal with the large number of junk e-mail messages received every day.

8) Most of the consumers of our company's products are young people, their age ranges from 15 to 25.

6. Translate the following sentences into Chinese.

1) 市场全球化要求商业伙伴及买卖双方在国际贸易工作中配合更加密切,交流更加频繁。但是他们通常都分布在世界各地,他们之间的信息交流常常需要穿越国界和时区。

2) 幸运的是高科技提供了更多的快捷便利的长途通信媒介,供人们选择。但这并不意味着你可以随便选择。

3) 为了提高沟通效率,有必要很好地选择沟通媒介。

4) 电子邮件信息可根据情况和读者灵活使用,它既可像信件一样正式,也可以像备忘录和便条那样不正式。

5) 文本信息经过分解、版面设计和顺序安排,供人们在线浏览。网页应按照世界各地不同的读者来编辑,通过网页中的某些窗口、菜单或电子邮件使读者能够输入他们的信息,以达到互动交流。

6) 网页可包含照片、图表和文本,提供有关公司、业务、产品规格、数量、价格、服务等的详细介绍。但是网页上的信息不是专为某一个人编辑的,而是为网络上的公众和目标群体编辑的。

7) 同时,超级链接能够使不同的读者在不同的地域最大限度地根据个人的取舍控制阅读内容。读者还可以下载和打印网页上提供的信息和文件。

8) 人们再也不会像过去那样只能依赖有线电话,互相写信或在紧急情况下发电报来进行沟通了。

Key to Lesson Three

2. Choose the best answer to complete the following statements.

1) D 2) C 3) A 4) B 5) A 6) B 7) A 8) A 9) C 10) A

3. Decide whether the following statements are true or false. Write "T" for true, and "F" for false.

1) F 2) F 3) T 4) F 5) F 6) T 7) F 8) T 9) F 10) T

4. Translate the following massage into English and write it in an appropriate letter format.

Dear Mr. Jones,

As you know, the Chinese Textile Exhibition will be held at the National Exhibition Centre, London, from October 14th – 30th. Should you or one of your colleagues wish to visit this interesting event, please let me know so that I will arrange to send a ticket.

Since I will not have an office at the centre throughout the exhibition period, if you would let me know in advance the date and approximate time of any intended visit, I will make arrangement to receive you.

Sincerely yours,

TIANJIN TEXTILE IMP. & EXP CORP. (LONDON OFFICE)

(*Signature*)

Zhang Shao-hua

Key to Lesson Four

2. Choose the best answer to complete the following statements.

1) D 2) B 3) C 4) A 5) D 6) B 7) D 8) D

3. Decide whether the following statements are true or false. Write "T" for true, and "F" for false.

1) T 2) T 3) T 4) F 5) F 6) T 7) T 8) T 9) T 10) T

4. Translate the following sentences into Chinese.

1) 如需要进一步信息请用下列地址与我联系。

2) 备忘录的主题应精炼,使忙碌的同事对信文内容一目了然。

3) 如果备忘录要用第二页,其标头的格式与信件相同。

4) 电子邮件可以如同正式的信件,也可以简单得像内部备忘录,你可自己选择。

5) 图文并茂比只有文字更吸引人。

6) 一个网站包含体现公司特点和性质的文字和艺术设计。

7) 新视野电力有限公司是1987年建成的,在证券交易所上市的公司,公司业务包括设计、制造、销售和安装再生能源设备。

8) 本公司是位于中国的再生能源公司,拥有富有经验和努力工作的员工。

Key to Lesson Five

2. Choose the best answer to complete the following statements.

1) A 2) B 3) C 4) C 5) D 6) C 7) A 8) D

3. Decide whether the following statements are true or false. Write "T" for true, and "F" for false.

1) F 2) F 3) T 4) T 5) T 6) F 7) T 8) T 9) F 10) F

4. Translate the following sentence segments into English.

1) An entry-level position responsible for computer programming

2) Administrative assistant to a high-level executive that needs the skill of short-hand and typing

3) A position that will give full play to my educational background in biology, and with a prospect of promotion

4) A position that utilize my ability of creative writing

5) Responsible for human resources management

6) A position in Foreign Trade Department, with opportunities for advancement to management position in the department

7) An administrative secretarial position where communication skills and a pleasant attitude toward people are assets.

8) A position as a design engineer in an engineering department

9) Seeking a position as a computer programmer in a medium-size firm

10) To serve as sales representative in a multinational corporation, willing to work short-term or long-term abroad at any time

5. Translate the following sentence segments into Chinese.

1) 管理的职位,该职位能充分发挥我的进取精神及创造能力

2) 行政助理的职位,能运用我在办公室管理方面的兴趣与经验

3) 为电器设备排除故障和修理损坏的部件

4) 财务或投资领域需运用分析技巧的职务

5) 从当会计见习开始,最后成为经理

6) 资料处理经理的职务,使我能够运用电脑系统的知识

7) 工商管理硕士和生物技术高等学位

8) 为人正直,有团队合作精神

6. Change the following sentences into phrases and sentence segments, adapting them to a résumé.

1) developed and conducted formal classes for groups of 50 to 500 people;
Gave lectures, used audiovisual aids, hands-on exercises, and extensive question-and-answer in my sessions

2) monitored job performance
gave on-the-spot training

3) writing sales and fund-raising letters for a variety of products
having organizing experiences for sales campaign

4) launched advertising campaign for Five Star pencils
presented the pencils in a fresh way to consumers
increased sale by 20%

5) set short-term goals to achieve manager's long-term goals
motivated employees to reach them
ordered parts for repair shop and sales department
assigned daily duties to store employees

6) analyzed available data to determine opponents' size, strength, capabilities, and plans
Received six months' intensive training in collecting, analyzing, and reporting data from multiple sources

Analyzed protocol, content, and electronic signature of radio signals to determine size, activity, type, and location of broadcasting unit

Key to Lesson Six

3. Decide whether the following statements are true or false. Write "T" for true, and "F" for false in the brackets.

1)F 2)T 3)F 4)F 5)T 6)F 7)F 8)T 9)F 10)T

4. Choose the best expression from each of the following groups of sentences of A, B, C and D for om application letter.

1)B 2)B 3)D 4)D

5. Choose the best answer to complete the following statements.

1)A 2)A 3)B 4)A

6. Translate the following phrases and make sentences with them.

1) to kindly grant me an interview
2) to attach (or enclose) a résumé
3) a copy of my transcript is enclosed
4) to apply for the position
5) to start at the bottom
6) to specialize in accounting at college
7) to fill in as one of your office staff
8) a letter of recommendation

7. Filling in the blanks with the words and phrases given below.

1) consultant 2) informed 3) leadership 4) position 5) demonstrate 6) candidate 7) experience 8) effectively 9) opportunity 10) contact

8. Translate the following sentences into English.

1) With reference to your advertisement in China Daily of May 2, I offer myself for the post of marketing research.
2) My fluency in English and French can be surely used for business negotiations and translation.
3) I have been in the business for the last ten years, and worked as the superintendent in the personnel department.
4) At school I won a scholarship and the first prize in speech contest.
5) I am a graduate of Hong Kong University, and have, in addition, a M. A. degree from UCLA (University of California, Los Angeles).
6) Enclosed please find my résumé and a letter of recommendation from my former teacher of English.
7) Throughout my college education, I have gained knowledge and experience in advertising both in the classroom and through work experience.
8) I would like to have an interview to go into greater detail about my abilities.
9) Being well acquainted with office works, I could contribute to your company should there be any vacancy requiring my services.
10) If you could give me an interview, I shall be on call at anytime between 11:00 a. m. to 10:00 p. m.

Keys to Lesson Seven

2. Choose the best answer to complete the following statements.

1) C 2) B 3) C 4) C 5) A 6) B 7) C 8) A 9) B 10) D

3. Decide whether the following statements are true or false. Write "T" for true, and "F" for false in the brackets.

1) T 2) F 3) F 4) F 5) T 6) F 7) F 8) F

4. Translate the terms and expressions from Chinese into English and use them in making sentences.

1) trade directory
2) financial standing
3) Chamber of Commerce
4) after-sale service
5) enter into business relations with
6) fall within the business scope of
7) leading exporter
8) place a trial order

5. Translate the terms and expressions from English into Chinese and use them in making sentences.

1) 打开市场,畅销
2) 商务参赞处
3) 另封邮寄
4) 商品交易会
5) 有意购买
6) 借此机会

6. Filling in the blanks with the words and phrases given below, and change the form when necessary.

1) learn 2) in the market for 3) falls/comes 4) enter 5) through 6) enjoy 7) acquaint 8) under 9) Upon receipt of 10) offer

7. Translate the following sentences from Chinese into English.

1) Your firm has been recommended to us by the Chamber of Commerce, London, England.

2) This is to introduce ourselves as one of the main exporter of Chinese textile goods having many years' experience in this particular line of business, and we hope to establish trade relations with you.

3) We thank you for your letter of September 10 and would like to discuss the possibility of initiating business on the following items.

4) We enclose a catalogue and a pricelist to acquaint you with our commodities now available for export.

5) Your letter addressed to the Commercial Counselor's Office of our Embassy in Pakistan has been forwarded to us for attention, as we exclusively handle the export of this article.

6) We are informed that you are potential buyers of Chinese Green Tea, which falls within the business scope of our corporation.

7) We owe your name and address to your Chamber of Commerce.

8) Our products are sold in many countries and enjoy good reputation on the world market.

9) Our company started its snack food in 1966 and now has become one of the largest multina-

tional snack food companies in the world with branches in more than 40 countries.

10) The company is one of the leading retailers of children's products in local area, specializing in toys, children's cloths and baby care.

8. Translate the following sentences from English into Chinese.

1) 我们从中国驻伦敦大使馆商会得到你公司的名称和地址。

2) 希望与贵公司在平等互利、互通有无的基础上建立贸易联系。

3) 约翰·史密斯先生向我们介绍,贵公司是你地区家具业的主要进口商。

4) 承蒙东方实业有限公司的介绍,我们了解到贵公司有意与我公司建立业务关系,以便进口我方的瓷器。

5) 我们专门经营远东地区的轻工业品出口,但与贵公司没有贸易联系。现给你方写信,希望建立直接业务关系。

6) 我们是高级衣料进口商,并且每年在欧洲市场有大量需求。

7) 我们公司与这里所有大的轻工业品经销商有良好的关系。我们确信如果价格适中,我们能够使你们的产品在市场上畅销。

8) 我们的业务银行是香港汇丰银行,他们可以向你方提供有关我方业务及资金的情况。

9. Translate the following passage of company introduction into Chinese.

约翰·迪尔

1837 年,约翰·迪尔创立了这家后来以他的名字命名的公司。1868 年,迪尔公司正式组建。今天,它已从只有一个人的铁匠铺发展为业务遍及全球并拥有约 47 000 名员工的跨国公司,成为美国历史上最为悠久的工业企业之一。

时至今日,公司仍然秉承其创立者约翰·迪尔所确立的核心价值:诚实、品质、信守承诺和创新。

Key to Lesson Eight

3. Choose the best answer for each of the statement.

1) D 2) C 3) A 4) D 5) D 6) C 7) C 8) A

4. Decide whether the following statements are true or false. Write "T" for true, and "F" for false in the brackets provided.

1) T 2) F 3) T 4) F 5) T 6) T 7) T 8) T

5. Translate the terms and expressions form Chinese into English.

1) status inquiry 2) credit reference 3) business extent 4) chamber of commerce

5) turnover rate

6. Translate the terms and expressions from English into Chinese.

1) 财务状况 2) 资信调查机构 3) 最大数目的赊账 4) 严格保密 5) 履行义务的信誉

8. Filling in the blanks with the words and phrases given below.

1) order 2) credit 3) reference 4) helpful 5) evaluate 6) appreciate 7) information

8) confidential 9) enclosing 10) reply

9. Translate the following sentences into Chinese.

1) 为了把风险降到最低,查询你打算建立业务关系的公司的资信情况是至关重要的。

2)若所提供的资信证明人为银行,你必须通过你的所在银行向相关银行进行调查。

3)如果您能够通过该银行给我们提供 James Smith & Co 的资信记录,我们将十分感谢。

4)主要情况将包括:Donna Gard 在花旗银行开立账户有多久,是否有任何未偿还的债务。

5)该公司有着一个相当好的资信记录,而且到目前,没有任何未偿债务。

6)我们已经收到我们一个客户的咨询,询问有关 VLD 有限公司的财务状况和经营信誉。

7)我们建议您通知您的客户与 Kasu Trading Corp 进行业务往来时一定要十分慎重。

8)所提供的上述情况仅供个人参考,我们对此不负任何责任。

9)供你参考,去年一年里我们曾同这家商行做过几笔半导体生意,全部用信用证支付。

10)我们相信,他们之所以能在我们地区批发商中享有盛誉,要归功于他们经营业务的稳妥和诚实。

10. Translate the following sentences into English.

1) Would you kindly send us the names of firms or a bank to whom reference can be made.

2) You may contact any Bank of Commerce in your city for information concerning our credit standing.

3) The above account has recently applied to our firm for credit terms, and listed you as credit reference.

4) As to our credit standing, we would like to refer you to the Bank of China.

5) We should be obliged if you could let us have your opinion on this firm's reputation and their financial standing.

6) We would appreciate your providing us with any relevant information you might have.

7) Would you kindly tell us your opinion of their reliability and the amount of credit which could be safely extended to them?

8) We can assure you that any information you may supply will be regarded as strictly confidential.

9) We enclose an addressed envelope for your reply and thank you for your favor.

10) This is a highly reputable and trustworthy firm with sound financial status and is punctual in payment. Any credit you extend to them will be safe.

Key to Lesson Nine

2. Choose the best answer to complete the following statements.

1)C 2)B 3)D 4)A 5)D 6)B 7)A 8)C

3. Decide whether the following statements are true or false. Write "T" for true, and "F" for false.

1)T 2)F 3)F 4)F 5)F 6)F 7)T 8)T

4. Translate the following terms into Chinese, and then explain them in English.

1)一般询价 An inquiry about the general information of a certain product.

2)具体询价 An inquiry about the specific information of a certain product.

3)询价单 A written document about the price and the purchase terms for certain products the buyer intends to buy.

4) 网上询价　An inquiry for the price and purchase of products made online.

5) 形式发票　An invoice for form's sake. It is issued before the buyer's payment for the goods mainly for the following purposes: (1) to serve as a formal quotation or as a price reference; (2) to enable the buyer to make the necessary preliminary arrangements, such as obtaining an import license for the goods he would like to order; (3) to inform the buyer of the amount payable for goods to be shipped.

5. Translate the following phrases into English.

1) after-sales service　　2) food ingredients

3) edible oil　　4) a full range of products

5) artificial leather　　6) substitute products

7) import license　　8) confirmed irrevocable letter of credit

9) business day　　10) most favorable price

6. Filling in the blanks with the words and phrases given below.

(1) exporter　interested　quotation　specifications　place

(2) inquiry　enter　reference　discount　sight

7. Translate the following sentences into English.

1) We have received your letter of October 23 and are glad that you are interested in our silk products. Attached please find a price list and catalogue as requested.

2) We allow a 5% discount for an order exceeding 100 units.

3) Please specify in the quotation the specifications of the products and other relevant information, and please mail the samples without delay.

4) We accept payment by L/C. Shipment will be made 20 days after receipt of the covering L/C at sight.

5) If your prices are more favorable than other competitors we shall send you our order.

6) Here is the catalogue of this season and it will give you a rough idea about our products.

7) Would you tell us the quantity you want so that we can work out an offer?

8) Please keep us informed of the latest quotations for the following items.

8. Translate the following sentences into Chinese.

1) 请报给我方伦敦到岸价的最低价格，并注明最早装运日期及你方所能给予的折扣。

2) 感谢你方5月15日询问我方空调产品的来函。但是很遗憾你方所要货物目前没有现货。

3) 由于此货物需求量很大，很难满足你方规定的发货时间。但是如果你方能在本周之内订货，我们可以保证4月15日前装运。

4) 如果你方能提供满足下列规格和品质的货物，我们可以定期大量订货。

5) 应你方7月4日来函要求，现寄去我方报价单及有关产品的具体信息和其他销售条件。

6) 这是我方纽约到岸价报价单。请注意单上所列价格的有效期于本月底结束。

7) 如果价格优惠我们可能会大量订货。

8) 感谢你方询价。随函附上我方最新的产品目录及上海到岸价报价单。

Key to Lesson Ten

3. Choose the best answer to complete the following statements.

1)A 2)B 3)B 4)C 5)D 6)B 7)B 8)C 9)A 10)B

4. Decide whether the following statements are true or false. Write "T" for true, and "F" for false in the brackets provided.

1)T 2)F 3)T 4)T 5)T 6)T 7)T 8)T 9)T 10)F

6. Filling in the blanks with the words and phrases given below. Change the form when necessary.

1) as follows 2) provided that 3) remain open 4) in line with
5) owing to 6) subjects to 7) to our regret 8) reduce
9) discount 10) acceptance

7. Translate the following sentences from Chinese into English.

1) In compliance with your request, we now quote you subject to our final confirmation for the following prices.

2) This offer will be withdrawn if not accepted within 7 days.

3) The offer is subject to your reply reaching us before the end of the month.

4) We find your quotation slightly higher than those we have received from other sources, and would ask you to reduce your price so as to make it competitive with other supplier.

5) Unfortunately we cannot accept your offer because other suppliers in your market offered us similar article at a price 3% lower than yours.

6) Your price is quite in line with the market, but the time of shipment is too distant.

7) It is in view of your long-standing business relationship with us that we make you such a offer.

8) Your counter-offer is much too low for an order of a small amount.

9) Our products are superior to similar products on the market and are very popular in recent years for its unique design, fashionable style, and reasonable prices.

10) You will enjoy 20% discount if your order exceeds 600.

8. Translate the following sentences from English into Chinese.

1)你在做价格对比时所参考的折扣价只适用于批量购买。

2)这些产品的利润很薄,任何降价都会使生意失去意义。

3)我们从此地的零售商处得知,本地大型百货商场的空调价格又下降了3%。

4)如果你们的订货量能翻一倍,我们将乐于与你讨论批量订货的折扣问题。

5)随函寄去我们的报价,此报价有效期仅为两周。

6)我们愿尽一切所能帮助你方开展新的业务,所以如你能在一个月内付款,我们准备给你方3%特别折扣。

7)感谢你方12月23日的来信,要求我方对2月运往新加坡的10000公吨标题小麦报盘。

8)我们收到了你方6月4日对我们电子玩具的询价,现向你方报盘如下,供你参考。

9)很遗憾,我们不能接受你方报盘,因为我们从其他渠道获得的类似质量产品的报价比你方的低6%。

10)考虑到我们所提供的箱子的质量,我们认为所报价格一点都不高,但是鉴于我们之间的长期业务关系,我们决定对你方超过2万美元的订货给予2%的特别折扣。

Key to Lesson Eleven

2. Decide whether the following statements are true or false. Write "T" for true, and "F" for false in the brackets.

1)T 2)T 3)F 4)T 5)T 6)T 7)T 8)F

3. Choose the best answer to complete the following statements.

1)C 2)A 3)A 4)D 5)B 6)D 7)A 8)A 9)A 10)A

4. Write out the full forms of the abbreviated payment methods and give the equivalent terms in Chinese.

Abbreviation	Full Form	Chinese
M/T	Mail Transfer	信汇
T/T	Telegraph Transfer	电汇
L/C	Letter of Credit	信用证
D/A	Document against Acceptance	承兑交单
D/P	Document against Payment	付款交单

6. Translate the following sentences into English.

1) We have carefully considered your proposal for easier payment terms. In view of the friendly relations of years of cooperation we decide to accept D/P at sight for the payment of the goods under your Order No. AC500.

2) As the stock is limited and the price is going to increase, please order as soon as possible.

3) We will be grateful if you could extend this favor to us.

4) Please get the following documents in order, so that we will be able to negotiate to the Bank of China.

5) We enclose the invoice for your Order No. 1456K which has been shipped per S. S. "Gold Star". Please give our draft due honor when presented to you by your bank.

6) According to the agreement between us, we have drawn on you at sight against this shipment through Bank of China here, please pay the draft upon presentation.

7) As the price of your leather shoes is acceptable, we are going to place a trial order with you if you agree with the terms of payment of D/P.

8) We accept the price in your offer for Men's Shirt, and now are applying for import license. We shall open the L/C soon after we receive the import license.

9) As the amount of money to be paid for the goods is large, it is difficult for us to accept pay-

ment by D/P, please accept L/C at 60 days sight.

10) Payment is to be made against sight draft drawn under a confirmed, irrevocable L/C for the full amount.

7. Translate the following passage into Chinese.

每个出口商都会遇到收款的问题,即使在富裕国家中也会出现买方不付货款的风险,如进口商破产,或政府不允许进口商购买支付货款所需的货币。此外,还有信贷风险,卖方要求预付货款,而买方没有资金,要求贷款。卖方必须提供好的(对买方有利的)支付方式,否则就会因客户寻求其他供应商而失去客户。汇率以及支付货币币值的变化也会导致问题,货币贬值,出口商就会赔钱。买卖双方都期待对方保证履约,出口商要求按时收到全部货款,进口商要求按时收到全部货物。解决这些问题的办法是让银行充当顾问。

Key to Lesson Twelve

2. Choose the best words or phrases to complete the following sentences.

1) A 2) B 3) A 4) B 5) C 6) D 7) B 8) C 9) B 10) A

3. Decide whether the following statements are true or false. Write "T" for true, and "F" for false in the brackets.

1) T 2) F 3) F 4) T 5) T 6) F 7) T 8) T

4. Translate the following sentence into Chinese.

1) 收到信用证后,出口商必须彻底检查所有的条款,以便确保他们与销售合同所规定的条款完全一致,因为任何的不符之处,甚至是很小的一些出入,如果不及时更正都有可能给出口方带来困难,或者不能够从议付银行得到货款。

2) 信用证是银行在进口方的要求下所签发的信函,在此函中,银行许诺在买方提交有关单据后付款。

3) 出口商审核信用证后才把出口货物交给承运人,承运人收到货物后出具提单。

4) 如果信用证可以由原受益人转让给另一个或几个人,那么这种信用证即为可转让信用证。原受益人称做第一受益人,接受转让的称做第二受益人。

5) 对于一笔具体交易来说,信用证不一定是最理想的付款方式。缔约双方应根据具体情况做出最好的选择。

6) 买方可能不了解卖方,而且卖方的商业可信度可能值得怀疑。

7) 由于贵方通常总是能够及时结清账目,而此次已逾期一月,我方仍然未能收到贵方上述账目的欠款,我们想知道是否有一些特殊的原因。

8) 付款方式灵活能够方便买方,同时也无疑会给你带来更多的订单。

9) 我们已完成对贵方5月18日来函提及的公司的各项调查,必须建议您审慎考虑与他们的任何交易。

10) 当出口方和进口方相互信赖,并且交易额不大时,可以考虑使用电汇方式付款。

5. Translate the following sentences into English.

1) Please send us the extended L/C before March 28 in order to ship the goods at the above time.

2) We are sorry that owning to the delay on the part of our suppliers at the place of origin, the captioned goods are not ready till the end of this month.

3) In international trade time is critical, so it is natural that the buyer usually insists that shipment be made before a specified deadline or within a period of time.

4) As the manufactures are heavily committed, we can only promise to effect shipment in March.

5) Our rules don't allow us to accept other payment terms except L/C, although the buyer has had two or three deals with us before.

6) The exporter, namely, beneficiary will make a careful examination of all the contents of the credit and will request the applicant to make amendments to any discrepancies in the credit so as to ensure safe and timely payment.

7) In executing a contract, both sides should abide by the stipulations in the contract. If one party fails to fulfill the obligations, it will bring inconvenience or even loss to the other party.

8) Either because the credit amount is too large, or because the exporter does not fully trust the opening bank, the exporter may sometimes require confirmed letter of credit

9) Letters of credit vary in form, length, language and stipulations depending on the different nature of the goods and the practice of different banks.

10) Time of shipment will be in July 15 ~ 18 provided the L/C reach the seller on/before June 15.

Keys to Lesson Thirteen

3. Choose the best answer to complete the following statements.

1) B 2) A 3) B 4) D 5) C 6) C 7) A 8) B 9) B 10) A

4. Decide whether the following statements are true or false. Write "T" for true, and "F" for false in the brackets.

1) F 2) F 3) T 4) T 5) F 6) T 7) F 8) F

5. Translate the terms and expressions and make sentences with each of them.

1) 野蛮搬运 2) 适合海运的 3) 中性包装 4) 防水的

5) 远离锅炉 6) 内衬 7) 易腐烂的 8) 唛头

6. Fill in the blanks with the words and phrases given below and change the form when necessary.

1) in perfect condition 2) rest assured 3) rough handling 4) be liable for

5) delay 6) appreciate 7) is lined with 8) catches the eye

7. Translate the following sentences into English.

1) Cartons, as a kind of container, have been widely used in international trade. Don't worry about the seaworthiness.

2) The towels under the captioned contract should be packed in plastic bags, each containing half a dozen in single color, 10 plastic bags to a cardboard box.

3) Your packing should be seaworthy and able to withstand rough handling in transit.

4) The packing should meet the preference of our market.

5) We have conveyed your opinion about packing to the manufacturer and they agree to adopt your suggestion for next shipment.

6) We have especially reinforced our packing in order to minimize possible damage to the goods.

7) The canned goods are to be packed in cartons with double straps.

8) On the outer packing, please mark the wording, "Handle with Care".

9) Unless otherwise instructed, please mark all the boxes as usual.

10) I'm afraid you have to pay extra expenses for your designated packing, as it needs more labor and cost.

8. Translate the following sentences into Chinese.

1)如果纸箱不够结实,恐怕大部分货物到达时都会破损。

2)所有唛头都应根据我方要求印刷。

3)除非我方另有指令,请用同上批货物一样的包装。

4)我方可以按你方要求用木箱包装,但额外包装费应由你方承担。

5)请在箱上按合同规定印上唛头。

6)机器包装必须防湿、防潮、防锈、防震。

7)你们对包装的意见将转达给厂商。

8)我们的包装可以与日本同行相媲美。

Key to Lesson Fourteen

2. Choose the best answer to complete the following statements.

1)D 2)D 3)A 4)B 5)A 6)C 7)C 8)D 9)C 10)D

3. Decide whether the following statements are true or false. Write "T" for true, and "F" for false in the brackets.

1)T 2)F 3)T 4)T 5)F 6)T 7)T 8)F 9)T 10)T

4. Translate the following letter into English.

Dear Mr. Simpson:

500 SEWING MACHINGS

We refer to Contract No. HK8899 between us on 12th March, 2010 for 500 SEWING MACHINGS, which is stipulated for shipment in May, 2010. However, up to now we have not received from you any information concerning this lot. As our end users are in urgent need of the machines, we intend to send our vessel S. S. "Sea Flower" to pick up the goods, which is expected to arrive at your port around the end of May. You are requested to let us have your immediate reply by fax whether you are agreeable to this proposal. If not, please let us know exactly the earliest time when the goods will be ready.

The delay in delivery has put us in great inconvenience. In case you fail to effect delivery by May, we will have to lodge a claim against you for loss and reserve the right to cancel the contract.

Yours sincerely,

5. Translate the following passage into Chinese.

在国际贸易中,海运是一种使用最普遍的运输方式。例如,我国80%以上的出口货物是由远洋船运输的。最重要的海运单据是提单。提单是由运载货物的船只的船长或其代理签署的一种单据,证明货物已收讫装船,状况良好,适合于提单规定的运输和交货。

货物装船后,船运公司的职员或代理签署提单,注明货物"收讫,表面完好无损"。换句话说,装船货物必须和提单上所写的毫无差别。装船的箱子必须没有损坏,如果有包或袋的话,不应有破损或脏污。装液体的桶不应碰瘪或渗漏。货物的件数和种类必须和提单上注明的相符。

如果提单上所写的和货物的实际情况有出入,船运公司就不得不在提单上加注批语,说明货物损坏和损失的实际情况。在这种情况下,提单不再是清洁提单,代表进口商的银行可能不接受这种提单,所以出口商的银行可能收不回货款。为此,必须不惜任何代价避免"不洁"或加有"批注"的提单,出口商必须确保货物抵达码头时完好无损。

Key to Lesson Fifteen

2. Decide whether the following statements are true or false. Write "T" for true, and "F" for false.

1)F 2)F 3)T 4)F 5)T 6)T 7)T 8)T 9)T 10)F

3. Choose the best answer to complete the following statements.

1)A 2)B 3)D 4)C 5)C 6)C 7)B 8)A

4. Translate the following sentences into English.

1) Risks other than All Risks and War Risks can be arranged, if the insurance company accepts, but the extra premium should be borne by the buyer.

2) Regarding insurance, the coverage is for 110% of invoice value up to the port of destination.

3) Generally we cover insurance WPA and War Risk in the absence of definite instructions from our clients. If you desire to cover All Risks, we can provide such coverage at a slightly higher premium.

4) Our present premium for the proposed shipment against all risks including war risks is 0.50% subject to our Ocean Marine Cargo Clauses, copies of which are enclosed for your reference.

5) Referring to our Order No. 3306 for 200 computers on CIF basis, we wish you to arrange All Risks insurance for us.

6) In our opinion, this type of coverage is necessary for the comparatively valuable and fragile cargo.

7) This is to acknowledge receipt of your letter dated March 6th, requesting us to effect insurance on the captioned shipment for 130% of the invoice value.

8) If you desire, we can arrange broader coverage on condition that the extra premium involved

is for buyer's account.

9) We regularly ship bottled beer to Singapore by cargo liner of the International Shipping Line. Will you please issue us an open policy on All Risks for the shipment?

10) We wish to know whether you can issue a special rate in return for our promise of regular monthly shipment.

5. Translate the passage into Chinese.

保险的历史可以追溯到12世纪,据说当时在意大利的北方已经存在着海运保险。在14世纪,意大利商人来到了英国,随之也带来了保护他们的船只和货物的保险制度。在那个年代,当然还没有保险公司;商人们总是聚在一起,共同保证偿付在风暴中遭受损失的或被海盗抢劫的船只或货物,并在保证书下面签字画押,这就是"underwriter"(在下面签署的人)一词的来源。如果船只沉没,经济损失由大家分摊,而不是由哪一个商人单独出资承担所有的风险。

Key to Lesson Sixteen

3. Choose the best answer to complete the following statements.

1)D 2)A 3)C 4)D 5)B 6)D 7)D 8)C 9)A 10)C

4. Decide whether the following statements are true or false. Write "T" for true, and "F" for false.

1)F 2)F 3)F 4)T 5)T 6)T 7)T 8)F 9)F 10)F

5. Fill in the blanks with the following words in their appropriate form.

1) breakage 2) loss 3) finding 4) inspector 5) shortage 6) examination 7) handling 8) storage 9) liability

7. Translate the following letter into Chinese and write a letter of reply to settle the problem.

布朗先生:

作为与贵公司合作三年的客户,看到贵公司为我们的宣传活动制作的印刷品,我们感到非常失望。

按照书面协议规定,我们期待得到全部彩色页面,并配以精彩的说明,可是我们发现活页宣传品中包括了黑白照片。

请派一名摄影师来为我们拍摄你们所承诺的彩色页面,不然就给我们退款。

此致敬礼

托马斯 R. 史密斯厂长

8. Translate the following letter into English.

Dear Sir:

The 100 Coffee Sets supplied to the above order were delivered yesterday. But we regret that 15 sets were badly damaged.

The packages containing the coffee sets appeared to be in good condition and we accepted and signed for them. We unpacked the boxes with great care and found there were not enough shock-proof pads. We assume this is the cause for the damage.

We hope you will replace the 15 sets as soon as you can. Meanwhile we have put the damaged coffee sets aside in case you need them to support a claim to your suppliers for compensation.

Yours sincerely,

Key to Lesson Seventeen

3. Decide whether the following statements are true or false. Write "T" for true, and "F" for false.

1)F 2)F 3)F 4)T 5)F 6)F 7)T 8)F 9)T 10)T

4. Choose the best answer to complete the following statements.

1)A 2)B 3)C 4)D 5)D 6)A 7)B 8)B 9)D 10)C

7. Translate the following sentences into English.

1) We found that the damage to the goods was caused by heavy rain during transportation.

2) If not for these difficulties, there is little doubt that the delivery terms would have been observed.

3) We regret to find that 85 bags of the goods delivered to you are not in conformity with the original sample.

4) Our company cannot be held liable to the matter of short weight, please file your claim to your shipping agency to cover the loss.

5) Please send us samples of the damaged goods for our detailed examination before we find a settlement to the matter.

6) We will take effective measures to prevent such things from happening again.

7) The cause of the damage to the goods cannot be proved for lack of evidence.

8) Only when both parties have agreed on all terms and conditions, can they sign the contract.

9) We assure you that we'll settle the claim equitably and fairly.

(or: We assure you of our just and fairness in settling your claim.)

10) We must apologize to you for not having given you news earlier about your present order.

8. Translate the following sentences into Chinese.

1)收到索赔信时首先要详细地分析和调查这个索赔是否合理,是否在你赔偿责任范围之内。

2)有时买方故意对货物挑毛病,因为他们不再想要这批货物,或者因为他们可以从其他地方买到更低价的。

3)至于380号货物,它们是用更薄的衣料制成的,更适合夏季穿着。如果你们有意销售,我们将提供特价,每件10美元。

4)该货物是在装船前两天由声望很高的ABC商检公司检验的,商检证书和清洁提单都表明货物装船时是完好的。

5)工厂罢工的确是我们无法预料的,而且我们也无法控制,所以我们不应当对此事负法律责任。

6)我们将立即给贵方更换发错的货物,即:发送365号货物来替换375号货物。货物在本月底前抵达旧金山。

7)我们很抱歉不能接受你方对咖啡器皿的索赔,因没有充分的证据证明你们的抱怨,即这项损坏是由于装卸不慎所造成的。

8)凡与执行本合同有关的一切争执,均应通过友好协商解决。

9)我们很抱歉不得不把此案提交仲裁。

10)争论要点似乎是延迟交货的原因是否应被看做是无法预料的情况。

Key to Lesson Eighteen

3. Translate the terms and expressions from Chinese into English.

1) sales letters 2) solicit business 3) potential customer 4) target customer

5) sales promotion

5. Choose the best answer for each of the statement.

1) D 2) D 3) A 4) C 5) D 6) A 7) D 8) B

6. Decide whether the following statements are true or false. Write "T" for true, and "F" for false in the brackets.

1) T 2) T 3) T 4) F 5) T 6) T 7) T 8) T

7. Translate the following sentences into English.

1) You are cordially invited to this session of fashion show, in which our latest collection of cashmere sweaters is displayed at No. 38 exhibition stand.

2) Now, all your troubles are over with the "Worldwide Encyclopedia" which has all the answers you'll ever need!

3) We will offer you 10% discount on the retail price of our radios. If your purchase is over 1,000 sets, we will consider offering you a higher discount.

4) Thank you for your friendly cooperation. Please fill in the questionnaire attached, and send it back to us in order for us to be informed of your customers' satisfaction.

5) We regret that nothing has been heard from you since your order of 500 cameras in July. If there are any difficulties in your sales please inform us. We'll do everything we can for your satisfaction.

6) Our new factory has started to produce electronic calculators, and we welcome inquiries and orders from you.

7) We trust that you will take advantage of this opportunity to offer your customers with first-class products.

8) Our illustrated catalogues, price-list and order forms are enclosed for your convenience.

8. Translate the following sentences into Chinese.

1)尽管我们3月9日给你们寄去了目录本,但却没有收到你方的订单。我们想知道你方是否需要了解有关我方产品的其他信息。

2)我请您特别注意我们的垂直档案存放系统,利用这一系统可将往来信息安全地放置在防尘、防火的抽屉里,又便于及时查找。

3)我们是本地区各种摩托车零部件的独家出口商,愿借此机会给您寄去现有的这类产品的报价单供你参考。希望您对此有兴趣。

4)为了推广这些产品,目录本中所有价格在5月份都可打10%的折扣。

5)你会注意到,由于你方在过去给予我们的支持,我们特别给你们做了降价。这种降价一周内有效。

6)为了支持你们的销售,我们特别准备了一些新产品的样本,另封邮寄,供你方参考。

7)为了你这样的老客户,我们愿意对每一部机器给5%的佣金,此外,对于在本月底之前收到的订单我们还给8% 的折扣。

8)我们很高兴随函寄给你方我们产品的最新设计式样,这些新设计质量高,价格适中,肯定会在你方市场畅销。

9. Rewrite the following sales letter with AIDA plan.

Dear Parents:

Do you spend hours trying to find a small piece of information for your children?

Now, all your troubles are over! THE WORLDWIDE ENCYCLOPAEDIA has all the answers you'll ever need!

It's easy! Just look in the large detailed index for the information you want. THE WORLDWIDE ENCYCLOPEADIA contains thousands of subjects. Your children can also use it quickly and easily. It has over 100 full color photographs, and at the back there are some useful tables covering all the countries of the world, their populations, capitals and sizes.

THE WORLDWIDE ENCYCLOPEADIA is a must for every family. There are two editions, a full three-volume set and a shorter edition in one volume. Get one for your home and you'll wonder how you managed without it.

Available now at UNIVERSAL BOOKS LTD. For purchase over 60 copies you'll get free transportation and prompt delivery.

Your sincerely,

UNIVERSAL BOOKS LTD.

Betty Wood

Sales representative

Key to Lesson Nineteen

2. Translate the following passage into Chinese.

(1)

正式报告通常有一个部分介绍情况或问题的历史背景。虽然现在的读者可能对报告的情况有所了解,但是报告是需要存档的,而且多年以后还会被查询。以后的读者可能不知道这些背景,而这些背景知识对于了解可能做出的选择是非常重要的。

(2)

开个网上商店对我公司来说是个重大决定。我们不具备那些比我们强大的公司所拥有的电脑人员,而且我们的商业运营已经很分散了。可是越来越多的人在网上购物,我们也不愿由于没有这种新的购物方式而落伍。经过几个星期的研究,我的结论是我们应该开发网店,但在实施方式上要谨慎。

3. Translate the following sentences into English.

1) Business report is a common and inevitable means of written communication for executive personnel during their work.

2) There are many kinds of business report, such as informational report, analytical report, recommendation report, etc.

3) A report must have a definite purpose; otherwise, it would be meaningless.

4) A report can be formal, or informal depending on your subject, your purpose, the culture of your organization, and your relationship with your audience.

5) A formal report must be written in line with a format, and use pronouns sparingly.

6) If the report is written to a large number of consumers, you'd better use a formal style, while to your assistant or colleague, you may use informal style.

7) Reports are helpful for you to present to your superiors the feasibility and progress of a project, as well as your ideas.

8) In writing a report, you may start with a table of contents, and develop each key word into a sentence, then use it as the first or last sentence in each paragraph.

Key to Lesson Twenty

3. Translate the following clauses from a sales contract into English.

1) The goods under this Sales Confirmation will be inspected by the China Commodity Inspection Bureau at the port of loading before they are shipped and the certificates of Quality and Quantity/Weight issued by the said Bureau shall be regarded as final and binding upon both parties.

2) The Buyers shall have the right to apply to the Import and Export Commodity Inspection Bureau of the People's Republic of China (CCIB) or China Import and Export Commodity Inspection Corporation (CCIC) for inspection after discharge of the goods at the port of destination.

3) Should the quality and/or quantity/weight be found not in conformity with the contract or invoice or quality certificate, the Buyers shall be entitled to lodge claims with the Sellers on the basis of CCIC's inspection certificate within 90 days after discharge of the goods at the port of destination, with the exception, however, of those claims for which the shipping company and/or the insurance company are to be held responsible.

4) In case of disputes, the parties should settle them through amicable consultation; when such attempt fails, they shall then be submitted to China Maritime Arbitration Commission for arbitration.

5) In case the Buyer fails to arrange insurance in time due to the seller not having a notification in time, the seller shall be responsible for the loss.

6) The normal daily working hours of the party engaged shall be 8 hours. For work done beyond the normal duty hours, overtime allowance shall be paid at 150% of the normal daily rate of

wages.

7) If the engaging party terminate the Contract, in addition to bearing the above-mentioned wages and benefits, it shall pay the engaged party three months' extra salary as compensation allowance.

8) The Contract comes into effect on the first day of the engaged party's arrival at the university and ceases to be effective at its expiration.

4. Translate the following part of an agreement into Chinese.

聘用协议

本协议于2005年3月1日由巴马科AA工厂(以下简称甲方)与张明(以下简称乙方)签订。

鉴于甲方愿意聘乙方,乙方同意应聘为甲方在巴马科的工程师,双方协议如下:

1)聘约为期二年,自2005年3月1日至2007年6月30日。自乙方抵达之日开始正式生效。乙方在完成两年工作后即返回本国。

2)乙方月薪为美金2 000元,由甲方在巴马科支付并由乙方随意汇往中国。在服务期间,乙方的住所由甲方供给。

3)乙方自广州到巴马科以及服务期满自巴马科回广州的飞机票,由甲方供给。

4)乙方应遵守马里的法律和规章。

5)本协议中英文本各二份,由双方签署并各执每种文本一份。

5. Rewrite the following sentences for exactness and free of ambiguity.

1) The Sellers shall deliver the goods on or before July 31.

2) Payment shall be made by Party B within 10 days.

3) Party A shall send technicians at Party B's expense to train Party B's personnel within 30 days after signing of the contract.

4) The goods are to be shipped by a steamer at a port on the West Coast as per bill of lading dated not later than April 30, 2010.

5) Shipment is to be effected twice a month at 600 metric tons each. (Shipment is to be effected every two months at 600 metric tons each.)

6) All activities of ABC Co. shall be governed by laws and pertinent rules and regulations of China.

Reference

1. Kitty O. Locker. Business and Administrative Communication. 5th edition. 北京:机械工业出版社,2000.
2. John V. Thill Excellence in Business Communication. 6th edition. 北京:北京大学出版社,2004.
3. Cheryl Hamilton. Communicating for Results. 6th edition. Wadsworth Thomson Learning,2000.
4. Management Communication Principles and Practice. 2nd edition. 北京:机械工业出版社,2004.
5. 王学成. 商务英语综合业务. 北京:中国商务出版社,2004.
6. 胡文仲,吴祯福. 实用英语写作. 北京:外语教学与研究出版社,1997.
7. 袁永友. 全国外销员统考外贸英语全真试题评析. 修订本. 北京:中国商务出版社,2006.
8. 王玉章. 国际贸易英语. 天津:天津大学出版社,1998.